THE EVERYTHING® JUMBO BOOK OF LARGE-PRINT CROSSWORDS

160 easy-to-challenging puzzles in large print

Douglas R. Fink

Adams Media
New York London Toronto Sydney New Delhi

Adams Media
An Imprint of Simon & Schuster, Inc.
100 Technology Center Drive
Stoughton, MA 02072

An Everything® Series Book.
Everything® and everything.com® are registered trademarks of Simon & Schuster, Inc.

First Adams Media trade paperback edition November 2018

ADAMS MEDIA and colophon are trademarks of Simon & Schuster.

For information about special discounts for bulk purchases, please contact Simon & Schuster Special Sales at 1-866-506-1949 or business@simonandschuster.com.

The Simon & Schuster Speakers Bureau can bring authors to your live event. For more information or to book an event contact the Simon & Schuster Speakers Bureau at 1-866-248-3049 or visit our website at www.simonspeakers.com.

Interior design by Heather McKiel

Manufactured in the United States of America

6 2023

ISBN 978-1-5072-0916-5

Contains material adapted from the following titles published by Adams Media, an Imprint of Simon & Schuster, Inc.: *The Everything® Large-Print Crosswords Book* by Douglas R. Fink, copyright © 2006, ISBN 978-1-59337-644-4 and *The Everything® Large-Print Crosswords Book, Volume II* by Douglas R. Fink, copyright © 2010, ISBN 978-1-4405-0367-2.

Contents

Puzzles / 5

Answers / 327

Puzzles

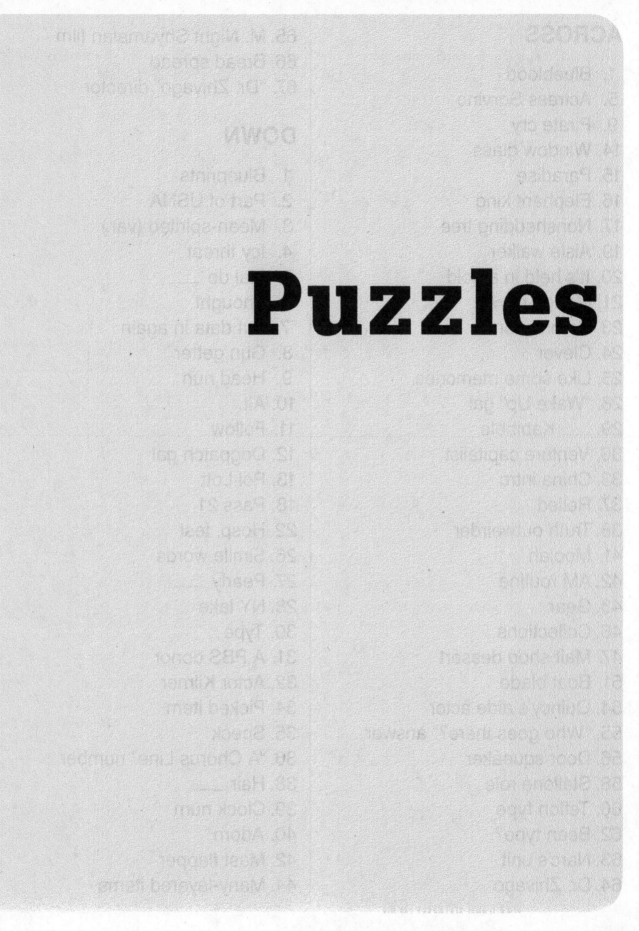

ACROSS

1. Blueblood
5. Actress Sorvino
9. Pirate cry
14. Window glass
15. Paradise
16. Elephant king
17. Nonshedding tree
19. Aisle walker
20. It's held in a hold
21. Manga movie
23. Commotion
24. Clever
25. Like some memories
28. "Wake Up" gal
29. ___ Kabibble
30. Venture capitalist
33. China intro
37. Relied
38. Truth outweirder
41. Moolah
42. AM routine
43. Gear
46. Collections
47. Malt shop dessert
51. Boat blade
54. Quincy's aide actor
55. "Who goes there?" answer
56. Door squeaker
58. Stallone role
60. Teflon type
62. Bean type?
63. Narc's unit
64. Dr. Zhivago
65. M. Night Shyamalan film
66. Bread spread
67. "Dr. Zhivago" director

DOWN

1. Blueprints
2. Part of USNA
3. Mean-spirited (var.)
4. Icy threat
5. Mal de ___
6. Thought
7. Put data in again
8. Gun getter
9. Head nun
10. Alt.
11. Follow
12. Dogpatch gal
13. Pol Lott
18. Pass 21
22. Hosp. test
26. Simile words
27. Pearly ___
28. NY lake
30. Type
31. A PBS donor
32. Actor Kilmer
34. Picked item
35. Speck
36. "A Chorus Line" number
38. Hair ___
39. Clock num.
40. Adorn
42. Mast flapper
44. Many-layered items

Give Peas a Chance

Solution on Page 328

1	2	3	4	■	5	6	7	8	■	9	10	11	12	13
14				■	15				■	16				
17				18					■	19				
20					■	21			22		■	23		
24			■	25	26						27			
■	■	■	28					■	29			■	■	■
30	31	32						■	■	■	33	34	35	36
37							■	38	39	40				
41				■	■	■	42							
■	■	■	43	44	45	■	46					■	■	■
47	48	49				50					■	51	52	53
54			■	55					■	56	57			
58			59		■	60			61					
62					■	63				■	64			
65					■	66				■	67			

45. Hood's piece
47. Some pens
48. Pong maker
49. Menu phrase
50. "Deep Space 9" VIP
51. Well-timed
52. Phobic front?
53. Survive the recount
57. Quaint poem
59. "*C'est Si* ___"
61. Kanga's kid

ACROSS

1. Like some carriages
10. Pram pusher
13. Ben Stiller mom
14. Will Smith title role
15. Carnivorous
17. Monty Python opener
18. Julia's "Ocean's Eleven" role
19. Hard red stone
21. A ___ formality!
22. Modesty
23. Razor residue
25. Counselor's domain
26. No ifs, ___, or buts
27. Green moths
28. Like the nineties
29. Will Shortz's st.
30. Jockey garbs
31. Tiny pest
32. Dependably
34. Like some ice cream
35. Igor's creator
36. Expressed
37. Fruit tool
38. Llama land
39. Philips rival
40. In to be sworn in
45. Dentist office sounds
46. Encounters
47. However
48. Chess capture without landing on the piece

DOWN

1. It's often cured
2. Countdown word
3. Cell letters
4. Some dogs
5. Some Arab rulers
6. A new ___ on life
7. Consumes
8. ___ Lanka
9. Punchlike drinks
10. Plane concern
11. Fight
12. Sentimental
16. Trashy trinkets
20. Cereal box stat.
21. Cradle of life
22. Like Brewster
23. Turnblad musical
24. "Wag the Dog" actress
25. Trench
27. Piano player with a candelabra
30. Witch trial city
31. Remainder getter
33. Suffering
34. Embrace
36. Kentucky college
38. Grandeur
41. Over thar
42. MPG gp.
43. Ball-and-chain kinda guy
44. Explosive stuff

All about Me

Solution on Page 328

1	2	3	4	5	6	7	8	9	■	■	10	11	12
13									■	■	14		
15									16	■	17		
■	■	■	18				■	19		20			
■	■	21				■	22						
23	24				■	25							
26				■	27					■	28		
29			■	30					■	31			
32			33					■	34				
35							■	36				■	■
37						■	38				■	■	■
39			■	40		41					42	43	44
45			■	■	46								
47			■	■	48								

ACROSS

1. "Sound of Music" peaks
5. Helps out
10. Be restless
14. Cheer
15. Politician Palin
16. Mr. Moto comment
17. Lead
19. Worn out, like a tire
20. Respond explosively
21. Pixies
23. Talks hoarsely
26. Farm moms
27. Talk a blue streak
30. Pretended
32. J. Low org.
35. Blackjack pro?
36. Story separators
37. Harry's Hogwarts' pal
38. Lose one's cool
39. Like a fork
40. Arrange
41. IPA part
42. Fern parts
43. Concerning
44. Sword beater
45. Bowling button
46. Singer Boyle
47. She-sheep
49. What newbies learn
51. Well-bribed
54. Anticipates
58. Stuttering actor
59. Eel catcher
62. Wedding SASE
63. Strikers, often
64. Unbleached fabric color
65. Replies
66. Bowling alley spots
67. He ___ she . . .

DOWN

1. They might be fine
2. Shark attack?
3. Pig's place
4. Far from first class
5. Trees or their burnt remains
6. Woolly welcome
7. Mess up
8. Labels
9. Big cane holders
10. Vaccine guy
11. Yuck!
12. Spot in the water
13. They go with cones
18. Guru
22. Beatty flick
24. Verandas
25. Picture taker
27. Subway handhold
28. Jonah's cage
29. Guest actor, often
31. Linked
33. In a way
34. Mr. Chekov
36. Aggravating
40. Bangers and mash need
42. Type of pass

Follow the Money

Solution on Page 328

1	2	3	4	■	5	6	7	8	9	■	10	11	12	13
14				■	15					■	16			
17				18						■	19			
20						■	■	21		22				
■	■	■	23			24	25	■	26				■	■
27	28	29			■	30		31			■	32	33	34
35				■	36						■	37		
38				■	39					■	40			
41			■	42						■	43			
44			■	45					■	46				
■	■	47	48			■	49		50			■	■	■
51	52					53	■	■	54			55	56	57
58				■	59		60	61						
62				■	63					■	64			
65				■	66					■	67			

46. Darned
48. Light plumes
50. They hurt
51. Paddles
52. Birth announcement opener
53. Actress Louise
55. Atahualpa, e.g.
56. Actress Hatcher
57. Cuff item
60. Do wrong
61. Shed item

ACROSS

1. Add one's two cents
7. Petty dictator
13. Pasta piece
14. Arrow poison
15. Pull from
16. Wine processes
17. Part 1 of quote (from Dickens's "Bleak House")
19. Fight schools
21. Sit for a picture
22. Got by
23. "CHiPS" star
27. But is it ___?
28. Part 2 of quote
30. Connect-it-carefully vid game
31. Some cars
33. Twist
34. Where "khaki" and "nabob" came from
35. Speak
36. Part 3 of quote
40. From the sticks
41. Some say it is everything
44. Do to do
45. Polar formation
46. Called
47. Piper rival

DOWN

1. Not Dem. or Rep.
2. Neither fish ___ fowl
3. She loves rock and roll
4. Title role for Johnny Depp
5. Blockades
6. Pitched item
7. Leafless, like a tulip
8. Maine's capital
9. More stale
10. Tirade
11. Jason's ship
12. Mexican moolah
18. Reveals
19. Adjective for Dr. McCoy
20. Gumbo pod
24. Water exercises
25. Earth
26. Car bar
28. Like some efforts
29. Not natural
32. Catch some rays
33. Start of a Woody Allen title
35. Shelved
36. Stage item
37. That hurts!
38. Simile words
39. Ear-related
42. A Bobbsey twin
43. Grad. student concern

What the Dickens?

Solution on Page 328

1	2	3	4	5	6	■	7	8	9	10	11	12
13						■	14					
15						■	16					
■	■	17				18						
19	20				■	21				■	■	■
22				■	■	23				24	25	26
27			■	28	29				■	30		
31			32				■	■	33			
■	■	■	34				■	35				
36	37	38					39				■	■
40						■	41				42	43
44						■	45					
46						■	47					

ACROSS

1. Hindu princess
9. What Horton heard
12. Retes, e.g.
13. Polloi preceder
14. Ranch aide
16. A bit off
17. Me too!
18. EVOO amt, say
19. "Common Sense" guy
21. 8th Greek letter
23. Irish moonshines
25. Sign of trouble
26. Shows fear
27. KP duty needs
29. Away from harbor
30. Earth tones
32. Sealy rival
34. Annual summit group, say
35. Close kin
36. Couldn't refuse
38. Rhoda's mom
39. Backstage adhesive
44. IRS concerns
45. Toothless
46. "Chorus Line" number
47. StubHub vendor

DOWN

1. Pitching stat.
2. Manila Thrilla
3. "And I Love ___"
4. Fireman's need
5. More red
6. Pallor
7. Tidy up
8. Ain't right
9. Chicken choice
10. Armrests?
11. Crankcase bases
15. Email address part
19. Pol's backup
20. Corroded
22. She played the Southern Good Witch in "The Wiz"
23. Water guru
24. Tower of London haunters
26. Italian WWII town
28. Basketballer Walker
31. Silver ___ (cloud seed)
33. Responses to masseuses
37. Pale imitator
40. Circuit switch, for short
41. Guy's date
42. Tribe that a state's name is based on
43. Simone's sea

Have a Ball

Solution on Page 329

1	2	3	4	5	6	7	8	■	■	9	10	11
12								■	■	13		
14								15	■	16		
■	■	■	■	17					■	18		
■	■	19	20				■	21	22			
■	23						24	■	25			
26						■	27	28				
29			■	30	31							■
32				33	■	34					■	■
35			■	36	37				■	■	■	■
38			■	39					40	41	42	43
44			■	■	45							
46			■	■	47							

ACROSS

1. Throw
5. . . . ___ of the emergency broadcast system
9. Diced side
13. Theatre award
14. Money man Greenspan
15. Mrs. Peel
16. It's to the side of the driver, usually
18. "___ Good Men"
19. "Spider-Man 3" being
20. Spot makers
21. Colorizer, say
23. ___ "Kookie" Byrnes
26. Garden variety
29. How's that for ___?
33. 54, e.g.
34. Crazy
35. Loathe
36. The most produced biochemical
38. "___ the ramparts . . ."
39. Boats' tipping points
42. Sweepy?
44. Medication
49. Fictitious second baseman
50. Rear mirror hanger, perhaps
51. Concerning
52. Out of the wind
53. Head swellers
54. Olympus denizens
55. Boston or Chicago
56. Bad stuff

DOWN

1. Duds
2. Follow
3. "The King and I" country
4. Slobodan Milosevic, e.g.
5. Big Chevy
6. Snobbery
7. Least risky
8. Wile E.'s weapon
9. Led
10. It's forward and to the side of the driver
11. Hook aide
12. She played Private Benjamin
17. Poitier title role
20. Eller and Em
22. RSVP holder
23. HOMES lake
24. Quite an impression
25. It's in front of the driver
27. Increase
28. Go-getter
30. Newborn gear
31. Dental filling
32. Appear
35. Resident
37. Crab, e.g.
40. Slept
41. Clever
42. Quick drink
43. Whoops!

By the Driver

Solution on Page 329

1	2	3	4	■	5	6	7	8	■	9	10	11	12
13				■	14				■	15			
16				17					■	18			
19								■	20				
■	■	■	■	21				22				■	■
23	24	25	■	■	■	26						27	28
29			30	31	32		■	33					
34						■	35						
36						37		■	■	■	38		
■	■	39						40	41	■	■	■	■
42	43				■	44				45	46	47	48
49				■	50								
51				■	52				■	53			
54				■	55				■	56			

45. Nice things to say
46. "Thank Heavens . . ." musical
47. Picture
48. Pool type
50. Like the Beatles

ACROSS

1. ___ au lait
5. Army rank
10. Circles
12. Some dresses
14. Bathtub item
15. Money back
16. Throw money around
18. Humorist
19. Chopper
20. Elmo's friend
21. Pet name stuttered in TV ads
22. Boring
24. ___ lines
25. Marble or clay, say
27. "I Remember Mama" star
29. Berlin's put-on?
30. I've had it ___ here!
31. Charlie's train
32. "Muppet Show" eagle
35. McBride of "Pushing Daisies"
36. Animal-talking doc
39. Chef hats
41. Like some battles
42. Soup sounds
43. Combined
44. Revered one
45. Call of ___

DOWN

1. St. ___
2. Up high
3. Revolutionary War instrument
4. And others
5. Homer's wife
6. Draft-dodging?
7. Forward sail
8. Spontaneously
9. Kind of value
10. Stew pot
11. Captain Marvel word
13. "Just Shoot Me" actor
17. Batter Clemente
21. "Vicky Cristina Barcelona" actress
22. Early Bond film
23. 66, e.g.
24. Skedaddle!
25. Classic
26. Slow way on
27. Spy movie conduits
28. Defend against critics
31. Unlike a rolling stone
32. Wilt, comparatively
33. Place so loud you can hear a pin drop
34. Vulcan mind ___
36. Part of NYPD
37. MP3 player
38. Commandment word
40. Jackson pal

Size Up

Solution on Page 329

ACROSS

1. Fab Four hairstyles
5. Pro-pet people: abbr.
10. Beaver barriers
14. Bread spread
15. Stocking stuff
16. Radiate
17. Radio couple
19. "Your Show of Shows" star
20. Tony musical role for LuPone
21. "Your Show of Shows" regular
23. Cozy spot
24. Cheerleader's supply
25. Those who run things
26. Tartare
27. Jargon
30. Prize funder
33. Tries to lose
34. Person of habit
35. Each
36. Blackjack cry
37. Loafing around
38. Lobster eater's attire
39. Doles (out)
40. "Young Frankenstein"/ "Everybody Loves Raymond" star
41. Tampa and Tacoma
43. Winter woe
44. Like a geek
45. Boffo Broadway letters
46. Scene chewer
49. Coupe's kin
51. Setting for "The Flintstones"
53. Engine hum
54. Dressler/Beery flick of '30
56. Verbal
57. Like a Pisan tower
58. Rorschach test pattern
59. Chest items
60. "Too many ___" ("Amadeus" complaint)
61. Darns

DOWN

1. Changed addresses
2. Greek salad item
3. Pie nut
4. Daytime drama
5. Philanthropist Mellon or Carnegie
6. Computer guru
7. Blueprint
8. Cape ___, MA
9. Funny story
10. Dishonesty
11. Comedy where Kingfish led in the jump from radio to TV
12. Shiny, flaky rock
13. Constellation point
18. Himalayan country
22. There are usually 20 in a fuse
25. Interruption sounds
26. Sales ___
27. Locations
28. Hiatus
29. Baby bouncer
30. Apprehends
31. Mayberry lad
32. Comedy duo for over 40 years

Twosomes

Solution on Page 329

1	2	3	4	■	5	6	7	8	9	■	10	11	12	13
14				■	15					■	16			
17				18						■	19			
20								■	21	22				
23			■	24			■	25					■	■
■	■	■	26			■	27						28	29
30	31	32			■	33					■	34		
35				■	36					■	37			
38			■	39					■	40				
41			42					■	43			■	■	■
■	■	44					■	45			■	46	47	48
49	50					■	51				52			
53				■	54	55								
56				■	57					■	58			
59				■	60					■	61			

33. Simple song
36. Flock tender
37. Chit
39. "Rise up so early in the ___ . . ."
40. Light wood shade
42. Oysters' output
43. Western sets, often
45. Hackneyed
46. ___ Selassie
47. Shining
48. Liquefies
49. Dog's name
50. Type of dollar
51. Huff
52. Lessens
55. O.J. judge

ACROSS

1. Man on a mountain
5. Appropriate
8. Open a bit
12. Yemeni port
13. Cassowary kin
14. Domain
15. Yellow sign?
17. Paula used to help judge it
18. "Different World" actress
20. Topmost
23. Ginger ___
24. Female assistant
28. Computer place, sometimes
31. Willing, once
32. Jam ingredient
33. Some paintings
34. B&B
35. Consipirator who failed
37. Bonding words
39. Armada
40. "Futurama" actress
45. Egg
46. Some dogs
50. Brouhaha
51. ___ you ready?
52. Put in stitches
53. Is outstanding
54. Rapid stock car boy of song
55. Out of the box

DOWN

1. Shiny substance
2. This means trouble
3. Director Brooks
4. Mutt ___
5. Iowa State's town
6. Bit of verse
7. "*Mon Oncle*" actor
8. The Little Mermaid
9. Like a movie critic
10. Baseball brother
11. Depend
16. "M*A*S*H" and "Gong Show" star
19. Aye negater
20. Wrinkled citrus
21. Ouchie
22. Cornucopia concept
25. Hosp. section
26. Sunlight hours
27. Sandy's plea
29. Shelter-ward
30. Ahem!
33. Wise
35. Gentile
36. Off yonder
38. They're for show
40. Drum of Japan
41. Swear
42. Celeb
43. Flying start
44. "Riders of the Purple Sage" author
47. It may be bitter
48. Get-up
49. Where swine dine

Guys and Gals

Solution on Page 330

1	2	3	4	■	5	6	7	■	8	9	10	11
12				■	13			■	14			
15				16				■	17			
■	■	■	18					19				
20	21	22			■	■	■	23			■	■
24					25	26	27		■	28	29	30
31				■	32			■	33			
34			■	35				36				
■	■	37	38		■	■	■	39				
40	41				42	43	44			■	■	■
45				■	46					47	48	49
50				■	51			■	52			
53				■	54			■	55			

ACROSS

1. Tends tables
6. Tow
10. Poems of praise
14. Pool problem
15. Word of understanding
16. Beatles hit
17. Radio/TV show signoff
20. Takes both sides
21. Use a soapbox
22. Multi-vol. ref. work
23. Cavorted
24. Mingus, for one
29. Time Warner buyer
30. ___ face!
31. Beseech
32. New Mexico resort
36. Johnny Mercer classic
40. Sushi serving
41. Contend
42. Gladiator's spot
43. Word in a long Woody Allen title
44. Goaded
46. They're grasped at
50. Tin Man's need
51. Susan Lucci role
52. As a rule
58. Marx Brothers film, with "A"
60. Theater award
61. Carnivore's craving
62. Body shop eliminations
63. Cincinnati swatters
64. Rock concert needs
65. Skedaddle!

DOWN

1. Funny lot
2. Muchly
3. Lab aide
4. Voila!
5. Email button
6. Pooh pal
7. Sat at the event
8. Allows
9. Part of a trip
10. Butler's love
11. Tooth ___
12. Crack
13. Velocity
18. Wedding words
19. ___ call
23. ___ fun at
24. Sonny and Cher's "I Got You ___"
25. Equal to the task
26. Satan's seeking
27. Prefers charges
28. ___ a living
29. Cinder
31. Chowed down
32. Car's "shoe"
33. Like some wine or cheese
34. "This can't be!"
35. Ollie's pal
37. Currier and ___
38. Put the kibosh on
39. Pester
43. Ruth's sultanate
44. Crazy ___ (card game)

Several Nights

Solution on Page 330

1	2	3	4	5	■	6	7	8	9	■	10	11	12	13
14					■	15				■	16			
17					18					19				
20									■	21				
■	■	■	■	■	22			■	23					
24	25	26	27	28			■	29			■	■	■	■
30					■	■	31			■	32	33	34	35
36					37	38				39				
40				■	41			■	■	42				
■	■	■	■	43			■	44	45					
46	47	48	49			■	50			■	■	■	■	■
51					■	52				53	54	55	56	57
58					59									
60				■	61				■	62				
63				■	64				■	65				

45. Singer's club
46. ___ Wences
47. Indian group
48. Fixed
49. They hurt
50. Readily available
52. One on a grocery list
53. Shows assent
54. Bigger than life
55. Gambling mecca
56. Jason's craft
57. Final
59. Doc flock

ACROSS

1. Each
5. Switch words
9. ___ donna
14. Road movie star
15. Holmes's find
16. One on horseback
17. Actor Guinness
18. Lawsuit limiter
20. Artie Shaw hit
22. Please continue . . .
23. Rustic mothers
24. "Try not to ___"
28. "Dragnet" star
30. TV co.
33. Oldsmobile model
34. Window ___
35. Breakfast, lunch or dinner
36. Artie Shaw hit
39. Writer Bagnold
40. Granada greeting
41. Severity
42. Used a pew
43. Stoke
44. Paper wasp
45. "But is it ___?"
46. Baby food
47. Artie Shaw hit
55. Crumby cover
56. Dust Bowl denizen
57. Early personal computer
58. Phaser setting
59. Planet Mongo man
60. Big name in Chicago politics
61. Pianist Dame Myra ___
62. "___ victory!"

DOWN

1. He had a great white hope
2. Actress Negri
3. Oil cartel
4. ¼ bushel
5. Fuel percentage
6. Golfer Ray ___
7. PETA people won't wear them
8. Jessica Fletcher's friend
9. Designed for easy assembly
10. Jazzman's lines
11. Matinee ___
12. Simple
13. Slot machine stand-out
19. Ali's "___ in the Jungle"
21. Passed or twirled stick
24. "___ in Toyland"
25. Actress Verdugo
26. On the level
27. Dry
28. Exert
29. Napoleon's isle
30. The ___ of Terror
31. Dugout
32. On one's toes
34. Casino deck holder
35. "The Ghost and Mrs. ___"
37. Iota preceders
38. Grasp at
43. "Dragnet" role
44. Safe places

Artie Shaw Hits

Solution on Page 330

45. Saying
46. Hocus ___
47. "My Friend ___"
48. Diamond or Sedaka of song
49. "Candy Is Dandy" author
50. Lyre kin
51. Crooner Perry
52. Likened
53. Dryer fuzz
54. Kid's building block
55. Like Leroy Brown

ACROSS

1. Let off
7. "___ Doubtfire"
10. Scoundrel
12. Sporty mazda
14. Silver surfer?
16. RSVP case
17. Signed kisses
18. Damp
19. Like the Gordian Knot
22. Camera concerns
24. Pirate drink
26. Ahead of schedule
27. Extra apartment
31. "Logan's Run" symbols
32. Carol starter
33. Hungarian, e.g.
35. Rhinestone holder
39. Teacher's org.
40. O.J., e.g.
42. Essayist Lamb
44. High-quality
48. Pick up on
49. Beneficiary
50. Narc's gp.
51. Atomic clock pieces

DOWN

1. They might be fine or liberal
2. "Yankee Doodle Dandy" guy
3. Chili con ___
4. Guideless
5. Sworn words
6. Royal flush low card
7. Hr. part
8. Plant that can be an allergen
9. Church bell spot
11. Harrison of "My Fair Lady"
12. Knot remover
13. Bohemian
15. Ump
20. Like some pens
21. MADD concern
23. Pan or chi preceder
25. "A-Team" actor
27. Irate
28. Kiev's country
29. ___ Beta Kappa
30. Sis or bro
31. Bee and Em
34. Wedding page word
36. Zs overseas
37. Pica alternative
38. Eye highlighter
41. Actor Kilmer
43. Ripens
45. RIF spot, e.g.
46. "Stand" band
47. Turk with a title

Easy As 1-2-3

Solution on Page 330

1	2	3	4	5	6	■	■	■	7	8	9	■
10						11	■	12				13
14							15					
16				■	■	17			■	18		
■	19			20	21	■	22		23			
■	■	■	■	24		25	■	26				
■	27	28	29				30					■
31					■	32			■	■	■	■
33					34	■	35		36	37	38	■
39			■	40		41	■	■	42			43
44			45				46	47				
48					■	49						
■	50			■	■	■	51					

ACROSS

1. Prairie critters
8. Loses temporarily
15. Emphatic words
16. West Indies island
17. Featured star ("Going My Way," "The Quiet Man," "How Green Was My Valley," etc.)
19. ___ Gay
20. Hat for Mike Hammer
21. ___ of passage
22. Recently
23. Enthusiasm
26. Long skirt
28. Frosty's mouthpiece
29. Meadow
32. "When You ___ Upon a Star"
34. Popeye, for one
36. 17 Across recreated his role of Orator for him
39. "Wooden Soldiers" action
40. The Red Planet
41. "___ kingdom come . . ."
42. Harrow rival
43. Burma neighbor
45. WKRP newsman
46. Tough tote
50. Get ready (for)
54. Sure thing
55. Type of trap or prize
56. Light comedy/romance starring 17 Across
60. Sheep, notably
61. Knickknack cabinet
62. The Gettysburg ___
63. Goes AWOL

DOWN

1. He taunts
2. Man from Muscat
3. He says he's all ears
4. Cotton Club locale
5. Irish folk singer
6. Literacy prog.
7. Overly starched
8. Miata maker
9. Metal bar
10. Cubic meter
11. Italian bread, formerly
12. ___ Khan
13. King portrayer
14. Blue
18. ___ Aviv
22. The O in H_2O
23. Flyboy
24. Era
25. Cheerful
27. Made speechless
28. Snapshot
29. Boutonniere spot
30. Make happy
31. Bushy dos
33. That guy
34. Fragment
35. Chan comment
37. ". . . dish ___ away with the spoon"
38. Skillful

Featured Star

Solution on Page 331

1	2	3	4	5	6	7	■	8	9	10	11	12	13	14
15							■	16						
17							18							
19					■	20						■	■	■
21				■	22						■	23	24	25
■	■	■	26	27			■	■	■	■	28			
29	30	31	■	32			33	■	34	35				
36			37					38						
39						■	40				■	41		
42				■	■	■	■	43			44	■	■	■
45			■	46	47	48	49			■	50	51	52	53
■	■	■	54						■	55				
56	57	58							59					
60							■	61						
62							■	63						

44. Moocher
46. Piglet
47. "Here ___ the Sun" (Beatles song)
48. Farm workers, sometimes
49. Fleur-de-___
51. With 52 Down, a Chicago film critic
52. See 51 Down
53. Big fires
54. Blofeld feature
55. 60 Across sounds
56. TKO org.
57. Yesteryear
58. Took control
59. ___ 66

ACROSS

1. Black and white
4. Butterfly catcher
7. Fancy spread
11. Little green men transport
12. Kwik-E-Mart man
13. Cambodian currency
15. Former Soviet satellite
16. What Beatniks beat
18. The Shah and others
20. Go too far
21. Crux
22. "Don't Bring Me Down" gp.
23. Ode's always
24. Concerned comment
26. Concerning, legally
27. Spiritual song
30. Quagmire
31. Seder month
32. Peak
33. Avoid the truth
34. Olympic symbol
38. John Wayne's first name
40. Pieces of eight piece
41. Fish portrayer
43. "___ Gang"
44. More devious
45. N. or S. state
46. Ebony
47. Latin being
48. Color
49. Chopping tool

DOWN

1. Curry spice, not a greeting
2. Blazing
3. Cleaning agent
4. Oreo maker
5. Long verse
6. Large cask
7. BYU city
8. Teammate
9. Earthen
10. Ones on the lam
14. Sweet sandwich
17. Automatons
19. Chaws
22. Bert's pal
25. Store overhang
26. "Are so!" retort
27. Can take shape
28. Fish hawks
29. Quick bread
30. Michelle and Cass
33. Orleans river
35. Spanish red wine
36. Gave hints
37. Budget rival
39. Singer Burl
40. Jazzy Anita
42. Peculiar

Divine Inspiration

Solution on Page 331

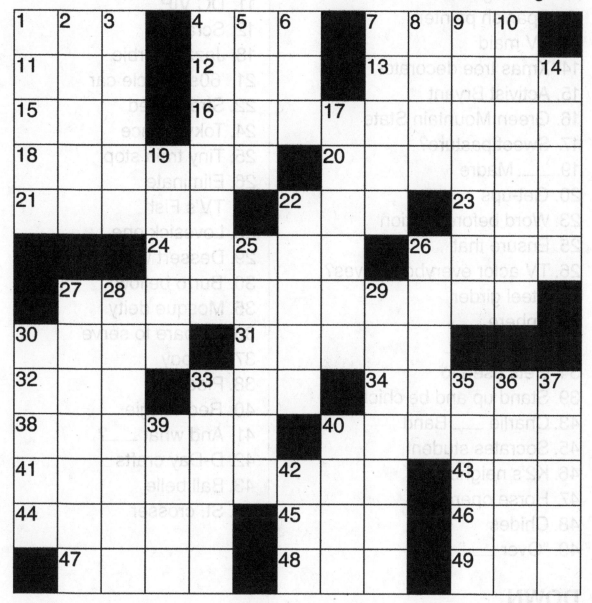

1	2	3	■	4	5	6	■	7	8	9	10	■
11			■	12			■	13				14
15			■	16			17					
18			19			■	20					
21					■	22			■	23		
■	■	■	24		25			■	26			
■	27	28						29				■
30				■	31					■	■	■
32			■	33			■	34		35	36	37
38			39			■	40					
41						42			■	43		
44					■	45			■	46		
■	47				■	48			■	49		

ACROSS

1. A Stooge
6. Spanish painter
13. TV maid
14. Xmas tree decorator
15. Activist Bryant
16. Green Mountain State
17. Sweet pasture?
19. ___ Madre
20. Get-ups
23. Word before ignition
25. Ensure that
26. TV actor everybody loves?
31. Steel girder
32. Sphere
33. Grateful ___
34. Gets used to
39. Stand up and be chicken?
43. Charlie ___ Band
45. Socrates student
46. K2's neighbor
47. Horse opera
48. Chides
49. "Over ___"

DOWN

1. Palindromic rulers
2. Hilton of film
3. "Slate," e.g.
4. Gauge
5. Tot spot
6. Smooth
7. Notion
8. Thin rope
9. War merchant
10. Whiter, in a way
11. DC VIP
12. Scrap
18. Jazzy Herbie
21. '60s muscle car
22. Strew seed
24. Tokyo, once
25. Tiny train stop
26. Eliminate
27. TV's Fish
28. Lovesick one
29. Dessert wine
30. Burro bellow
35. Mosque deity
36. Prepare to serve
37. Bellboy
38. Pledged
40. Red veggie
41. And what ___?
42. D-Day crafts
43. Ball belle
44. St. crosser

Pain at the End

Solution on Page 331

1	2	3	4	5	■	6	7	8	9	10	11	12
13					■	14						
15					■	16						
17					18						■	■
19						■	■	■	20		21	22
■	■	■	■	23		24	■	25				
26	27	28	29				30					
31					■	32			■	■	■	■
33				■	■	■	34		35	36	37	38
■	■	39		40	41	42						
43	44						■	45				
46							■	47				
48							■	49				

ACROSS

1. ___ Jean (Marilyn, by birth)
6. Chef's amt.
10. Belafonte refrain
14. "Cats" man
15. What a diva does
16. Actress Thompson
17. Profiled director
20. Aggravate
21. Barkers
22. Gumbo pods
23. I'll ___ you, and raise you . . .
24. West of Brooklyn
25. "___ Miniver"
26. "The Thin Man" costar
27. Dizzy baseballer
29. Apprehend
32. ___ kitchen
35. Get through hard work
36. Cole Porter's birthplace
37. 17 Across film set on a train
40. . . . and not a ___ more!
41. Eye part or camera part
42. HAL's last song
43. "___ Pinafore"
44. Newspaper page
45. Teacher's ___
46. Double-decker or crosstown vehicle
47. Lodging rater
48. Supply weapons to
51. They're good for lounging
54. Insult
56. Ernie's wife
57. Title, secretive group in a 17 Across film
60. Green Gables gal
61. ___ India Company
62. ___ and dreams
63. Lead role's last name in a long-running film franchise
64. Hot tubs
65. Data ___

DOWN

1. Approaches
2. Stan's pal, or Kukla's pal
3. Hunter's weapon
4. "Encore!"
5. Noshed
6. Resort lake
7. Navy lockup
8. Makes a lap
9. ___-10
10. They fill shoes in casinos
11. Bing Crosby hit
12. Village People hit
13. Acorns' ambitions
18. When America went to war
19. Trumpet
24. Da Vinci's Lisa
25. Public education pioneer
26. Jaunty rhythm
27. He married Dora, by Dickens
28. Significant periods
29. Radar's purple drink
30. War god
31. Bee-like?
32. Draw with acid
33. Excuse me!
34. Till fill
35. Rochester's love

He's in His Films

Solution on Page 331

1	2	3	4	5	■	6	7	8	9	■	10	11	12	13
14					■	15				■	16			
17					18					19				
20				■	21				■	22				
23			■	24			■	■	25			■	■	■
■	■	■	26			■	27	28			■	29	30	31
32	33	34			■	35				■	36			
37					38					39				
40				■	41				■	42				
43			■	44				■	45			■	■	■
■	■	■	46			■	■	47			■	48	49	50
51	52	53			■	54	55			■	56			
57					58					59				
60				■	61				■	62				
63				■	64				■	65				

36. Jr.'s exam
38. Short swims
39. Concept
44. Throw out
45. Flay fruit
46. Exposed
47. Bee and Em
48. Skilled
49. Less green
50. Not neat
51. Pierce
52. "This can't be!"
53. Twain's rafter
54. Ginger cookie
55. Eva, on "Green Acres"
56. School for 63 Across
58. Proposal answer
59. "___ Wore a Yellow Ribbon"

ACROSS

1. Of the Vatican
6. Automaker Iacocca
9. Western
14. "Maria ___"
15. Corn serving
16. ___ ho!
17. Baseballer Stengel
18. ___ Khan
19. Made a booboo
20. Is well-studied
23. Telephone button
24. Gun lobby
25. "Leave It to Beaver" family name
29. Hair salon worker
33. Seabiscuit or Secretariat
34. From where Charlie never returned
35. EMS skill
36. Up the creek
41. "___ Miserables"
42. Part of PRNDL
43. Arab bigwig
44. "Highly unlikely!"
47. Sticklers
49. Kid's pie material
50. It's a long story
51. Gangster film comment
59. Corridors
60. Watched the kids
61. Rodeo rope
62. Actor Davis
63. Paid expert
64. Musician Jones
65. Hubcap's place
66. Desire
67. Ohio or Iowa

DOWN

1. Peter Piper's pick
2. Money expert Greenspan
3. Mexican moolah
4. All over again
5. Stops at on a flight leg
6. Good throw in horseshoes
7. Chomping at the bit
8. Notable periods
9. Famed storyteller
10. TV antenna
11. Poi base
12. Fairly matched
13. Cincinnati team
21. Unseal, in poetry
22. Like some beer
25. Kid
26. Hermit
27. Rub out
28. Dangerous snake
29. Pig's place
30. FDR's Interior Secretary
31. Skedaddle
32. Journeys
34. Cable channel for rock fans
37. Wear away
38. Bowling pin count
39. Kibbutz workers
40. Tai ___

Burger Time

Solution on Page 332

1	2	3	4	5	■	6	7	8	■	9	10	11	12	13
14					■	15			■	16				
17					■	18			■	19				
20					21				22					
■	■	■	■	23				■	24			■	■	■
25	26	27	28				■	29				30	31	32
33					■	■	34			■	■	35		
36					37	38				39	40			
41			■	■	42			■	■	43				
44			45	46			■	47	48					
■	■	■	49			■	50				■	■	■	■
51	52	53				54					55	56	57	58
59					■	60			■	61				
62					■	63			■	64				
65					■	66			■	67				

45. French film of 2001
46. Seafood staple
47. Battle of the Bulge leader
48. Yuck!
50. Look at intently
51. Dog or food
52. Meat and potatoes
53. Alternatively
54. Culp/Cosby show
55. Play people
56. Workplace watchdog
57. Teen's big exam
58. A few

ACROSS

1. Accumulated, as a tab
6. Kramer's real name
11. Golf stat
14. Dress style
15. Change
16. Color
17. One star of the film
19. ___ in the bag!
20. Beatle wife
21. Skedaddle!
22. Story stirrer
23. Pinocchio's growth agent
26. Taxing org.
28. Tunnelers
30. Findable
33. Whitewater ___
36. Repeated "Ring Around the Rosie" word
37. Mine cars
39. Carmaker Iacocca
40. High-schooler
41. Ethiopia's Selassie
42. Office shape
43. "2001" villain/victim
44. Music genre, for short
45. In what place
46. Clown Kelly
48. Walking on air
50. Build
52. Curly's assaulter
53. "Desk ___" (Hepburn/Tracy film)
54. "M*A*S*H" star
56. Harley cycle
58. And so on
60. Provide weapons to
61. One star of the film
66. ATF's cousin
67. Jazzy Shaw
68. Jubilate
69. ___ Andreas Fault
70. Russian refusals
71. Richards of tennis

DOWN

1. Castle collider
2. Spinks sparrer
3. Nothing
4. Do ___ others . . .
5. Showy flowers
6. Scatter Calloway
7. Bread spread
8. Sweep the strings
9. The Velvet Fog
10. It's mined
11. One star of the film
12. Large ferry passenger
13. Take a load off
18. "Cheers" cry
22. Spirit
23. Detest
24. Tailor's concern
25. One star of the film
27. Old Nick
29. "Viva ___ Vegas"
31. Coop clucker
32. Lion's group
34. Honey
35. Choose
38. Vinyl in an envelope

It's a Mad, Mad, Mad, Mad World

Solution on Page 332

41. Coop
42. Taunting cry
44. Map abbr.
45. "___ 'tis nobler . . ."
47. Stray away
49. Pound, for one
51. Linzer ___
54. They come and go
55. Neighborhood
57. "True ___"
59. "Unforgettable" singer
61. M&M color until recently
62. Certainly!
63. "Chico and the ___"
64. ___ crow (was humbled)
65. Spot

ACROSS

1. Wealthy
5. Horn sound
10. ___ roast (meat cut)
14. Monty Python troupe member
15. Upsets
16. Gotcha
17. Capp character
20. Utilizes
21. From that place
22. Spots
23. Some riot gear
24. Big desert
28. Soda ___ (malt shop workers)
29. British school
30. TV Raymond's mom
31. Recipe amt.
34. Capp character
38. Brat
39. Haven
40. Do a doctor's work
41. Discernment
42. Gracie's guy
44. Hurts
47. Stool pigeon
48. Oohs and aahs
49. Takes another turn for the worse
54. Capp character
56. One against
57. Party ___
58. Bear or bat's hangout
59. Not so nice
60. He did "Chicago" and "Cabaret"
61. "The Man Who ___ Too Much"

DOWN

1. Breach
2. Concept
3. Applaud
4. Towel word
5. Rhoda's sister
6. Rosters
7. "The Sun ___ Rises"
8. Ump
9. Rather obscure
10. Fare payers
11. Imposing upon
12. Pilgrimage destination
13. Little dogs
18. Fibber
19. Trembles
23. ___ and conditions
24. Big rig
25. Smallest bit
26. Basketball goal
27. Actress Sothern
28. Actor Farr of "M*A*S*H"
30. Ship poles
31. Level
32. Sticky wicket
33. Soccer great
35. Gets on
36. Cools it
37. "___ goes there?"
41. Watch
42. In abundance
43. Yadda-yadda, in a bibliography
44. Belief of over a billion
45. Nary a soul

Li'l Abner

Solution on Page 332

46. Cabal
47. Collected collateral
49. Guns, as an engine
50. "Roman Holiday" actor
51. Check through
52. Icicle holder
53. Goulash
55. Big Red

ACROSS

1. Strip
5. Collect
10. Shadowbox
14. Stewpot
15. Cleansing acid
16. "Soap" family
17. Gibberish
19. Down under finds
20. "Strange Magic" band
21. "Wurst" humor
22. Film type started in 1927
24. Paleontological fake
27. Spirits
30. Baker Lee
31. Wrong
32. Rommel ambusher
37. Speed event
38. Sharp ridge
39. Ring above the collar
40. Transversely
42. Like the motel in "Cars"
43. A.D.'s A.
44. Magnet alloy
45. Self-titled rap hit of 1995
50. Tatooine tyke
51. Thumbs-down review
52. Hwy. crosser
55. Wee monkey
56. Family tree adjective
60. Pain
61. Through mom
62. CD's D
63. Dregs
64. Went out
65. "Logan's Run" symbol

DOWN

1. Fleshy fruit
2. Tishri lead-in
3. Fiery saint
4. "Monster Mash" work site
5. Disavow
6. Diamond head?
7. Supply weapons
8. Sis or bro
9. Way to get off
10. Vodka, slangily
11. Winter coat
12. Got delivery
13. Stopwatch button
18. Fiery gems
23. Growth aid
24. Court collection
25. Words to a tot or a kitty
26. Crash diets
27. Singer Anthony
28. Actor Epps
29. *Con mucho dinero*
32. Pipe cleaner
33. Scant beach attire
34. Rajah's wife
35. He played Obi-Wan
36. Fuss
38. Like many a shop
41. 34 Down garb
42. Stick
44. Waned

At Large

Solution on Page 332

1	2	3	4	■	5	6	7	8	9	■	10	11	12	13
14				■	15					■	16			
17				18						■	19			
20			■	21			■	■	22	23				
■	■	■	24				25	26						
27	28	29				■	30				■	■	■	■
31					■	32					33	34	35	36
37				■	38					■	39			
40				41					■	42				
■	■	■	■	43				■	44					
45	46	47	48					49				■	■	■
50						■	■	51			■	52	53	54
55				■	56	57	58				59			
60				■	61					■	62			
63				■	64					■	65			

45. Birth-related
46. Back-burnered
47. 10% levy
48. '30s drifters
49. Sudden burst
52. Buggy brake
53. Chore
54. Carve
57. Gen. letters
58. Mangia!
59. Nut. qty.

ACROSS

1. Amscray!
4. Edgar ___ Poe
9. ___ Marie Presley
13. "The wolf ___ the door"
15. Inexperienced
16. Singer Clapton
17. Manly rite of passage
19. Flame attractant
20. Flinch
21. "60 Minutes" closer
23. Aroma
24. Rotate
25. Military command
29. Baby bringer?
33. Cinema souvenir
37. Well-ventilated
38. Hatch from Utah
39. "She ___ a Yellow Ribbon"
40. Go berserk
42. Relax
43. Part of WASP
45. Hidden name in art
46. Actress Sommer
47. Triangular sign
48. Pola of the silents
50. ___ hither
52. ER request
57. Appeal
60. Type of blouse
63. Psychic
64. Type of firework
66. Chicken ___
67. Timex rival
68. Japanese sport
69. Japanese drink
70. Skin soothers
71. CPA's forte

DOWN

1. "227" star
2. Hayes of song
3. Parisian pie
4. Feed the kitty
5. ___ Susan
6. Like early TV
7. Ms. Gardner
8. Indira Gandhi's dad
9. Peter, Paul and Mary song
10. Monopoly piece
11. Space
12. In need of a chiropractor
14. Eliot Ness, for one
18. Take ___ custody
22. Approximately
24. These are ___ times
26. Urban music
27. Senator Feinstein
28. Tennessee ___ Ford
30. Like some medicines
31. World takeover game
32. Banjo's place
33. Influence
34. Author Morrison
35. Coax
36. Student grade evener
41. Jam ingredient
44. Awful aroma

Slots

Solution on Page 333

49. Unpalatable
51. Hadj's destination
53. Chemists' places
54. It's ___ time!
55. "Throw ___ from the Train"
56. Cayman Islands bus. address, often
57. Requests
58. "Star Wars" princess
59. Potato soup veggie
60. Carlos's coin
61. HOMES lake
62. Love personified
65. Linden who was Barney Miller

ACROSS

1. Play part
4. Pup's cry
7. Cry
10. Tarzan's pal
13. Like sushi
14. Big Band ___
15. Flightless bird
16. Expense
17. Spoon-bender Geller
18. Heavy weight
19. Cushion
20. Night bird
21. Like Jesus
25. Capable
26. Blemish
27. Little bit
29. Russian classic
34. ___ face
37. Airport acronym
38. ___ speak (as it were)
39. Become the champ
40. Ancient
42. Summer in Paris
44. Guidry or Darling of baseball
45. Seaweed
47. Food scrap
49. White weasel
51. Rushed around
54. Bluenose
55. Tue. preceder
56. Hard to find
60. New
64. "Much ___ about Nothing"
66. Use a chair
67. UN labor arm
68. HQ
69. Costello, but not Abbott
70. Yalie
71. Genetic letters
72. Wedding page word
73. Mil. rank
74. NYSE regulator
75. Blockade
76. Building add-on

DOWN

1. Resort near Venezuela
2. Chocolate substitute
3. Spin
4. Abominable Snowman
5. Press
6. Hat or Canal
7. Divide
8. Muscat is its capital
9. Small parrot
10. All the more
11. Church seat
12. Electric fish
22. "Hud" Oscar winner
23. Create
24. Ages and ages
28. Playwright Chekhov
30. Modern prefix
31. Stocking stuff
32. AAA or EPA
33. Jim-dandy
34. Deck mop
35. "Psycho" star
36. Naive

Al Hirschfeld Tribute

Solution on Page 333

1	2	3	■	4	5	6	■	7	8	9	■	10	11	12
13			■	14			■	15			■	16		
17			■	18			■	19			■	20		
21			22				23				24		■	■
25				■	■	26			■	27			28	■
■	■	■	29	30	31				32					33
34	35	36				■	37			■	38			
39			■	40		41	■	42		43	■	44		
45			46	■	47		48	■	49		50			
51				52				53				■	■	■
■	54				■	55			■	■	56	57	58	59
■	■	60			61				62	63				
64	65		■	66			■	67			■	68		
69			■	70			■	71			■	72		
73			■	74			■	75			■	76		

41. Highly emotional
43. To ___ is human
46. Soon
48. Holier-than-___
50. Vidal's Breckinridge
52. Wading birds
53. Release
57. Do penance
58. Act like Teflon
59. Henry Ford's son
61. Cleopatra's river
62. Longest arm bone
63. Wander
64. Cakes and ___
65. Comic Knotts or Rickles

ACROSS

1. TV or movie follower
4. Pub quaff
7. Apprehend
10. "Eat here—get ___"
13. Keatsian work
14. Arlo, to Woody
15. Rocks, at the bar
16. Stand in ___
17. Super-secret spy gp.
18. "If I Only ___ a Brain"
19. Struggle
21. He was the Beaver
24. As well
25. Parking place
26. Weight
30. The Beaver's big brother
35. Annoyance
38. What a ham hams up on
39. Honest one, on the five
40. Skedaddle!
42. ___ diem
43. ___ Moines
44. Wine info
46. They're fetching
48. 30 Across's smarmy friend
51. Cozy home
52. Hoodwink
53. Used item sale sign
57. He played the Beaver's dad
62. Serengeti leaper
65. Sound device
66. In the style of
67. Army R&R provider
68. Rhyme ___ reason
69. Polka ___
70. Cauldron
71. Fight ending initials
72. Tummy muscles
73. Broadway hit letters
74. Meadow mama

DOWN

1. Skater Henie
2. Automaker's son
3. "___ of a Clown"
4. Like a campfire
5. Rich soil
6. The ultimate
7. "Want to come up to my place for a ___?"
8. "God's Little ___"
9. Goldilocks surpriser
10. Space
11. Hole-punch tool
12. Match, in poker
20. Fiddlesticks!
22. They cross columns
23. Yo-yo or Slinky
27. Steer clear of
28. Peggy Lee hit
29. Plait
31. Pond scum
32. "Psycho" costar
33. Feudal lord
34. Swashbuckling Flynn
35. Sanctuary
36. ___ by the rules
37. Puts in the mail
41. Lesson planners

Leave It to Beaver

Solution on Page 333

1	2	3	■	4	5	6	■	7	8	9	■	10	11	12
13			■	14			■	15			■	16		
17			■	18			■	19			20			
21			22				23					■	■	■
24				■	■	25			■	■	26	27	28	29
■	■	■	30	31	32				33	34				
35	36	37				■	■	38						
39			■	40		41	■	42			■	43		
44			45				■	■	46		47			
48							49	50				■	■	■
51				■	■	52			■	■	53	54	55	56
■	■	■	57	58	59				60	61				
62	63	64					■	65			■	66		
67			■	68			■	69			■	70		
71			■	72			■	73			■	74		

45. Church's 10%
47. Flim-____ man
49. Cry
50. De-airs, as dough
54. White table wine
55. One related by marriage
56. ____ of the Union
58. Arm bone
59. Dollop
60. Bing Crosby bestseller
61. "So, what have you been ____?"
62. Emotional place?
63. Make a request
64. Where beside a crossword to find gnus

ACROSS

1. Type of shark
5. Major league
12. ___ that special?
13. Endless
14. Home on the range, variantly
15. Carbon dating concern?
16. Nonrepeat performance
18. Li'l piggies
19. Slurp silently
20. Fool!
23. Number 5's need
25. Bridge expert
28. Harry Potter's Quidditch role
30. Vito Corleone portrayer
33. "Last week on . . ." featurette
35. Multiple roles for Sally Field
36. Comment to Dolly
38. "What happened next?"
39. Flying pest
43. Says it's so
45. Comment to a li'l darling?
48. "Who's on First," e.g.
49. African stork
50. Kind of wave
51. Mosey
52. MIT grad, often

DOWN

1. Division to multiply
2. Silly
3. Something to sneeze at
4. Lex Luthor abettor
5. Michael Jackson hit
6. Hairy cousin
7. Golly!
8. Jogging gait
9. Data
10. Created
11. Benevolent brothers
15. Bar
17. State-of-the-art
21. Sphere
22. Trunks
24. Luau lute
26. Now I ___ me down to sleep . . .
27. "C of Love" actress?
29. Comedienne Charlotte
31. Making an impression?
32. Senior
34. Dental concern
37. D-Day craft
39. Places for reps
40. Couples' cruise manager
41. Special glow
42. Trolley car
44. Brutus's being
46. Recede
47. CD mailer

A Couple of Letters

Solution on Page 333

1	2	3	4			5	6	7	8	9	10	11
12						13						
14					15							
16				17					18			
19				20			21	22				
23			24			25			26	27		
28					29		30				31	32
		33				34		35				
				36			37			38		
39	40	41	42			43			44			
45				46	47				48			
49									50			
51									52			

ACROSS

1. Pizzazz
6. Slot insertions
10. ___ the hogs
14. Trunk need
15. Depressed
16. "Music Man" setting
17. Bar fixture
18. "Candid Camera" star
20. They hire narcs
22. Author Harte
23. The IRS, hopefully
28. "Time Machine" author
32. Smart one?
33. Corrida cry
34. Make beloved
35. Hauled
37. Concur
39. Tango quorum
40. Requires
42. Fidel's pal
45. Comes together
46. Shadowboxes
51. Race car
53. 4 o'clock drink
55. Ratio words
56. Old Peruvian
57. Simon's partner
59. Ike's ex
61. "___ Jazz Singer"
62. Mouseketeer of film
67. 180
71. ___ I didn't know!
72. Inheritor
73. Hoarse cries
74. Depend
75. Culp/Cosby show
76. Scent

DOWN

1. CIA forerunner
2. Select
3. March man
4. Veggie dept.
5. 1,000 ship launcher
6. Not-yet-scheduled abbr.
7. 100%
8. Garden plantings
9. Psychic
10. Prepped flour
11. Baseballer Gehrig
12. Possess
13. Tricky Dick's wife
19. Recency
21. Hubbub
23. Polonius, audibly, to Hamlet
24. "Don't Bring Me Down" rock gp.
25. Not many
26. Lift one's spirits
27. Boat event
29. Permit
30. There oughta be a ___
31. Packed-in-like-sardines abbr.
34. Slippery fish
36. Evil
38. Choir stand
41. Actor Beatty or Pro pitcher Garver
42. Greek X
43. Dearie

Ain't We Got Fun?

Solution on Page 334

44. Yadda-yadda
47. George Brett's bat substance
48. Request
49. 66, e.g.
50. La preceder
52. Enact
54. Astern
57. Storms
58. Sulu shipmate
60. Radar's drink
62. Distant
63. Take advantage of
64. Nothing
65. Golf cup edge
66. Jazz kid
68. Troop troupe
69. 33, 45, or 78
70. Hush-hush org.

ACROSS

1. Hope/Crosby destination
5. Stick in a meat thermometer
9. Feature record part
14. Once ___ a time
15. Actress Turner
16. A social one
17. Civil rights heroine
19. Actress Hayward
20. "Casey at the ___"
21. Stringy candy
23. One more time
26. Psychic
27. Uno y uno
28. Like Hammett's falcon
30. Dire
33. A long time ___ . . .
34. Stereo attachment to keep the room quiet
37. "Honeymooners" actress
42. Like some flights
43. Kept out of sight
45. Imaginary
48. Go down
51. Mapplethorpe funder
52. Part of 51 Across
55. The mating game
56. Enterprise for Enterprise
59. Chinese path
60. Gardening tool
61. "Blazing Saddles" director
66. Get another base
67. Foots the bills
68. "M*A*S*H" star
69. Sculptor's product, often
70. Procedure part
71. The ___ of the earth

DOWN

1. Natural sticker
2. Mil. address
3. Angeles lead-in
4. Soon
5. Window shutter part
6. ___ and feather
7. It gets wet when you wade
8. Musical count
9. In addition
10. Sweet and ___ pork
11. Not outdoors
12. Church official
13. Author Hemingway
18. Part to look through
22. It's more than a battle
23. Koop gp.
24. Head over heels
25. Baseball brother
26. Ciao!
29. It finishes
31. Roulette bet
32. '60s Pontiac model
35. Presidential daughter in the '70s
36. Mr. who went to town
38. AES beater, twice
39. New Deal org.
40. Carnival ride cry
41. There are seven deadly ones

Natural Settings

Solution on Page 334

1	2	3	4	■	5	6	7	8	■	9	10	11	12	13
14				■	15				■	16				
17				18					■	19				
■	■	■	20			■	21		22					
23	24	25			■	26				■	■	27		
28					29		■	■	30	31	32			
33			■	■	34		35	36				■	■	■
■	37		38	39								40	41	■
■	■	■	42							■	■	43		44
45	46	47				■	■	48		49	50			
51			■	■	52	53	54		■	55				
56			57	58				■	59			■	■	■
60					■	61		62				63	64	65
66					■	67				■	68			
69					■	70				■	71			

44. Tooth pro's deg.
45. Civil ___ (riot)
46. Must
47. The Lone ___ (Silver's rider)
49. Surgery mark
50. Elect
53. Highway ons or offs
54. Halloween option
57. 4 o'clock events
58. He sang about Alice
59. Cook's qty.
62. Drain cleaner
63. Hold the deed to
64. Billy the ___
65. They cross rds.

ACROSS

1. Dieter's concern
6. Vamoose
11. Auction action
14. Return
15. Isle with Edam
16. Jonny Quest role
17. Boat girl?
19. Emer.
20. Some Scandinavians
21. Large rock
23. Break up
26. Meadowsweets
28. Singer/singer
30. Angle
31. Bog
32. Negative
34. Head
35. Cygnus star
37. Chatty bird
39. Li'l piggies
41. Venus's sister
43. NASDAQ deb
46. Marble, maybe
48. Fast watch
50. Most mean
52. Villainous grimaces
53. Service at four
54. Rose oil
56. Jr.'s jr.
57. Place for functions?
62. Dropped item
63. A little of this, a little of that
64. Ballerina bar
65. 911 people
66. Li'l brats
67. 'til now

DOWN

1. Surfer's domain
2. Collection
3. Hairy cousin
4. Deem proper
5. Casey Jones, e.g.
6. Hewed
7. Like some wires
8. Bananas Foster need
9. Counters
10. Chalets
11. Actress's telegram?
12. Skua's live there
13. Hates
18. Naiads' kin
22. Slot car wood
23. Weird Al movie
24. Born
25. Bikini help?
27. Ready to go
29. Sleeps it off
33. Rummy kin
36. Colorado park
38. Popular wax
39. Type of sensation
40. Belief in Shrek?
42. Ack-ack
44. Mini-golf goal
45. HQ
47. Chooses

Just Add Water

Solution on Page 334

1	2	3	4	5	■	6	7	8	9	10	■	11	12	13
14					■	15					■	16		
17					18						■	19		
■	■	■	20					■	21		22			
23	24	25				■	26	27						
28						29			■	30				
31			■	32					33	■	34			
■	■	35	36				■	37		38			■	■
39	40			■	41		42				■	43	44	45
46				47	■	48					49			
50					51			■	52					
53						■	54	55				■	■	■
56			■	57		58						59	60	61
62			■	63					■	64				
65			■	66					■	67				

49. Latin lands
51. Actor Hawke
55. She's guarded, at the movies
58. GI address
59. Jazzy kid
60. It lacks refinement
61. Made, like a deadline

ACROSS

1. Ad abuser
8. Just do it
11. Blueblood's concern
12. Some salmon
14. Hackneyed
16. ___ get you for that
17. Fish/fowl joiner
18. Take into custody
19. Brosnan role
21. Italia seaport
23. Colorful fish
25. ___ weevil
26. Karamazov creator
30. Midrange run
31. Beak part
32. Hebrew prophet
34. In attendance
39. Picked item
40. Cheerleader cry
42. Old German coin
43. Model train set piece
46. Straphangers' lack
47. Slip-on shoes
48. Unwet
49. Missile type

DOWN

1. Salt victims
2. Wine grape
3. + end
4. Actress Oberon
5. One-piece swimsuit
6. Seder plate item
7. Bridle strap
8. Time Warner mergee
9. Warm wind
10. That was ___ awesome!
12. "Fame" singer
13. TV role with lots of personality
15. Willy Loman, e.g.
20. Eral
22. "Mystery!" airer
24. Boat vote?
26. In demand
27. Running wild
28. Flat foot?
29. Of the belly
30. Lightens or darkens
33. Performing ___
35. Israeli seaport
36. Charcoal wood
37. Girlfriend to Chaplin and Valentino
38. Gown
41. Fab Four film
44. Pigs digs
45. Derisive cry

Spanish Count

Solution on Page 334

1	2	3	4	5	6	7			8	9	10	
11								12				13
14							15					
16						17				18		
19					20		21		22			
				23		24			25			
	26	27	28					29				
30				31								
32				33			34		35	36	37	38
39				40		41		42				
43			44				45					
46						47						
	48					49						

ACROSS

1. Short run
5. All-thumbs sort
8. Fabric
11. Song syllables
13. Dodged
14. Zimbabwe's capital
16. Was more than bipolar
17. Parisian star
18. Sore subject?
19. Crystals hit of '63
21. Ctrl-___-Del
22. Thin spaces
23. ___ annum
24. Poetry event
26. Etiquette expert Baldrige
30. Top priority
35. Eviction
36. Telephone book eater
37. Jack Horner's last words
38. Eggs
41. Women's ___
42. Not quite random in layout
47. Collection
48. Cream of ___
49. Less klutzy
51. Sitcom about J.D. and Elliot Reid
52. "Concentration" puzzles
53. "Christian Year" author
54. Clapped items, once
55. Singer Snider
56. Dregs

DOWN

1. Ravage
2. Rink leap
3. Walked
4. Offer?
5. Choral work
6. Duelist Burr
7. Penchant
8. Actress Bankhead
9. Yorkshire city
10. Taro root
11. Contract word
12. Alice's chronicler
15. Darktime
16. It's beyond one's control
20. Write-in section
25. Charlie's downfall
26. "Summer Girls" band
27. Experian's old name
28. Golden Calf worshipers
29. Nonchalance
31. Escapable
32. Regret
33. Buckeye State
34. Imprison
38. Less normal
39. SAT part
40. Enliven
42. Half qts.
43. Santa's bag
44. Screwed up
45. Lab item, not online videos
46. Steak order
50. Gotcha

Hidden Doors

Solution on Page 335

ACROSS

1. Assist
5. Inscribed pillar
10. It will live on in infamy
14. Milano money, once
15. Pulsate
16. Cunning
17. Trojan War fighter
18. Saharan stops
19. Armchair QB's channel
20. Ovine comedian
23. Granola-ish cereal
24. Land's End rival
27. Cupid's mo.
29. Ans.
30. ___ Beta Kappa
31. Recipe amt.
35. Ovine politician
38. Orally
40. Hide ___ hair
41. "Card, please"
42. Ovine cartoon
45. Porgy's love
46. NY time
47. Menagerie
48. Dip
50. Propped (up)
52. It'll test your chops
57. Ovine singer
61. Horror movie monster of '58
63. It's a long story
64. Horus's mom
65. Exact points
66. Silent film vamp
67. Nuh-uh
68. Eliot Ness, e.g.
69. "The Maids" playwright
70. German car

DOWN

1. It may be raised
2. Quaint trinket
3. Wipe out
4. One of two certainties
5. More poker-faced
6. Holier-___-thou
7. Celtic
8. "I Do" singer
9. Half a Faulkner title
10. Nerd
11. Infamy
12. Cleo's biter
13. Kobe cash
21. TV E.T.
22. Koran focus
25. Throat clearings
26. Frasier's bro
28. Alabaman knee-sitter
29. Peasants
31. Domesticates
32. Get red
33. Quietly
34. Place
36. Miny follower
37. Pen tip
39. Twelve
43. Auction action
44. Ad-libbed

I Love Ewe

Solution on Page 335

49. Open space
51. Batman's buddy
53. African charger
54. "The Fox and the Grapes" fable teller
55. Balderdash
56. Henry Ford's son
58. Seeking shelter
59. Sandwich man's garb
60. Tortoise rival
61. Deli order
62. He played Inspector Dreyfus

ACROSS

1. Hope/Crosby destination
5. Look out ___!
10. Chair
14. Arab title
15. Petite "SNL" comedienne
16. Pallid
17. Well-honed
19. Love expert
20. Grandmamas
21. Shoelace hole
23. Arrives
26. "Car 54" officer
27. Half of a WWII movie title
28. CNN newsman
31. Practice fights
32. Perfect Sleeper seller
33. "Less Than Perfect" actress
34. Go down
35. Goes for flies
36. Twain hero
37. Lit. is part of it
38. Use a debit card
39. "American Pie" star
40. Least trusting
42. Frat wannabe
43. Helpers
44. Illuminated
45. Smooth material
47. "Today Show" chimp
48. "Comprendo"
49. Golly!
54. Not sweet
55. Annoy
56. "___ la Douce"
57. 54 make a game, usually
58. Pretentious
59. Bird abode

DOWN

1. Lawyer's test
2. "I ___ Rock"
3. Fashion's Claiborne
4. Gate or sword, e.g.
5. Sarajevo's land
6. Actor Hawke
7. Meadows
8. Bobby the Bruin
9. Surfboard stinkers
10. Bikini brand
11. Daybreak
12. Vera's intro
13. Exam
18. Some files
22. Luke's teacher
23. German astronomer
24. Wolfish
25. Medium alarm
26. Rich cake
28. Vaulted
29. Stretchy rope
30. Picked up on
32. Holey cheese
35. Honeypie
36. Some drumheads
38. Party
39. Amish craft
41. Rosie's bits

That Smarts

Solution on Page 335

1	2	3	4		5	6	7	8	9		10	11	12	13
14					15						16			
17				18							19			
			20						21	22				
23	24	25						26						
27							28						29	30
31						32						33		
34					35						36			
37				38						39				
40			41						42					
		43						44						
45	46						47							
48					49	50						51	52	53
54					55						56			
57					58						59			

42. Southpaw's opposite
44. "Star Wars" maker
45. Corleone VIP
46. Jacob's twin
47. Newsman Lauer
50. Face stick-out
51. Palindrome preposition
52. 911 people
53. ___ King Cole

ACROSS

1. I've had it ___ here!
5. Like some seeds
9. Garbage hauler
13. Excuse ME!
14. Honshu hound
16. Spelling on TV
17. Drinking actor?
19. A distance
20. Does dock work
21. Cast
23. Sci-fi pioneer
26. Prize
27. Talks
28. One way to play
31. Ship post
32. Hull area
33. ___ carte
34. S-shaped molding
35. Small mesa
36. All over again
37. Screw up
38. Water holes
39. Peppy dance
40. Helicopter inventor
42. Search
43. Double curves
44. Colleague
45. Forever
47. Iraqi religion
48. Sari wearer
49. Drinking rocker?
54. ___ of Evil
55. Allay
56. ___ springs eternal
57. Heaved oh
58. French state
59. Hopper

DOWN

1. Car folk
2. ___ Beta Kappa
3. Bowling pin count
4. Eggy dish
5. Home helpers
6. Dust Bowl denizens
7. Toupees
8. To the ___ degree
9. Sculpture
10. Drinking politician?
11. Like some hygiene
12. Thin
15. Missing
18. Curly cabbages
22. Actress Sommer
23. Tramps
24. African charm
25. Drinking actor?
26. Battery units
28. One-A
29. Sworn thing
30. Twain's Tom
32. Masses
35. Is worthy of
36. Like some alibis
38. Songbird
39. ___ Doone
41. Mean and ugly

Choice of Beverage

Solution on Page 335

1	2	3	4	■	5	6	7	8	■	■	9	10	11	12
13				■	14				15	■	16			
17				18						■	19			
■	■	■	20					■	21	22				
23	24	25					■	26					■	■
27						■	28						29	30
31					■	32					■	33		
34				■	35					■	36			
37			■	38					■	39				
40			41					■	42					
■	■	43					■	44						
45	46					■	47					■	■	■
48				■	49	50						51	52	53
54				■	55					■	56			
57				■	■	58				■	59			

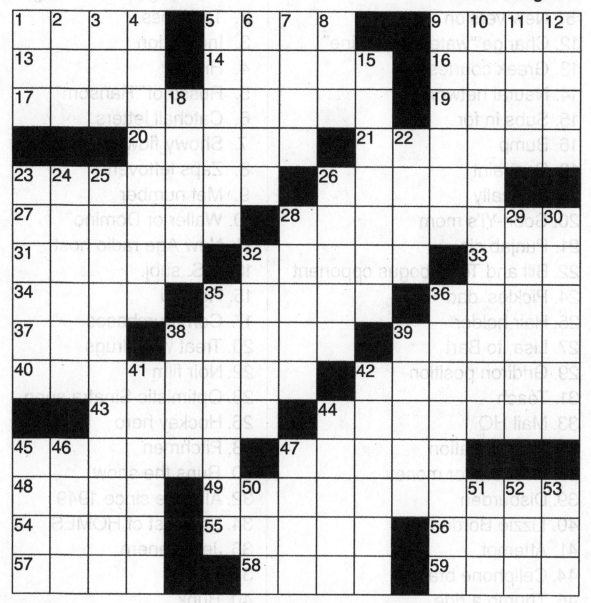

42. Plane type
44. Genuine
45. Time periods
46. Hirsch show
47. Stilelike piece
50. French isle
51. Glop
52. MPG raters
53. Code color

ACROSS

1. Bastes
5. New version
12. Change "water" into "wine"
13. Greek courtesans
14. Neural network
15. Subs in for
16. Bump
18. Restraint
19. Basically
20. Soon-Yi's mom
21. Punjab city
22. Bill and Ted's bogus opponent
24. Pickles' dad
25. Hair holder
27. Lisa, to Bart
29. Gridiron position
31. Teach
33. Mail HQ
35. Concentration
37. Redeem for money
39. Disburden
40. Lizzie Borden item
41. Attempt
44. Cellphone brand
45. Thumb a ride
47. Copycat
48. Possible pluck
49. Roz from "Frasier"
50. Coastal
51. Co. sued by Standard Oil

DOWN

1. Cliffhanger shows, e.g.
2. Toothless
3. Inquisition
4. Hi-fi
5. Russo of "Ransom"
6. Catchall letters
7. Showy flower
8. Zaps leftovers
9. Met number
10. Waller or Domino
11. New Age radio host
13. H.S. subj.
15. Reared
17. Corn purchases
20. Treat with drugs
22. Noir film
23. Optimistic Sinatra song
26. Hockey hero
28. Pitchmen
30. Runs the show
32. Alliance since 1949
34. Smallest of HOMES
36. Jew's enero
38. Brawl
40. Bunk
41. Therefore
42. Ready to pick
43. ___ girl!
44. Karaoke need
46. Brick holder

HH

Solution on Page 336

1	2	3	4	■	■	■	5	6	7	8	9	10	11
12				■	■	13							
14				■	15								
16				17				■	18				
19							■	20			■	■	■
21						■	22				23	■	■
24			■	25		26			■	27		28	■
■	29		30	■	31				32	■	33		34
■	■	35		36			■	37		38			
■	■	■	39			■	40						
41	42	43			■	44							
45					46				■	47			
48								■	■	49			
50							■	■	■	51			

ACROSS

1. Jack Horner's fruits
6. Iraqi port
11. RN's forte
14. Fable teller
15. Deplete
16. So there!
17. Beethoven work
20. Haphazard
21. Meter or liter
22. Be a snoop
25. ___ the line
26. Familiarize
28. In a bit
30. Framework
33. Evaluate
34. Endeavor
36. First airline to use a hub city with spokes
38. "You're My Greatest Love" was its theme song
43. Perfect
44. Strike this, for instance
45. Corn "tree"
48. Like some cars
50. Mrs. Peel who is needed
51. Rooftop rabbit ears
53. Get in one's sights
55. Elect
56. "Shall we?" response
57. Gets together
61. My sweetheart, in an old song
66. Poetic adverb
67. Act part
68. Prop or jet
69. "L.A. Law" actress
70. ___ Wences
71. Actor who wrote speeches for Nixon

DOWN

1. Actress Dawber
2. Hugmeister Buscaglia
3. Troop troupe
4. "Who's the Boss?" mom
5. Divorce
6. Taps player, often
7. 1975 Wimbledon champ
8. Kits
9. "In the Line of Fire" actress
10. GI addr.
11. Scottish lords
12. Lady of Spain
13. Like a yenta
18. Comic Coca
19. Pest
22. Alley cry
23. Portnoy's creator
24. Long ago
27. Boca ___
29. Anarchy
31. Pastoral poems
32. Clinton or Carter
35. Gimlet ingredient
37. None too quiet
39. ___ de Cologne
40. "Blondie" tyke
41. ___ roast

Moon Music

Solution on Page 336

42. Chair
45. Like some nuts
46. Little laugh
47. Vein opposite
49. Egg hunt time
52. Jouster's stick
54. Track events
58. Demeanor
59. ___ Domini
60. Porno
62. Biblical beast
63. It lacks refinement
64. Sash
65. Persona ___ gratis

ACROSS

1. Salon job
5. "___ Miniver"
8. Pouffy-hatted one
12. "Be it ___ so humble . . ."
13. Koala's home
14. Shore find
15. Pup or circus follower
16. Command to Fido
17. Like Silent Cal
18. "Able was I ___ I saw Elba"
19. Vendor
21. Dr. Ruth's subject
22. Crystal ball user
24. Sports judge
26. Played the first card
28. Call-in show employee
33. Judge
36. ___ Xing
38. Irritate
39. Lodge member
40. Postal Creed word
42. Hut preceder
43. Run in the wash
46. "Harper Valley PTA" actress
47. "Over here!"
48. "Piccolo Pete" bandleader who launched Perry Como's career
50. Stick in the ground
52. Big foot?
53. Split ___
56. Econ. yardstick
59. Bar giveaway
64. And so on
66. "Chico and the Man" actress
68. "___ Were Expendable"
69. Run away
70. Actress Burstyn
71. Hand over
72. First name in stunts
73. Happiness
74. Pinafore head
75. Sobbed

DOWN

1. "Our Gang" dog
2. Medgar of civil rights
3. Actress Zellweger
4. "A-Team" star
5. '60s TV horse
6. Walter ___ Hospital
7. Bear's advice
8. "Evita" role
9. Towel word
10. Or ___ what?
11. Bend
13. Common title start
14. "Out of Africa" star
19. Before, appearing before
20. Go astray
23. Shady tree
25. Fare
27. Tooth-driller's deg.
28. Kernels
29. Manitoba tribe
30. New Jersey NBA team
31. 12/24 and 12/31
32. "La Boheme" update
33. Paid one's ___ to society
34. Vogue rival
35. ___ out a living (got by)

Life of Es

Solution on Page 336

1	2	3	4	■	■	5	6	7	■	■	8	9	10	11
12				■	13				■	14				
15				■	16				■	17				
18			■	19					20		■	21		
■	22		23		■	■	■	■	24		25	■	■	■
■	■	■	26		27	■	28	29				30	31	32
33	34	35		■	36	37			■	38				
39			■	■	40				41	■	■	42		
43			44	45	■	46				■	47			
48					49			■	50	51		■	■	■
■	■	■	52			■	■	■	■	53		54	55	■
56	57	58	■	59		60	61	62	63		■	64		65
66			67		■	68				■	69			
70					■	71				■	72			
73				■	■	74			■	■	75			

37. Grade sch.
41. Explosive letters
44. She-sheep
45. Intensify
47. Sword beater
49. Poetic adverb
51. Electric fish
54. Probe
55. Like a ravine
56. Diver Louganis
57. Dickens's "Little ___"
58. Soccer great
60. Engrave
61. Those, there
62. British enders
63. Hurricane part
65. Highland Scot
67. Comprehend
69. Not many

ACROSS

1. Random ___ of kindness
5. Speak out against
9. Air apparent?
13. Belch
14. "Mutual of ___'s Wild Kingdom"
16. "And away ___!" (Gleason line)
17. Neither wins nor loses
19. Pound of poetry
20. Egg style
21. In awe
23. Hot tub chemical
24. Ninotchka portrayer
25. ___ takers?
26. Purse protective spray
27. Neither/___
30. "___ Yankees"
33. Skating figure
34. Likeable fellow?
35. GI's address, often
36. Typesetters and oarsmen work there
38. Heston's org.
39. Offensive time?
40. Truly stinks
41. Board, in "bed and board"
42. Bat wood
43. Bat paths
44. Bikini part
46. ___ up (clean one's plate)
48. Cleans
52. Rhododendron
54. Emulate Hamill
56. Jeff's partner
57. Shed some pounds
59. Bread spread
60. Where the sun doesn't reach
61. Without ice
62. Constellation constituents
63. Was in debt
64. Early Bond flick

DOWN

1. Monastery head
2. Bend
3. Skier's hazards
4. Athenian's foe
5. Penance unit
6. "Rag Mop" brothers
7. Bean or blue
8. Common title starter
9. Perspiration
10. Seating locale
11. Fairy-tale baddie, before "Shrek"
12. Spur on
15. Chaos theory?
18. Quick-witted
22. Sport events
24. Odometers, etc.
26. ___ it for all it's worth
28. Gumbo veggie
29. Actual
30. Info
31. Boulle planet dwellers
32. Like a holey jacket
33. Vote in
36. Prep Parmesan
37. Cable TV replaced them

End Count

Solution on Page 336

1	2	3	4	■	5	6	7	8	■	■	9	10	11	12
13				■	14				15	■	16			
17				18						■	19			
20								■	21	22				
23						■	■	24					■	■
■	■	■	25			■	26				■	27	28	29
30	31	32		■	■	33					■	34		
35			■	36	37						■	38		
39			■	40					■	■	41			
42			■	43				■	44	45		■	■	■
■	■	46	47				■	■	48			49	50	51
52	53					■	54	55						
56				■	57	58								
59				■	60					■	61			
62				■	■	63				■	64			

41. ". . . giant leap for ___"
44. Used a still
45. Stand up
47. Some saxes
49. Less unwise
50. Patriot Allen
51. Fight
52. Andy's radio pal
53. Bantu people
54. "___ Mommy Kissing Santa Claus"
55. Surrender
58. "I've got you now!"

ACROSS

1. Bikini item
6. Z3 maker
9. "Evita" narrator
12. Sound, but not safe
13. Jamie Foxx biopic
14. Embrace
15. It takes work to drop one
17. Some work
18. Dollar, from bits
19. Beachhead craft
20. UPC code, e.g.
23. March events?
25. Ones who Google
27. Bob Marley fan
30. Couples' cruise destination
31. "Trading Spaces" climax
32. Flat flattener
33. Medal trim
34. All ___ go!
36. It sells, they say
37. Rick's "Casablanca" love
39. Madras moolah
41. Feel remorse
42. Type of incense
46. Honest one
47. Mighty Joe Young, e.g.
48. Take a bow?
49. Therefore
50. Uh-huh
51. Noodles

DOWN

1. "It ___ to Be You"
2. Pricker
3. Tribute
4. Bento box item
5. Brown fruit
6. Prickers
7. Its symbol looks like wings in a ring
8. Flux capacitor shape
9. They have 32 pieces
10. Injured
11. Quiche needs
16. Begin
19. Get out!
20. Russian ruler
21. Kirlian photograph, e.g.
22. Sown-in-lawn
24. Uses the costume box
26. Norse Eros
28. London gallery
29. "Clockwork Orange" antihero
31. Frolics
33. Adapts for something else
35. Figure of speech
37. Bush "Axis of Evil" nation
38. Grease job
40. Sicilian spewer
42. His hour moved up in 2009
43. Part of TGIF
44. Camp aide
45. Mauna ___

Triple SSS

Solution on Page 337

1	2	3	4	5	■	6	7	8	■	9	10	11
12					■	13			■	14		
15					16				■	17		
■	■	■	18					■	19			
20	21	22	■	23				24			■	■
25			26				■	27			28	29
30						■	31					
32					■	33						
■	■	34			35				■	36		
37	38			■	39				40	■	■	■
41			■	42						43	44	45
46			■	47			■	48				
49			■	50			■	51				

ACROSS

1. Pols with pull
4. Trunk sealer
8. Trumpet accessory
12. Hole in the ground
13. Stanford rival
14. And others
15. One-spot
16. Like some gains
18. Ogre hue?
20. Pick up on
21. ___ Rica
24. Response to cafeteria mystery meat?
28. Giant wait
31. Pod person?
32. Pasture
33. Massive uprooting?
38. Spot of tea
39. Mathematician who sounds like an athlete
43. Sweet smell?
47. Toilet material
49. Waitress reward
50. "I think I goofed!"
51. Out of harm's way
52. Beatle love
53. Freight weight
54. Repair
55. Trapeze safety

DOWN

1. "Too rich for my blood!"
2. Cubbyhole
3. All-media king?
4. He'll keep his ears peeled
5. Cyrus song title word
6. Trudge
7. Incredible surname
8. Sky flash
9. Tool
10. Sailor
11. Freddy's street
17. Part of MIT
19. New York time
22. Links peg
23. Alias
25. ___ finance
26. ___-haw!
27. Animal pouch
28. And so on
29. Tulsa sch.
30. Kidney part
34. Times
35. Lessen
36. Spaced out
37. Litigate
40. Pretended
41. "Slate," e.g.
42. Plant again
44. Cowboy actor
45. School that made many presidents
46. Gaston's good
47. Place
48. Leered comment

Write In, You Say?

Solution on Page 337

1	2	3	■	4	5	6	7	■	8	9	10	11
12			■	13				■	14			
15			■	16				17				
18			19								■	■
20					■	■	■	21			22	23
■	■	■	24		25	26	27					
28	29	30	■	■	31			■	■	32		
33			34	35				36	37	■	■	■
38					■	■	■	39		40	41	42
■	■	43			44	45	46					
47	48								■	49		
50				■	51				■	52		
53				■	54				■	55		

ACROSS

1. Actor Sharif
5. Yippie Hoffman
10. Cruising
14. Artist Magritte
15. Move like a baby
16. Hatfields or McCoys
17. Topps bubble gum kid
19. It's on an ear to be nibbled
20. Roth ___
21. Eagle launcher
22. Agatha Christie heroine
24. Strategies
26. Boost
27. 21 Across affirmative
28. Rochester's love
31. Louisiana cuisine
34. Penny loafer stuffers
35. Doodle
36. Plunder
37. Halloween needs
38. Just eh
39. The loneliest number
40. Yummy
41. "My Bonnie Lies over the ___"
42. Mensa types
44. Swine ___
45. Peeve
46. Monkee whose mom made Liquid Paper
50. Make wet
52. Hay block
53. ___ is me!
54. Office shape
55. Three-time Super Bowl MVP
58. Actress Moreno
59. "Sleeper" star/director
60. Like some books
61. Pale
62. Enjoys a book
63. Burghoff of "M*A*S*H"

DOWN

1. Celestial path
2. Stiller's partner
3. "Waltzing Matilda" singer
4. ___ Speedwagon
5. Antiaircraft fire
6. Herb Alpert's Tijuana ___
7. California peninsula
8. ___ Jima
9. Silver and gold
10. Accumulate
11. Diner special that stains
12. ___ Fatha Hines
13. Diarist Frank
18. It has many layers
23. Rock of ___
25. Like a tug-of-war rope
26. Tall and thin
28. Jokes
29. Civil rights leader Parks
30. James Bond's school
31. Pipe problem
32. Topnotch
33. Pro footballer of pantyhose ads
34. Jones or Stengel
37. Pickler's container

A Cup of Joe

Solution on Page 337

1	2	3	4	■	5	6	7	8	9	■	10	11	12	13
14				■	15					■	16			
17				18						■	19			
20			■	21				■	22	23				
24			25				■	26					■	■
■	■	■	27			■	28						29	30
31	32	33			■	34					■	35		
36				■	37					■	38			
39			■	40					■	41				
42		43					■	44				■	■	■
■	■	45					■	46				47	48	49
50	51					■	52				■	53		
54				■	55	56					57			
58				■	59					■	60			
61				■	62					■	63			

38. Lowlife
40. “I can name that ___ in two notes”
41. Workmate of Kent and Lane
43. Live, in sports
44. More than petty criminals
46. Labeled
47. Tabloid movie title start
48. Printer need
49. Giddy
50. The first Mrs. Copperfield
51. Enterprise rival
52. First name in early horror films
56. Bullfight cry
57. Yank

ACROSS

1. Cone of silence?
9. Female GI
12. Popular movie series
13. Driller's org.
14. Late-night host
16. Craggy hill
17. Angler's hope
18. Palindromic preposition
19. Texas A&M player
22. Polonius's place
24. Bears the cost of
26. Burial sites
27. Missionary Moon to China
28. Consignment transaction
29. Regions
30. Less tidy
31. ___ to you!
32. John who played Gomez
33. Weapon
34. Last words
36. Vid-game scripting language
37. Rita of song, e.g.
43. Web addr.
44. Unique one
45. Wednesday dot
46. Calls a spade a heart

DOWN

1. One way to the Net
2. Sport ___
3. Rebel Turner
4. PC screen type
5. Flock female
6. Union follower
7. Warring parties
8. Jr.'s test
9. Big pipe
10. Cute
11. Huggy type
15. Least slovenly
19. TV spinoff of '83
20. Suggested
21. Gus of NASA
23. Martini partner
24. Star of 19 Down's predecessor
25. Precedes
28. Those on break
30. Tropical drink
35. Mound
38. "What EEZ it man?" pooch
39. CEO's deg., often
40. Goal
41. Fury
42. 13 Across member

Terminology

Solution on Page 337

1	2	3	4	5	6	7	8	■	■	9	10	11
12								■	■	13		
14								15	■	16		
■	■	■	■	■	17				■	18		
■	■	19	20	21			■	22	23			
24	25						■	26				
27						■	28					
29					■	30						
31					■	32					■	■
33			■	34	35			■	■	■	■	■
36			■	37				38	39	40	41	42
43			■	■	44							
45			■	■	46							

ACROSS

1. Journey to Mecca
5. Hit show that switched networks
9. S.F. hill
12. Twistable cookie
13. Sigh!
14. Bruins' #4
15. Balderdash
17. Court assembly?
18. Took a pew
19. Flashbulb giveaways
21. Went in a bit
22. What a good scout does
25. Atahualpa and others
28. One of the Three Tenors
30. Shed
32. Questionable critter
33. High praise
35. Dust devil dust, perhaps
36. Enjoys a French dip
37. Sicced
39. Like a pageant winner
41. The way
44. Paving material
46. Balderdash
48. "Grey's Anatomy" amnesiac
49. "Peter and the Wolf" duck
50. Eyesore of a fruit
51. Kind of talk or rally
52. One who drinks sake?
53. Scoundrel

DOWN

1. Bikers' wheels
2. Met piece
3. It precedes Chapter 11
4. Occupation
5. Acted like a spooked horse
6. Left out
7. Biopic words
8. A whiter shade of pale
9. Balderdash
10. "Sleeper" prop
11. '60s burner
16. Worked on a crossword?
20. The Wizard of Menlo Park
21. '60s dance
23. Protection (var.)
24. Bambi's mom and others
25. Rugrats
26. ___ contendere
27. Balderdash
29. Tune
31. Bare oneself
34. The ___ Dome Scandal
38. Prairie home
40. Each
41. Like a takeout order
42. Rights defenders
43. "Grapes of Wrath" extra
44. Dance type
45. Maria's lead-in
47. Mongrel

Balderdash

Solution on Page 338

1	2	3	4	■	5	6	7	8	■	9	10	11
12				■	13				■	14		
15				16					■	17		
18			■	19					20		■	■
■	■	■	21					■	22		23	24
25	26	27			■	28		29				
30					31	■	32					
33						34	■	35				
36				■	37		38			■	■	■
■	■	39		40					■	41	42	43
44	45		■	46					47			
48			■	49				■	50			
51			■	52				■	53			

ACROSS

1. "Little" snack maker
7. They went from L.A. to St. Louis
11. Go from L.A. to St. Louis, e.g.
12. '80s airline merger
14. Showy stuff
15. ". . . Oz" actor
17. Memory traces
18. Pay for
19. Quaked
20. Archeological site
21. Retention concern
24. Actor Baldwin
25. Rocky foe, then friend
30. Big Red guy
31. Flub
32. With feeling
33. LAX letters
34. Disencumber
35. His bio was called "At the Center of the Storm"
37. Tag sale condition
39. Gave a thumbs-down review
40. Hamlet or Prometheus
43. "Casablanca" star
47. Racing
48. Root veggie
50. "Says you!", say
51. Without words
52. Eco verb
53. Emcees, e.g.
54. WWII gun
55. Part of Robitussin-DM

DOWN

1. Wild Aussie dog
2. Chinese appetizer
3. Thespian wish
4. Beer scum
5. Disease ending
6. Big foot?
7. Clinton T-man
8. United
9. Asian peninsula
10. Railyard workers
11. Ho Chi ___
13. Do a demo
14. ___ Paul
16. One who used to be called a "regular"
18. Film category
20. "All's Well That Ends Well" count
22. Fleshy fruit
23. Cesta, e.g.
25. Aquarium need
26. Title role (with "The") for Patrick McGoohan
27. Commands
28. Smooth
29. Obstacle
36. TV's Lou Grant
38. Hit the trail
41. In and of itself
42. Like Cheerios
44. Emcee's chatter
45. Goose eggs
46. Mole, e.g.

I'm a Believer

Solution on Page 338

■	■	1	2	3	4	5	6	■	7	8	9	10	■	■
■	11							■	12				13	■
14								■	15					16
17							■	18						
19					■	■	20							
■	■	■	21		22	23			■	■	24			
25	26	27							28	29	■	30		
31			■	32							■	33		
34			■	35							36			
37			38	■	■	39						■	■	■
40				41	42			■	■	43		44	45	46
47							■	48	49					
50						■	51							
■	52					■	53							■
■	■	54				■	55						■	■

48. Sherlock Holmes prop
49. Daniel mourned him on "Ugly Betty"
51. Lay down the lawn

ACROSS

1. Iroquois Indian
5. Banned pesticide
8. Reach
14. Baking ___
15. Chit
16. Daydream design
17. Senor Wences phrase
19. Salesman
20. Daring words
21. AP rival
23. Finale
24. WWII craft
26. Where to rest your butt
29. Senor Wences phrase
34. Naked
35. Spanish sun
36. Put it another way
39. Rod and reel woe
41. Lip
43. Killed, biblically
45. Shimmer
47. Common tower
49. Throw into the pot
50. Curly comment
53. Actress Holm
56. Rue Morgue murderer
57. An ex of Frank
58. In the past
60. Like some llamas
65. Playful pet
68. Curly comment
70. Hire
71. That girl
72. For votes
73. Pool people
74. Spots
75. "I'll ___ ya—last one there is a rotten egg!"

DOWN

1. Exxon, abroad
2. Crowd sound
3. Python person
4. Royal guy
5. Journals
6. Play-___
7. Bishop Desmond
8. Ickes or Meese
9. ___ the line
10. Homework unit?
11. Slide rule or abacus
12. Actress Massey
13. Like a geek
18. The Emerald ___
22. Launch ___
25. Thunder god
27. Farm tools
28. Dewey's defeater
29. Eye network
30. "Metropolis" director
31. ___-B (dental co.)
32. Peaceful
33. 2000 news name
37. Walkman maker
38. "___, Brute?"
40. Wise rival
42. Author Angelou

Two Bits

Solution on Page 338

1	2	3	4	■	5	6	7	■	8	9	10	11	12	13
14				■	15			■	16					
17				18				■	19					
20						■	21	22		■	■	23		
■	■	■	■	24		25	■	26		27	28			
29	30	31	32				33					■	■	■
34				■	35			■	36			37	38	■
39				40	■	41		42	■	43				44
■	45				46	■	47		48	■	49			
■	■	■	50			51				52				
53	54	55					■	56			■	■	■	■
57			■	■	58		59	■	60		61	62	63	64
65			66	67		■	68	69						
70						■	71			■	72			
73						■	74			■	75			

44. Cry from atop a chair
46. Changes genetically
48. Tot tenders
51. Cask kin
52. Planet byline
53. Bistros
54. Spectacular
55. Giant
59. Work watchdog
61. Pet
62. Irish singer
63. Actor Guinness
64. AMEX rival
66. Vied for office
67. Alter ___
69. Brit. ref. books

ACROSS

1. Like some windows
6. Demand
12. Anoint, once
13. Must
14. One with mouth wide open
15. False rumors
17. Hockey game start, perhaps
19. Nabokov heroine
20. Expand
21. Saxy musician
24. Darth Vader, as a kid
25. Went, like Kirk
27. A shot can prevent it
29. Sirs of Spain
30. Jewel
33. Man about the house
35. Put at ease
38. Mud bath spot
39. Garbage spots
40. Like some drums
44. Icicle sites
45. Ink spewers
46. Obliterate
47. ___ scholar
48. Chills

DOWN

1. Gong site
2. Aleve alternative
3. Katmandu sort
4. Dorsey's "Maria ___"
5. Pied Piper verb
6. Native Peruvian
7. PBS benefactor
8. Dodd or D'Amato (abbr.)
9. Rhoda's mom
10. Enisle
11. Hot rum drink
16. Droop
18. Borrower
21. Dorothy's home
22. Rod Hull's bird
23. Former Genesis competitor
26. Jug handle
27. Bus. card no.
28. Acapulco-Miami dir.
29. Rice or potato
30. Tropical fruits
31. Author Hemingway
32. Pigpens
33. "Be prepared" gp.
34. Agreeable to
36. See-through
37. Frighten
39. Black cuckoos
41. O.J. judge
42. Food fish
43. One way to go

Can-Do

Solution on Page 338

<table>
<tr><td>1</td><td>2</td><td>3</td><td>4</td><td>5</td><td>■</td><td>6</td><td>7</td><td>8</td><td>9</td><td>10</td><td>11</td><td>■</td></tr>
<tr><td>12</td><td></td><td></td><td></td><td></td><td>■</td><td>13</td><td></td><td></td><td></td><td></td><td></td><td>■</td></tr>
<tr><td>14</td><td></td><td></td><td></td><td></td><td>■</td><td>15</td><td></td><td></td><td></td><td></td><td></td><td>16</td></tr>
<tr><td>17</td><td></td><td></td><td></td><td></td><td>18</td><td></td><td>■</td><td>■</td><td>■</td><td>19</td><td></td><td></td></tr>
<tr><td>20</td><td></td><td></td><td></td><td></td><td></td><td>■</td><td>21</td><td>22</td><td>23</td><td></td><td></td><td></td></tr>
<tr><td>24</td><td></td><td></td><td>■</td><td>■</td><td>25</td><td>26</td><td></td><td></td><td></td><td></td><td>■</td><td>■</td></tr>
<tr><td>■</td><td>■</td><td>■</td><td>27</td><td>28</td><td></td><td></td><td></td><td></td><td></td><td>■</td><td>■</td><td>■</td></tr>
<tr><td>■</td><td>■</td><td>29</td><td></td><td></td><td></td><td></td><td></td><td>■</td><td>■</td><td>30</td><td>31</td><td>32</td></tr>
<tr><td>33</td><td>34</td><td></td><td></td><td></td><td></td><td>■</td><td>35</td><td>36</td><td>37</td><td></td><td></td><td></td></tr>
<tr><td>38</td><td></td><td></td><td>■</td><td>■</td><td>■</td><td>39</td><td></td><td></td><td></td><td></td><td></td><td></td></tr>
<tr><td>40</td><td></td><td></td><td>41</td><td>42</td><td>43</td><td></td><td>■</td><td>44</td><td></td><td></td><td></td><td></td></tr>
<tr><td>■</td><td>45</td><td></td><td></td><td></td><td></td><td></td><td>■</td><td>46</td><td></td><td></td><td></td><td></td></tr>
<tr><td>■</td><td>47</td><td></td><td></td><td></td><td></td><td></td><td>■</td><td>48</td><td></td><td></td><td></td><td></td></tr>
</table>

ACROSS

1. Gambling letters
4. Least fresh
11. P-town neighbor
13. Possible pub order
14. Aromatic oil
15. Shade provider
16. Hairy sci-fi guy
18. Old cheer
19. He played Mr. Chekov
20. Bigger than a breadbox, say
21. Pool tester
23. Raja's wife
24. Hairy title movie role
27. Modern memo
29. Guy's honey
30. Univ. mil.
31. Noodle choices
36. French friend
37. Hairy TV role
40. Coastal perennial
42. Remove a suit
43. Peace pact
44. Wonderful
45. Some sound systems
46. Double curve

DOWN

1. Dental brand
2. Pupil
3. Strength
4. According to ___
5. Soft stone
6. Singer Gluck
7. Permit
8. Mother's temptation to a baby
9. Vulgarity
10. Little laugh
11. Zigzag at sea
12. Like satellites
17. Entranced
20. ___ Paolo
22. Humpty Dumpty, e.g.
23. "Divided Self" author
24. Fill
25. Sot's squawk
26. Runs at the mouth
27. Wipes out
28. Instant
32. Sleep soundly?
33. Bathroom floor, perhaps
34. U.S. rocket series
35. Don't change
37. French film
38. Atop
39. Luau lutes
41. Byword?

Hirsute

Solution on Page 339

■	1	2	3	■	■	4	5	6	7	8	9	10
11				12	■	13						
14					■	15						
16					17				■	18		
19						■	■	■	20			
■	■	■	■	21		22	■	23				
■	■	24	25				26				■	■
27	28				■	29			■	■	■	■
30				■	■	■	31		32	33	34	35
36			■	37	38	39						
40			41				■	42				
43							■	44				
45							■	■	46			■

ACROSS

1. Waste maker
6. Smart one?
10. Wicked
14. Laud
15. Fibber
16. Singer Simone
17. "M*A*S*H" specialty
20. Gloom
21. Rouses
22. Makeshift bed
25. Comic Sothern
26. Got in one's sights
31. Got up
34. ___ and every
37. Astonishedly
38. Can fans
40. Woody's ex
41. Movie genre
44. Haul
45. Pulls
46. ___ on a true story
47. A Great Lake
49. Biggest continent
50. Strict
51. Snatch
53. Recipe amt.
55. Lennon classic
59. Quartz and feldspar
64. Financing options
68. Actress Falco
69. Bun's spot
70. Perfect
71. Pekoe and oolong
72. Wojo's gp.
73. Wee

DOWN

1. Clothing line
2. Fired
3. Celebrity
4. Haul
5. Exile isle
6. Entire
7. Diamond ___
8. "___ on Down the Road"
9. Gist
10. V6 or V8
11. Tet celebrant
12. Concerning
13. Wise rival
18. Circle segment
19. Color TV pioneer
23. Church instruments
24. Handyman's set
26. ". . . and save us the ___ seats"
27. Acquire
28. Fine print, of sorts
29. She-sheep
30. Like a morning lawn
32. Tex-Mex dips
33. List ender
35. Mulled drink
36. Austrian composer
39. Weeps
42. Sheepish sound
43. Wrestling pad
48. "Where ___ Dare"

Keep Your Eye on the Ball

Solution on Page 339

1	2	3	4	5	■	6	7	8	9	■	10	11	12	13
14					■	15				■	16			
17					18					19				
■	20					■	■	21						
■	■	■	■	■	22	23	24	■	■	25			■	■
26	27	28	29	30	■	31		32	33	■	34		35	36
37					■	38				39	■	40		
41					42						43			
44			■	45					■	46				
47			48	■	49				■	50				
■	■	51		52	■	■	53		54	■	■	■	■	■
55	56				57	58	■	■	59	60	61	62	63	■
64							65	66						67
68				■	69				■	70				
71				■	72				■	73				

52. Life story
54. Snoop
55. Hedger's add-in
56. Created
57. High time?
58. The green monster
60. Leave out
61. Relinquish
62. Banjo place
63. Baseballer Musial
65. Cheerleader's need
66. "What happened next?"
67. Crafty

ACROSS

1. Angle
5. Mrs. Peel's successor
9. Latin "ditto"
13. Met number
14. Colorful computer
15. "Fame" actress
16. "Stupid Pet Tricks," say?
19. "___ It Romantic?"
20. They're catching
21. Tightening tool
23. Living loops
24. Deli purchase
25. Sets mood lighting
26. Rotating car parts
28. Bridges the gap
30. Ashtray filler
31. Tin Man's need
32. Or ___
33. Doctor office concern
34. Surface tension?
35. ___-jongg
36. Waits impatiently
37. Enjoyed
38. Routine places
40. Drum type
41. Declarations
42. "Blue's Clues" cry
43. Israeli government
44. Mouseketeer of note
48. Wash
49. Bait willing to make the sacrifice?
51. Saudi VIP
52. Auction cry
53. Smallest bit
54. They're shocking!
55. Ogled
56. Green mystic

DOWN

1. They come and go
2. "If ___ the Zoo"
3. Hindu deity
4. Recession sufferer
5. Euphrates neighbor
6. Collect
7. Aries, e.g.
8. Worsens
9. Hard-to-prove murder weapon
10. Showy haircut?
11. Lily Tomlin role
12. Newsman Lauer
17. Considers
18. All ___ Day
22. Wide keyboard keys
25. What Van Helsing did?
26. They might get blown
27. It has runners
28. Trucker's truck
29. Nice, e.g.
30. Kind of pass
33. Beseeched
34. Path through
36. Camera downloads
37. Antipsychiatrist
39. Choir stands
40. Locked out

Assistant D.A.

Solution on Page 339

1	2	3	4	■	5	6	7	8	■	■	9	10	11	12
13				■	14				■	■	15			
16				17				18		■	19			
20						■	21			22				
■	■	■	23			■	24							■
■	■	25			■	26								27
28	29			■	30					■	31			
32			■	33					■	34				
35		■	36					■	37					
38		39					■	40				■	■	■
■	41					■	42					■	■	■
43						■	44				45	46	47	
48				■	49	50								
51				■	■	52				■	53			
54				■	■	55				■	56			

42. Orono's state
43. Last name in surrealism
45. Purloined pooch
46. Walked upon
47. Peel that's needed
50. Singer Orbison

ACROSS

1. Tusked ones
6. Letter opener
10. Each
14. Tie type
15. Lewd look
16. Canyon edges
17. Nose, like Durante's
19. Wad of Washingtons
20. Chinese "path"
21. "Anything ___"
22. Son, in "Sanford & Son"
24. What glaciers cause
26. Purple bloomer
27. ___ *Etats-Unis*
28. Seep
29. Tai ___ (martial art)
32. With natural gravy
35. Montezuma, e.g.
36. Attila fan
37. Reason to go to Plan B
38. Storylines
39. Tickled color
40. And so on
41. Pipe cleaner
42. Hard-to-get weed parts
43. Hunky-dory, at NASA
44. City not built in a day
45. Flat hat
46. Flamboyant sprinter of the '80s
48. Fort
52. Tight situation
54. First name of Eleanor Roosevelt and Patty Duke
55. Int'l carrier, once
56. What strongmen pump
57. Train's nose
60. Fail to win
61. G
62. Out in front
63. Elects
64. Single fish?
65. Ex-manager Bradshaw

DOWN

1. Moisten the bird
2. Academy Award
3. Explosive sound
4. Actor Glass of "Barney Miller"
5. Cheap cigars
6. Egg quantity
7. They might be inflated
8. Every
9. Becomes aware of
10. Scent
11. His nose shows his lies
12. Seer's sign
13. Hey, come here!
18. Animal houses?
23. Actor Guinness
25. Snail kin
26. Gambling game
28. Endangered layer
30. "The ___ for Red October"
31. They came in wells
32. Sailing
33. "Do ___ others . . ."
34. Nose nipper

The Nose Knows

Solution on Page 339

1	2	3	4	5	■	6	7	8	9	■	10	11	12	13
14					■	15				■	16			
17					18					■	19			
20			■	21				■	22	23				
24			25				■	26					■	■
■	■	■	27			■	28				■	29	30	31
32	33	34			■	35					■	36		
37				■	38					■	39			
40			■	41					■	42				
43			■	44				■	45			■	■	■
■	■	46	47				■	48				49	50	51
52	53					■	54				■	55		
56				■	57	58					59			
60				■	61				■	62				
63				■	64				■	65				

35. Enterprise rival
38. Things to work on
39. "___ and Circumstance"
41. Steep decline
42. Tommy gun sound
45. Salad fish
47. Bowling alleys
48. When expected
49. Turn the ___ cheek
50. Say "*$@#!"
51. Late to class
52. Missile or grain holder
53. Farm yield
54. GI gone
58. Taunting cry
59. Amigo of Fidel

ACROSS

1. Pump ratio
7. Lucasfilm, e.g.
10. Giant closer
13. Like Dorothy's slippers
14. Eureka!
15. Maria's intro
16. Voyeuristic Hitchcock film
18. All U.S. presidents so far
19. Stiff cilia
20. Water nymph
22. Crowd cries
25. Albanian currency
26. Tumbles
27. Knocks
29. Sorcery
31. Not pricy
33. Pulled up stakes
36. Dumpster diver
38. Big Three site
39. Word-for-word
41. Animal, vegetable, or mineral
42. RNA sugar
44. ___ sequitur
46. Stalemate
47. Greek market
48. Dickens's Drood
50. Winter woe
51. Hitchcock's first film, based on a du Maurier work
56. Cargo unit
57. Slot machine pull
58. Gentile gal
59. Bit of land
60. Crucial
61. For this reason

DOWN

1. Bruins' #4
2. Kind of ball or card
3. TV grid's "?"
4. Is broadcast
5. Banister post
6. Revised
7. Ore score
8. But (var.)
9. Underhype
10. Hitchcock's last film (a comedy!)
11. Concerning a colored spot
12. Fixes
17. Less clad
21. Flyboy
22. Gygax heavies
23. Li'l laugh
24. Hitchcock film in an asylum
26. Attack!
28. Rescuer
30. Open porch
32. Wheel man
34. Tiny case
35. Hamlet, e.g.
37. Gosh!
40. Near bottom
42. Rapids transits
43. Nanook's nook
45. Pigeonhole
48. Daytime TV award

Hitch

Solution on Page 340

1	2	3	4	5	6	■	7	8	9	■	10	11	12
13						■	14			■	15		
16						17				■	18		
■	■	■	19					■	20	21			
22	23	24	■	25			■	26					
27			28	■	29		30					■	■
31				32	■	33						34	35
36					37			■	38				
■	■	39						40	■	41			
42	43					■	44		45	■	46		
47					■	48				49	■	■	■
50			■	51	52						53	54	55
56			■	57			■	58					
59			■	60			■	61					

49. Neet rival
52. “You ___ There”
53. ETO commander
54. POTUS advisors
55. Turner who was revolting?

ACROSS

1. Singer Lane
5. Foreigner hit
11. Oahu Os
12. Protector of sorts
13. Beatle film
14. Daily grind
15. Stock deb
16. Word with in or lip
17. Bowling pin count
18. Post observer
20. Woman's word
21. One who'll give it a go
22. "I love" in Latin
24. Like one quartet
26. Dueler Burr
30. Comes together
33. They say it is a potent cup of tea
35. Mentalist Geller
36. Tie
37. Former orbiter
38. Like some grapefruit or slippers
40. Original mike-roving talk show host
41. Hoopla
42. Lake rumored to have Bessie
43. Race watch spot
44. Insurance claim

DOWN

1. "Java" player
2. Doctor's item
3. Blue Neil Simon site
4. Second sight
5. Idi Amin's country
6. U. mil. prog.
7. Needlefish
8. Make happy
9. Less mean
10. Prom crowd
14. Seeded or unseeded bread
16. Doris Day's "will be"
19. Judges
20. Frozen dew
23. Liq.-concerned gp.
25. Prickly shrubs
27. Joker portrayer
28. Isis's hubby
29. Jitteriness
30. Ones in the know
31. Gush
32. Astral balance
34. Completion
36. Thin nail
39. Not hither
40. Comic Brooks

RR Crossing

Solution on Page 340

1	2	3	4	■	■	5	6	7	8	9	10
11				■	■	12					
13				■	14						
15			■	16				■	17		
18			19				■	20			
21				■	22	23			■	■	■
■	■	■	24		25	■	26		27	28	29
30	31	32		■	33	34					
35			■	36				■	37		
38			39				■	40			
41						■	■	42			
43						■	■	44			

ACROSS

1. Motto
6. Gave in
11. 49 Across predecessor
14. "Nevermore" quother
15. Topnotch
16. The Plastic ___ Band
17. Pestered
18. Singer Sherman
19. Pest
20. Funny opening?
22. Notable period
23. Gobs and gobs
24. In vogue
25. Yeses
26. 49 Across's command
28. Deli hanger
32. Bus
35. Pirate song
38. Nay negater
39. One-spot
41. Rd.
42. I have you now!
43. For almost nothing
46. '73 resigner
48. Petrol units
49. See 26 Across
50. Shafts of light
52. "___ Fine Day"
54. Tubby prez
58. Crone
59. Bird crossed with a goat?
63. Famous NHLer
64. Desert eden
65. Gobbled with gusto
66. Female deer
67. Whole ___ bread
68. Path
69. ___ takers?
70. Rude
71. Paid up

DOWN

1. Slither
2. 2:1, e.g.
3. Occurrence
4. Salty site
5. Aware of
6. End
7. Oval
8. ___ pickle
9. And others
10. Turn away
11. Woo?
12. Trap
13. Greek garb
21. ___ am I?
25. Doc bloc
27. Land parcel
29. Senior gp.
30. D-Day lander
31. Up yonder
32. Dancer Charisse
33. Circle of life
34. Worry sign?
35. Psychic
36. Dropped title word
37. Ouch!

Y Me?

Solution on Page 340

40. "Evita" role
44. Third word of "America"
45. Egocentric
47. Begin
49. Reading spot
50. Sitcom with la lyrics
51. Composer Copland
53. Vicious
55. Native Alaskan
56. Tootled thing
57. Used keys
59. Pulls along
60. Hawaiian isle
61. Netizen
62. Silent screen vamp

ACROSS

1. Kobe companions
8. Sad news
14. Aircells
15. They're often silenced at movies
16. Catch more z's
17. Fathers
18. Dating event
20. Norse trickster
23. First name in architecture
24. Yup!
25. NASCAR figure, often
28. Warning or revelry sign
29. Powder or beer holder
30. This ship
33. Recipe amt.
34. Verizon purchase of 2006
37. Follow, as a tip
39. Local malt shop
42. "Titanic" dance
45. Alice's chronicler
46. Sky bear
47. Baggage
50. Dude ranch divider
51. Emphatic comment
55. Plaza pest
56. Resurrect a computer
57. Costner film title start
58. Where to keep your arms

DOWN

1. It might be pumped
2. Building afterthought
3. "___ Got a Secret"
4. More squalid
5. Mesa dweller
6. Put in a row
7. Preacher's target
8. Say yes
9. Caviar source
10. Blowhard's fill
11. Regarding
12. Parisian's thanks
13. Slalom turns
19. "CHiPs" star Estrada
20. Artist's space
21. Wise birds
22. Sack opening
26. Hero Williams
27. My word!
30. Avoid lumps
31. Start appetizers?
32. New Age singer
35. Baby spots
36. Concerning
38. With good reason
39. Priest
40. City near Binghamton
41. Rent payer
42. Turned to bits
43. It dropped the bomb
44. Renamed field
48. Tear down
49. Monstrous loch?
52. ___ sequitur
53. Simple ___
54. Bus. card abbr.

Nerd Alert

Solution on Page 340

1	2	3	4	5	6	7	■	8	9	10	11	12	13
14							■	15					
16							■	17					
■	■	■	18				19						
20	21	22		■	23				■	24			
25			26						27		■	■	■
28					■	■	29			■	30	31	32
33			■	34	35	36	■	■	37	38			
■	■	■	39				40	41					
42	43	44		■	45				■	46			
47				48					49		■	■	■
50						■	51				52	53	54
55						■	56						
57						■	58						

ACROSS

1. Silk center
6. Subway hold
11. Party line
12. Aussie girl
13. I've had it up to here!
15. Lean toward
16. Certain cadet
18. It may contain an MO
20. Cel mate?
21. Rake in
23. "Ooh, you make me so mad!" guy
28. Alice's chronicler
29. Unagi fishes
30. Corrida scene
35. Answers, in "Jeopardy!"
36. "Orinoco Flow" singer
37. Hive head
38. Economic stat
44. Drink name meaning "good"
45. Enjoys
48. Speedy Gonzales's cry
49. Gemstone
50. ". . . and ___ a good night"
51. Peeve

DOWN

1. "Alrighty then" guy
2. III, to II
3. Go from bad to worse
4. Big chill
5. GQ and O
6. Reduce in the wash
7. Idol or angel
8. Split
9. Toward shelter
10. Incredible family surname
12. The Tick's mighty cry
14. URL letters
17. Mushy dish
18. Swift steed
19. Llama land
22. D.C. denizen
24. Pro vote
25. He had a Band of Renown
26. Actress Sommer
27. Latin being
31. Old drugstore chain
32. Concave body part
33. Big Apple sch.
34. Molls might have long ones
38. ___ my wit's end!
39. iPod ___
40. ___ double take
41. Yada yada
42. It's south of San Diego
43. Balanced
46. ___ Speedwagon
47. Cunning

Fingered

Solution on Page 341

1	2	3	4	5	■	■	■	6	7	8	9	10
11					■	■	12					
13					14	■	15					
■	■	16				17						
18	19		■	■	20				■	■	■	■
21			22	■	23				24	25	26	27
28				■	■	■	■	■	29			
30				31	32	33	34	■	35			
■	■	■	■	36				■	■	37		
38	39	40	41					42	43		■	■
44						■	45				46	47
48						■	■	49				
50					■	■	■	51				

ACROSS

1. Coll. entrance exam
5. The Little Mermaid
10. Belt or window part
14. Freedom fighters: abbr.
15. Infernal writer?
16. Alliance since '49
17. Another TV role for the original Clarabell
20. Thespian group
21. Spyglass user
22. It's just a stage
25. Monopoly fees
26. Artistic judgment
30. Like sails or some elections
33. Actress Massey
34. Region
35. Drink like a cat
38. Cagney/Keeler flick of '33
42. "Ain't We Got ___?"
43. Takes to court
44. "On the Waterfront" director
45. Prep leftovers
47. Things
48. Born-again's adjective
51. Coed's lodging
53. Refrain sounds
56. Ridiculous
61. "White Christmas" lead actress
64. Cleric's closer
65. Take another base
66. Penalty
67. Verb tense
68. Statesman Kissinger
69. Western actor

DOWN

1. Covenant
2. Feature shared by Harriet Tubman, Harrison Ford, and Harry Potter
3. Kal-Kan rival
4. 1984 Peace Prize recipient
5. Farewell
6. Sought office
7. It's black or red in finance
8. List catchall
9. Carson's successor
10. Used a plumber's tool
11. He finished with 755 homers
12. Portly
13. Owl calls
18. Mass or sex follower
19. "Earth in the Balance" author
23. Czech capital
24. Dimwit
26. Spat
27. Baseball brother
28. In a bit
29. Explosive letters
31. Reaches
32. Space
35. Loll
36. Actor Arkin
37. Animal holders
39. Comic Kabibble
40. With hands on hips
41. Cagney's dirty addressee

OO!

Solution on Page 341

1	2	3	4	■	5	6	7	8	9	■	10	11	12	13
14				■	15					■	16			
17				18						19				
20						■	■	21						
■	■	■	■	22		23	24	■	■	25				
26	27	28	29		■	30		31	32			■	■	■
33					■	34				■	■	35	36	37
38					39					40	41			
42			■	■	43				■	44				
■	■	■	45	46					■	47				
48	49	50			■	■	51		52		■	■	■	■
53					54	55	■	■	56		57	58	59	60
61							62	63						
64				■	65					■	66			
67				■	68					■	69			

45. Let up
46. Dutch cheese
48. Rein or watchband
49. Scent
50. Flower holders
52. Make a comeback
54. Eye hair
55. Comic Johnson
57. Couch
58. Army group
59. Philosopher Descartes
60. Makes Easter eggs
62. Nikkei currency
63. You put things in its trunk

ACROSS

1. Spheres
5. Arturo's agreement
9. It's just a ___ he's going through
14. O'Hara home
15. Crackerjacks
16. Telecast
17. Computer image
18. Seasonal change symbol
20. Homestead hunters
22. Keep
23. Waste maker
24. Window section
25. Perspiring
27. Lack of faith
31. Sounds the alarm
32. ___ and regs
33. Postal creed word
34. Gumbo veggie
35. Lendable singer?
36. Undesirable spots
37. New Deal org.
38. James Dean flick
39. Gyrating dances
40. Gateway
42. Spuds
43. Revise text
44. Barber's tool
45. Nervous
48. Beatle hit
51. Miner's strike
53. Latin love
54. "This ___ a drill!"
55. Phone button letters
56. Hull haulers
57. "___ Entertainment!"
58. Worthless one
59. Standard Oil sued them to change their name

DOWN

1. Mayberry sot
2. "The Great ___" (with Lemmon as Professor Fate)
3. College film with Reagan, Eddie Albert, and Wayne Morris
4. Seat of Orange County
5. ___ first!
6. Concerned words
7. Stage decor
8. Kyser's Kabibble
9. Moms and dads
10. No-___ (perfectly pitched game)
11. Opera solo
12. Big rig
13. "East of ___"
19. It's clapped at school
21. D-Day crafts
24. Aviator
25. Took an oath
26. Get up
27. She was nominated 5 times for Best Actress
28. Fictional storyteller
29. Sub's sense
30. Braid

It's All Relative

Solution on Page 341

1	2	3	4	■	5	6	7	8	■	9	10	11	12	13
14				■	15				■	16				
17				■	18				19					
20				21				■	22					
■	■	23					■	24				■	■	■
25	26					■	27					28	29	30
31					■	32					■	33		
34				■	35					■	36			
37			■	38					■	39				
40			41					■	42					
■	■	■	43				■	44					■	■
45	46	47				■	48						49	50
51						52				■	53			
54					■	55				■	56			
57					■	58				■	59			

32. Do a double take
35. Less big
36. Computerize
38. Gizmos
39. Fog
41. Cinnamon-flavored candy
42. ___ puzzle (stumper to untie or separate)
44. Cowboy contest
45. Leave out
46. Munch
47. Italian volcano
48. Easy gait
49. Footsies
50. Approximately
52. Sever

ACROSS

1. TDs and TKOs
6. Lackluster
10. Items in a pod
14. Take by force
15. Hard to find
16. Concerning
17. Romanian Comaneci
18. Actress Samms
19. Legend
20. "Seventh Seal" character
22. Trash bag maker
23. Flat hat
24. Helps to pay for
26. Cameos
31. Hank Aaron is still the career leader in this
32. Vocalist Adams
33. Like Felix Unger
35. Spin doctor's concern
39. Elvis song "___ Be Cruel"
40. Took notice
42. The biggest continent
43. Wood strips
45. Measly
46. Funny stuff
47. However
49. Trap that Indy would hate
51. "I" problem
55. ___ bono (free)
56. Barbra's "Funny Girl" costar
57. "Sing, Sing, Sing," "Just a Gigolo," and "When You're Smilin'" creator
63. H.H. Munro's pen name
64. Spree or songbird
65. ___ over (studied)
66. "Let ___ eat cake"
67. Periphery
68. WWII buy
69. Vic's radio wife
70. Hair colorers
71. ___ a hand (helps out)

DOWN

1. "Song ___ Blue"
2. Kremlin autocrat
3. Autobahn auto
4. Cut to size
5. Athens' rival
6. Olympics basketball group
7. Highway entrance/exit
8. ___ and dangerous
9. The ___ of bad news
10. Hadj, e.g.
11. ___ Gay
12. Matrix
13. They're sown
21. Takes home
25. G-man's group
26. Garden plots
27. Matinee ___
28. Pop singer Turner
29. Gangster's humble beginnings
30. Oversatisfies
34. Highways
36. Stat!

Rim Shots

Solution on Page 341

1	2	3	4	5	■	6	7	8	9	■	10	11	12	13
14					■	15				■	16			
17					■	18				■	19			
20					21					■	22			
■	■	■	■	23			■	24		25				
26	27	28	29				30	■	31			■	■	■
32				■	33			34	■	35		36	37	38
39				■	40				41	■	42			
43				44	■	45				■	46			
■	■	■	47		48	■	49			50				
51	52	53				54	■	55			■	■	■	■
56				■	57		58				59	60	61	62
63				■	64				■	65				
66				■	67				■	68				
69				■	70				■	71				

37. “Thank Heavens for Little Girls” musical
38. ___ India Company
41. Boscs and Bartletts
44. Told ya so!
48. Plowed
50. “Nightline” name
51. Expenses
52. Mutual of ___
53. Without clothes
54. Sycophant
58. Plead
59. Nightgown
60. Pressing need
61. Darn
62. Appends

ACROSS

1. Sousa genre
6. Nile nippers
10. Not all, not none
14. Blessing preceder, often
15. Ginger cookie, say
16. Ski lift part
17. Docile
18. She played Inga in "Young Frankenstein"
19. Gymnast Korbut
20. Comic Martin
21. Plumbing problems
23. Capes
25. Sonja of skating
26. Dawdled
29. Dawdle
30. Slow mover
31. Postpone
34. Buttons on the machine sides control them
40. Stout
41. Milton's Muse
42. Like a nervous heart
46. Like bootleg software
48. Rapidly
49. Kane's model
51. Aquarium needs
53. Adamant
57. Spewer in Sicily
58. Double curve
59. Seiko rival
60. Rug, or cut a rug, '30s-style
61. Jury member, they say
62. Some women
63. Use a keyboard
64. Screws up
65. Novel developments

DOWN

1. Marian, e.g.
2. Undesirable spots
3. Carla on "Cheers"
4. Bin
5. Dog or chocolate preceder
6. On top of
7. ___ preview
8. Where to get plastered?
9. Rotate
10. Like kisses or bases
11. Rectangle
12. Smith who played Miss Jean Brodie
13. Pencil end
21. "Meet John ___"
22. Birds
24. Dogpatch denizen
26. Recipe amt.
27. Darth Vader, as a kid
28. Sprinted
29. Luau loop
32. Gee preceder
33. Sticky sheets
35. Chicken request
36. Physical comedian's standard
37. Consume
38. "___ 66"
39. Grass section

Fancy Footwear

Solution on Page 342

42. Least cooked
43. Indifference
44. Siesta
45. When mammoths roamed
47. Tax agcy.
49. More big
50. Arab prince
52. Vatican VIP
54. Simile words
55. Civil uprising
56. Rolling stone's lack
59. Toy gun ammo

ACROSS

1. Gabor of "Green Acres"
4. Assists in a crime
9. Lewis with Lamb Chop
14. "Runaway" singer Shannon
15. Singer Iglesias
16. Adores
17. ___ Lanka
18. Burns' partner
19. Bumbling
20. Famous ventriloquist
23. Dryer collection
24. Epics
27. Jazzman Davis
32. Like some coalitions
34. Fitting
37. Martin's partner
39. Middle Easterner
41. One dummy for 20 Across
45. Become weary
46. Cereal scooper
47. Ginger ___
48. Is idle
51. Rock
53. Forest members
55. Factory watchdogs
59. Famous ventriloquist
64. Fake
68. Name in millennium news
69. Hill dweller
70. Military screwup
71. Check the sum
72. AT&T rival
73. Fable teller
74. ___ out (serves)
75. Part of MPG

DOWN

1. Failed Ford
2. Opera composer
3. Place evenly
4. Slightly open
5. Idea indicator
6. "Vogue" rival
7. Layer
8. They're sung
9. ". . . ___ and arrows of outrageous . . ."
10. Darlin'
11. ___ Maria
12. Not Dem. or Ind.
13. Follower's suffix
21. Money dispenser
22. ___ de Cologne
25. Discontinued apple spray
26. Sealy rival
28. Sick
29. Flower garland
30. She-sheep
31. Knuckleheads
33. Wonka's maker
34. Do something
35. Comic Silvers
36. Seer's cards
38. Highlander
40. Cheerio
42. Raise
43. Bill and ___

Ventriloquism

Solution on Page 342

1	2	3	■	4	5	6	7	8	■	9	10	11	12	13
14			■	15					■	16				
17			■	18					■	19				
20			21						22		■	■	■	■
23				■	■	■	■	24			25	26	■	■
■	■	■	27	28	29	30	31	■	32				33	■
34	35	36	■	37				38	■	■	39			40
41			42						43	44				
45				■	■	46					■	47		
■	48			49	50	■	51				52	■	■	■
■	■	53				54	■	■	■	■	55	56	57	58
■	■	■	■	59			60	61	62	63				
64	65	66	67		■	68					■	69		
70					■	71					■	72		
73					■	74					■	75		

44. Columnist Landers
49. Tell all
50. Notice
52. It's a long time
54. Another dummy for 20 Across
56. Rascal
57. Therefore
58. Moving
60. Butter substitute
61. Iranian currency
62. Walk through water
63. Means justifier?
64. "Be Prepared" gp.
65. The loneliest number
66. ___ guzzler
67. Flying saucer

ACROSS

1. Euro-replaced coin
6. 911 people
9. Sympathy's companion
12. Language that gave us "marimba"
13. Actor Kilmer
14. Safe cracker?
15. Village People hit
17. Gangsta ___
18. Chaps
19. Shop ___ you drop
20. Some switches
24. Down in the mouth?
26. Intros
28. Kind words
29. Power in Hollywood
30. Made it a White Christmas
33. Dimple
34. Equation symbol
35. Blue hue
38. Splitters
39. "Star Wars" role, with 42 Across
40. Make legal
42. See 39 Across
43. "School of Rock" actor
48. Erhard movement
49. Nocturnal one
50. Mideast peninsula
51. Sculling letter?
52. Comb user
53. Factory

DOWN

1. Mulder's employer
2. Kurosawa classic
3. Hill resident
4. Utmost
5. Like lights or actors
6. Dodges
7. Old pro
8. Woodstock singer
9. Car polish maker
10. Spam, perhaps
11. Register
16. Gentle prod
20. Elect
21. Word with pan or stir
22. A U.S. subcompact
23. "John B." of song
25. Love love LOVE
27. Training type
30. Dot
31. Louisville-Albany dir.
32. Deg. in calculus?
34. "Matrix" role
35. Johnny Appleseed, e.g.
36. Put to shame
37. Amazed
41. Recipe amt.
44. ___ Abner
45. Santa ___ winds
46. Kick the ___
47. ". . . old ___ bag and smile, smile, smile"

Bean There, Done That

Solution on Page 342

1	2	3	4	5	■	6	7	8	■	9	10	11
12					■	13			■	14		
15					16				■	17		
■	■	■	■	18					■	19		
20	21	22	23	■	24				25			
26				27			■	28			■	■
29						■	30				31	32
■	■	33			■	34						
35	36				37			■	38			
39			■	40				41	■	■	■	■
42			■	43					44	45	46	47
48			■	49			■	50				
51			■	52			■	53				

ACROSS

1. It Girl Bow
6. Fight
11. "I've ___ a Secret"
14. Head lights?
15. Main artery
16. Slugger's stat
17. Radiates
18. Witch city
19. Shocking fish
20. Robert Young sitcom
23. Sea plea
24. Melodies
25. Most senior
29. Increases personnel
32. Nick's tec partner
33. "Unsafe at Any Speed" author
34. ___ operative
37. Caesar/Coca TV series
41. Money dispenser: abbr.
42. Walrus standouts
43. One way to run
44. Quarries
45. Fraternal group
47. Shaw of jazz
50. Elect
51. Early anthology TV series
59. The loneliest number
60. Inelegant laugh
61. Hi or goodbye
62. Put to good ___
63. Kovacs of comedy
64. Fills to the gills
65. "___ Miserables"
66. Sidetrack
67. History paper, say

DOWN

1. Head cook
2. Monk
3. Touched down
4. ___ IRA
5. Size up
6. Wine barrels
7. Savings and ___
8. Woodstock name
9. Soup that's a meal
10. Guinea pig's kin
11. Inexperienced
12. Having lots to lose
13. Pinball no-nos
21. Go bad
22. Ralph Kramden's workplace
25. Irish new-ager
26. Bandit's take
27. Bongo or tom-tom
28. Lent body part
29. Pro war bunch
30. Wedding words
31. Sports judge
33. Meddlesome
34. "It's Impossible" singer
35. Champion's cry
36. Answers, in "Jeopardy!"
38. On edge
39. Color
40. Possesses
44. Bakery item

Classic TV

Solution on Page 342

1	2	3	4	5	■	6	7	8	9	10	■	11	12	13
14					■	15					■	16		
17					■	18					■	19		
20					21						22			
■	■	■	■	23			■	■	■	24				
25	26	27	28			■	29	30	31			■	■	■
32				■	■	33					■	34	35	36
37				38	39						40			
41			■	42					■	■	43			
■	■	■	44					■	45	46				
47	48	49			■	■	■	50			■	■	■	■
51					52	53	54				55	56	57	58
59			■	60					■	61				
62			■	63					■	64				
65			■	66					■	67				

45. Speed in the U.S.
46. Relax, ROTC
47. Run ___ of the law
48. Dentist's command
49. Skiing danger
50. Weaselly swimmer
52. Concerning
53. Parent's word
54. Part of HOMES
55. A word to Yorick
56. Rugrats
57. Carla's portrayer
58. "Five ___ Pieces"

ACROSS

1. Huck Finn's crafts
6. Shadowbox
10. Moon personified
14. Fool's month
15. Seek alternative
16. Type of hygiene
17. Whipped dessert
20. Female relative
21. Writer Asimov
22. Funny-nosed plane last flown on 11/26/03
23. Flightless birds
24. Toilet paper concern
25. Portends
27. ___ generis (unique)
28. Cocktail lounge
31. ___ of note
33. Well-read folks
35. Milkshake needs
39. eBay events
40. Scottish isle
41. To the ___ degree
42. Long time
43. Assists
46. Deli order
47. ___ ghanoush
48. TV initials for the seventh World Series game
51. D.C. subway
54. Sailboat
56. Like some hair
58. ___ cats and dogs
59. Implore
60. Senegal's capital
61. Trudge
62. Title
63. Anoint, once

DOWN

1. Dishwasher rollouts
2. Garden pest
3. Parliament spokespeople
4. Nervous twitches
5. Applied the brakes
6. Tec
7. Pockets
8. Arabian gulf
9. Sleep cycle
10. Terrible
11. Minor or Major constellation
12. Moon conqueror
13. Actor Guinness
18. Togo's capital
19. Slicker
24. It's less than a drive
26. Leave out
27. Half dozen
28. Swimming style
29. LL.D. holder
30. Yeast verb
31. Lendl of tennis
32. Without slack
33. Broadway's "___ Miserables"
34. File
36. Avoid calling attention
37. Ill-gotten gains
38. Actress Jillian

The Neapolitan

Solution on Page 343

1	2	3	4	5	■	6	7	8	9	■	10	11	12	13
14					■	15				■	16			
17					18					19				
20									■	21				
22			■	23				■	24			■	■	■
■	■	25	26				■	27			■	28	29	30
31	32			■	■	■	33				34			
35				36	37	38								
39								■	■	■	40			
41			■	42			■	43	44	45			■	■
■	■	■	46			■	47				■	48	49	50
51	52	53			■	54					55			
56					57									
58				■	59				■	60				
61				■	62				■	63				

43. Animosity
44. Auction site
45. Kappa follower
46. Mark animals
47. Scow
49. Trite
50. Agassi of tennis
51. Car dealer's initials
52. Yadda-yadda
53. Magi, e.g.
54. Canary's nose
55. King of comedy
57. Lou's partner

ACROSS

1. Store sign
5. Mete out
10. Earwax picker
14. Bun's spot
15. Bond portrayer
16. Chan's comment
17. Beatles song
19. Reqm't
20. Straddling
21. Ruffles have 'em
23. Gets another base
24. Zombie glass drink
26. Profit
27. Spheres
28. NBA stats
31. Markers
34. It takes a big bow
35. Squad or rally starter
36. Enterprise rival
37. "All That Jazz" guy
38. Simple
39. Chicken choice
40. High-class
41. Gert's villainous role
42. Not Dem. or Rep.
43. Hill's partner
44. Be under the weather
45. O'Neill comer
47. Slogans
51. Swiss
53. Dependable
54. Transfixed
55. Jack Frost, e.g.
58. "Of ___ I Sing"
59. Dealt with
60. Actress Olin
61. Flubs up
62. October gems
63. Swirl

DOWN

1. Jerked drinks
2. Pirate's cry
3. WWII gulf
4. Competitors
5. Between
6. Easy gait
7. Chop (off)
8. Smeltery input
9. Awful
10. Pressroom forum
11. Reagan role
12. Gotcha!
13. Spacecraft components
18. Gets one's goat
22. "___ Wonderful Life"
24. Wet
25. Came up
29. She played Mrs. Mr. Mom
30. Job detail, briefly
31. Melted watch painter
32. Tied
33. Popular array of stars
34. There you have it!
37. Lively Spanish dance
38. Repeated
40. Ancient garden

Zipper Closing

Solution on Page 343

1	2	3	4	■	5	6	7	8	9	■	10	11	12	13
14				■	15					■	16			
17				18						■	19			
20							■	■	21	22				
23						■	24	25					■	■
■	■	■	26			■	27				■	28	29	30
31	32	33			■	34					■	35		
36				■	37					■	38			
39			■	40					■	41				
42			■	43				■	44			■	■	■
■	■	45	46					■	47			48	49	50
51	52					■	■	53						
54				■	55	56	57							
58				■	59					■	60			
61				■	62					■	63			

41. Garlicky sauce
44. Edits
46. Quotes
48. Not live
49. Upright
50. Dogcatcher's catch
51. Comic Johnson
52. Bolger costar
53. Screening room item
56. Alley ___
57. Evian, for one

ACROSS

1. Drinks daintily
5. Farmer's place
9. Verne or Wells genre
14. Jacob's twin
15. Peter Gunn's girl
16. Reindeer or cleanser
17. O.K. shooter
18. Fountain treat
19. They're shown when training
20. Of this, I'm certain
23. Like a ghost
24. Moll's leg
25. Bill
28. Flower
32. See red
33. Dioxin-concerned gp.
36. "thirtysomething" actor
37. Make one's own
38. California crack
42. Uses a straw
43. List ender
44. I told ya so!
45. Fishing, perhaps
46. Surveillance verb
49. Uh-huh
50. "Mystery!" airer
51. Syrup source
55. One way to learn
60. Like a seance
62. "Be it ___ so humble . . ."
63. Sweet and ___ soup
64. Bat an eye
65. Ripped
66. Still the non-U.S. name for what we call Exxon
67. It's so loud you can hear a pin drop
68. It falls quietly
69. ___ Xing

DOWN

1. Has the look
2. Apple-observant Newton
3. Winterwear
4. Fab
5. Mock-up
6. Red-rind cheese
7. '53 Caron musical film
8. "Move it, already!"
9. "Move it, already!"
10. Moore's sidekick in British movies
11. Rash
12. User ___
13. "___ De-Lovely"
21. Flyboy's gift for his gal
22. Woolen cap
26. More than adequate
27. Midler or Davis
29. The good ___ days
30. Knight's title
31. Villain's look
32. Med. watchdog
33. English assignment
34. Hiatus
35. Like a totem pole
37. Burning

Goofy

Solution on Page 343

1	2	3	4	■	5	6	7	8	■	9	10	11	12	13
14				■	15				■	16				
17				■	18				■	19				
20				21					22				■	■
23					■	■	■	24			■	25	26	27
■	■	■	28		29	30	31			■	32			
33	34	35	■	36				■	■	37				
38			39					40	41					
42					■	■	43				■	44		
45				■	46	47					48	■	■	■
49			■	50			■	■	■	51		52	53	54
■	■	55	56				57	58	59					
60	61				■	62				■	63			
64					■	65				■	66			
67					■	68				■	69			

39. Alias
40. Chewed up
41. Used a pew
46. TKO gp.
47. Puddle-jumper destinations
48. Took apart, grammatically
50. Devoutness
52. Text
53. Bad apple
54. Mistake
56. Sushi need
57. Bard's place
58. Fiery fiddler
59. Fought, Old West–style
60. Century 21 rival
61. Sushi fish

ACROSS

1. Market wagon
5. "___ Here to Eternity"
9. Mistake
14. Baseball brother
15. Rack ___
16. Get out!
17. Cut closer
18. Chooses
19. Rims
20. Consider
23. Proofreader's ^
24. Command to Spot
25. Process flour
28. Lawrence's place
33. Siam visitor
37. God with a bow
39. Computer click-ons
40. Pre-employment routine
43. Net communication
44. "When You Wish Upon a ___"
45. Historical periods
46. Use for support
48. Hot tubs
50. Like some scientists
52. Unpretentious
57. Trip
63. Ancient Peruvian
64. Blame bearer
65. ⅓ of a WWII movie title
66. Beginning
67. BMW rival
68. "Rio Lobo" actor
69. Sculpture segment, often
70. According to ___
71. Blockades

DOWN

1. Prickly plants
2. Comedian Sherman
3. Castles
4. Student
5. Unsettled region
6. Transfixed
7. Chancellor Bismarck
8. Flattops
9. Type of blanket
10. Change over
11. Prego rival
12. Kiln
13. Musical break
21. CPA employer
22. Bush Sr. once headed it
26. To's and ___
27. Promotes
29. Pang
30. Afrikaner
31. Machu Picchu builder
32. Queries
33. First victim
34. Moniker
35. March Madness org.
36. Related
38. Rice Krispies sound
41. Attach
42. Theatrical
47. A Bobbsey twin
49. Note before la

You Can Bank on It

Solution on Page 343

1	2	3	4	■	5	6	7	8	■	9	10	11	12	13
14				■	15				■	16				
17				■	18				■	19				
20				21					22					
23						■	■	24			■	■	■	■
■	■	■	■	25		26	27	■	28		29	30	31	32
33	34	35	36	■	37			38	■	39				
40				41					42					
43					■	44				■	45			
46					47	■	48			49	■	■	■	■
■	■	■	■	50		51	■	■	52		53	54	55	56
57	58	59	60				61	62						
63					■	64				■	65			
66					■	67				■	68			
69					■	70				■	71			

51. Painter of ballerinas
53. Seen
54. ___ Gay
55. Vamoose
56. Tigers and Cubs
57. Inventory
58. Atop
59. Surgery reminder
60. Antony wanted them lent
61. Andy Warhol can type
62. Offered

ACROSS

1. Tells Spot to attack
5. Mata ___
9. Camden ___
14. Assessment, for short
15. Aware of
16. The same
17. Central points
18. Load cargo
19. Singing cowboy of film
20. The Chairman of the Board
23. Fork-taker Berra
24. Prior to, to poets
25. Brit. ref.
28. Rat Pack member
33. Clergy robe
36. Ralph Kramden's vehicle
37. Lost
38. Proceed
41. Type of bag
43. Hate
44. Laundry bubble
45. Paris when it sizzles
46. Rat Pack member
51. Double curve
52. It needs refinement
53. Lack of difficulty
56. First person to call them "Rat Pack," perhaps
61. Koran creator
64. List ender
65. The Golden ___
66. Casio rival
67. www.themecrossword.com, e.g.
68. Singer Redding
69. "Roots" author
70. Used a club and a stick
71. Untouchable head

DOWN

1. ___-esteem
2. Coast or tower start
3. Chocolate source
4. ". . . ___ and arrows of outrageous fortune . . ."
5. Serenade the villain
6. One opposed
7. Andy and Mickey
8. Toward the center
9. "Same Time, Next ___"
10. Sea color
11. Well-traveled sign
12. Patriotic org.
13. Cunning
21. Korean carmaker
22. Boston Harbor jetsam
25. Actor Davis
26. Toss out
27. Male duck
29. CEO, often
30. Kid's pie material
31. Alt. spelling
32. "___ beginning to look a lot like Christmas"
33. Held open
34. Pieces of one's mind
35. Thai coins
39. Santa's farm command?
40. Miscue

Rat Pack

Solution on Page 344

41. ___ Wiedersehen
42. Altar words
44. Lambikins
47. Bud's buddy
48. "You're under ___!"
49. "Crying Game" actor
50. Polyester fabric
54. Recipe verb
55. Pianist Marsalis
56. Ladd costar in "This Gun for Hire" and "The Blue Dahlia"
57. Howdy, sailor
58. Archibald of the NBA
59. Ran in the wash
60. Minus
61. Cinder
62. Meadow
63. Diamond ___

ACROSS

1. ___ one's heels
6. Buffalo Bill ___
10. Smooch
14. Jazz player Shaw
15. Fluffy hairstyle
16. Taken ___ custody
17. "Ain't Misbehavin'" artist
19. March Madness org.
20. Ran away together
21. Give an answer in "Jeopardy!"
22. Schmutz
23. Haley hit
25. Ladies men
26. Hotel door posting
30. Boll ___
32. Awakening
35. Pension puller
39. Steep item
40. Make public
41. Lampoons
43. Moms and dads
44. Barnum "attraction"
46. "Broadway Danny ___"
47. Investigation
50. Accumulate
53. Thomas accuser
54. Winter woe
55. It's fate
60. "M*A*S*H" star
61. He led his Five Pennies
63. Hide and ___
64. Jason's ship
65. Type of bear
66. Bronte heroine
67. Computer person
68. Mortgage burner

DOWN

1. ___ au lait
2. Like some exams or medicines
3. Statesman von Bismarck
4. Thay thpeech like thith
5. Ed Norton's workplace
6. Terse President
7. Recently
8. Bedroom item
9. Title role for Cooper
10. Wah-wah originator
11. Bring upon oneself
12. Ben E. King's "___ by Me"
13. Stays in the tub
18. Shakespeare's problem
24. Night bird
25. Soda unit
26. Charlie Brown curse
27. Locality
28. Suits me ___
29. "I'm Just Wild About Harry" composer
31. Miles of "Psycho"
33. Beetle Bailey boss
34. Time, notably
36. Divorce city
37. Swallows
38. What ___ is new?
42. Primer coats, often
43. Bicentennial Minute, e.g.

All That Jazz

Solution on Page 344

45. Crossword erasure, often
47. Process part
48. “The Life of ___”
49. More mature
51. Do cross-country
52. Perv
54. ___ Blucher (“Young Frankenstein” role)
56. Display
57. Haunted house sound
58. 5 rival
59. Peter or Ivan
62. Hide ___ hair

ACROSS

1. Tirades
6. WWII turning point
10. In ___ (stuck)
14. Comment to the audience
15. Bank collection
16. Minstrel's strings
17. "To Market" comment
19. Hemsley series
20. Pluses
21. Uncle Sam's country
22. Ball-throwing game
23. Dizzying designs
25. Jumps around, like a record
26. ___ California
30. Like Poirot
32. Delinquent
35. Have lunch, say
36. Mandible
39. Clay beat him in '64
40. "Absence of ___"
42. Orthodontist's deg.
43. Banned pesticide
45. Obtains by reasoning
46. Overeat
49. Nuisance
50. Toy soldier
52. CD preceder
55. Spoken
56. Pie ___ mode
57. Bamboo eaters
62. Domesticated
63. "Ulysses" author
65. Comic actor Roscoe ___
66. Skin soother
67. Met event
68. Mrs. Dick Tracy
69. Uncommon
70. Bowler's button

DOWN

1. Indian prince
2. Used item sale sign
3. Stints
4. Advantage
5. Take care of
6. Alcohol-free
7. According to law
8. One of a biblical dozen
9. Exercise discipline
10. "Northern Exposure" locale
11. Jazz classic
12. Enjoyed
13. Darns
18. Recipe amt.
24. Actor Vigoda
25. Indian instrument
26. Daring
27. Excited
28. Outlaw played by Roy Rogers
29. Actor Carney
31. Chess or charades
33. Elude
34. Word processor button
37. "___ High"
38. Greeley's direction
41. Rim
44. Refrain sounds

J.J.

Solution on Page 344

1	2	3	4	5	■	6	7	8	9	■	10	11	12	13
14					■	15				■	16			
17					18					■	19			
20						■	21			■	22			
■	■	■	■	23		24			■	25				
26	27	28	29	■	■	30			31				■	■
32				33	34		■	35			■	36	37	38
39						■	■	■	40		41			
42			■	43		44	■	45						
■	■	46	47				48		■	■	49			
50	51				■	52			53	54	■	■	■	■
55				■	56			■	57		58	59	60	61
62				■	63			64						
65				■	66				■	67				
68				■	69				■	70				

45. Society gal
47. ___ than (at least)
48. Allure
50. Hinted
51. Angry
53. FedEx rival
54. Army rank
56. Not quite closed
58. Uh-uh
59. Colorers
60. Realty amount
61. Chair
64. Wide width

ACROSS

1. Brainstormer's cry
4. Race car loops
8. Anticipates
14. Patriotic org.
15. The Buckeye State
16. Monster, affectionately
17. Volleyball path
18. Sailing
19. Huey, Dewey or Louie
20. Take an action with finality
23. "Don't take that ___ with me, young man"
24. Jimmy Carter's daughter
25. "2001" computer
28. Talk a blue streak
30. Throw into the pot
32. Horserace chasee
33. Whoops!
35. "Moonstruck" actor
37. Princeton prez who signed the Declaration of Independence
42. Know-it-all
43. Lendl of tennis
44. Dud
45. Quote
47. Forumwear
52. Nourished
53. Orr's org.
54. Mr. Disney
55. Bobby Darin hit
60. Holy city?
63. Columbo or Cohan
64. Heston's gp.
65. Soon
66. Workmate
67. Cry at a mouse
68. Airport city in New Jersey
69. Like two ___ in a pod
70. Orthodontist's letters

DOWN

1. Gets used to
2. The Blonde Bombshell
3. Like runes
4. Bread or meat block
5. Facetious "I see"
6. It's on the waterfront
7. Drench
8. Jerry Stiller's partner
9. Like a tearjerker
10. Cleo's biter
11. ___ Kabibble
12. Fancy restaurant requirement
13. Darn
21. "___, though I walk . . ."
22. Dine
25. Ring above the collar
26. Alice's chronicler
27. Fighter Spinks
29. Audience lines
30. Farm or army member
31. Like seven Nolan Ryan games
32. ___ cat
34. Profiled director
36. Ain't behaving well
37. Actor Goldblum
38. Leer
39. The engine's under it
40. Tuck's partner

Setting Pieces

Solution on Page 344

41. Actress Arden
46. Kind
48. "A League of Their___"
49. Acquired
50. First name of 34 Down
51. Carnivore's orders
53. Presidential candidate of 2000 and 2004
55. Arizona city
56. Golf hazard
57. Golf goal
58. Scatter Fitzgerald
59. Janitor's heavyweight
60. Can metal
61. The loneliest number
62. Long-armed thing

ACROSS

1. Gloom
6. Actor Ray
10. Immediately!
14. "The ___ has landed"
15. Chick's comment
16. Otello, for one
17. Classic big band song
20. African desert
21. It clangs
22. Hatfields or McCoys
25. Commercials
27. Consumed
28. Muggy
30. Immediately, ensign!
32. Small feat wrap-up
36. Be less introverted
38. Baseball brother
40. Siesta
41. Classic big band song
44. Close
45. Biblical brother
46. "The Phantom Empire" or "The Rocketeer"
47. Activist Parks
49. According to ___ (as planned)
51. Scorch
52. Common article
54. Tapped fluid
56. Roscoe of old flicks
57. Join a sit-in, say
61. The ___ of the wild
63. Classic big band song
68. Noted nights
69. And so on
70. "The ___ Professor"
71. "I'm No Angel" actress
72. Desert mount
73. When prompted

DOWN

1. Social newbie
2. Title role's middle name for Sally Field
3. Quiche base
4. Arranging
5. Clinton's Attorney General
6. Plant pests
7. Civil War figure
8. Credit card balance
9. Lily Tomlin's Ernestine and others
10. Good-luck charm
11. Dirt
12. Welk start
13. The hunted
18. "TV Guide" blank
19. "I've ___ a Gal in Kalamazoo"
22. Snug adornment
23. "High Sierra" actress
24. They're made in apology
26. Heavy art pieces
29. Bamboozle
31. Pub pint
33. Sprinkle with oil
34. Injure
35. Bobbing for ___
37. Like Regan in "The Exorcist"

Classic Big Band Songs

Solution on Page 345

39. 1,001 ___!
42. Seance sound
43. Test drive
48. Swear
50. Witch's laugh
53. Fat Albert's opening word
55. Chum
57. "That was close!"
58. Bush aide
59. Till filler
60. Dancer's duds
62. Carson's replacer
64. Half a dance?
65. Like some stocks: abbr.
66. Actor Erwin
67. CBS symbol

ACROSS

1. Like Tuesday?
4. 11/11/18 ender
7. Agita
12. Doc bloc
13. Long time
14. In a way
15. Turner channel
17. Bottleneck
18. Like a takeout order
19. "On Language" writer
21. Sot's seat
23. NATO mem.
24. Simple signatures
27. Quiz show guy Charles Van ___
29. Chandler's dukedom
30. Charles de ___
33. Agita
35. Neck part
36. Not noir
38. D.C. influence gp.
39. Opie's aunt
40. Fawned over
44. Take into the station
47. Casino city
48. Love love LOVE
50. College admissions concern
52. His touch was deadly
53. Night before
54. Basis of a Steve Martin song
55. Gorilla garbage
56. Place for quiet, sometimes
57. That's not fair!

DOWN

1. Real data
2. "Are so!" preceder
3. Two-person dance
4. Li'l
5. Amazes
6. Crazy
7. Moving
8. "DOA" genre
9. Coll. test
10. Beatle Sutcliffe
11. Sapsucker?
16. Ziti or penne
20. "Ulee's Gold" star
22. Netizen's guffaw
25. Time period
26. Clever
28. What conformists don't do
29. Accompany
30. Econ. fig.
31. Common tower
32. It's scanned in stores
34. Not Dem. or Rep.
37. Rents
39. "God ___ America"
41. Gear parts
42. Follow
43. Eccentric
45. Like dental hygiene
46. All-night party
48. Roadie gear
49. It's cast
51. Asian party time

Say It Again

Solution on Page 345

1	2	3	■	4	5	6	■	7	8	9	10	11
12			■	13			■	14				
15			16				■	17				
18				■	19		20				■	■
21				22	■	23			■	24	25	26
■	■	■	27		28			■	29			
30	31	32				■	33	34				
35				■	36	37				■	■	■
38			■	39			■	40		41	42	43
■	■	44	45				46	■	47			
48	49				■	50		51				
52					■	53			■	54		
55					■	56			■	57		

ACROSS

1. Gullet
4. Winglike
8. Puts on rushedly
12. Yale bulldog
13. Descartes who was
14. Sub in a tub
15. Frequent
16. Sinatra standard
18. Baby bawl
19. Shining
20. Loose cannon
22. Flight from justice
25. Hi, Bligh!
27. Inciters
29. Lead source
32. Undercover operations
33. Fireman's faucet
35. Torme's milieau
36. Jawboned biblical animal
37. Stain
40. Filled pastry
41. Towel word
44. Diner
47. The loneliest number
48. Festival
49. Fed
50. Soccer mom's vehicle, for short
51. Uh-huh
52. Rational
53. "Twilight Zone" guy

DOWN

1. Cat call
2. Romeo lead-in
3. Keeps back
4. Nirvana reacher
5. "GWTW" actress
6. Trig concern
7. Readies leftovers
8. Misfortune
9. Peak
10. Bonnet buzzer
11. HELP!
17. Was fed up
21. ___ and terminer
22. Noon to one, often
23. Pond scum
24. Fog
25. Turkish VIP
26. "Airplane!" actor
28. "Little ___ Sunshine"
30. "Of course!"
31. Counterparts
34. Big shock
38. Passover month
39. Actress Pappas
40. Teletubby greeting
42. Fascinated by
43. Future plant
44. "What the?"
45. Hatchet
46. Renewal site

All Wet

Solution on Page 345

1	2	3	■	4	5	6	7	■	8	9	10	11
12			■	13				■	14			
15			■	16				17				
18			■	19						■	■	■
■	■	20	21						■	22	23	24
25	26			■	■	27			28			
29				30	31	■	32					
33						34	■	■	35			
36			■	37			38	39			■	■
■	■	■	40						■	41	42	43
44	45	46							■	47		
48				■	49				■	50		
51				■	52				■	53		

ACROSS

1. Actress Verdon
5. It's in them thar hills
9. Trouper
14. On vacation
15. The Buckeye State
16. Curly-haired non-talking funny guy
17. Like a sage
18. Part of SRO
19. Pig places
20. Oscar role for Ginger Rogers
23. Prohibitions
24. Blubber uncontrollably
25. Friends by mail
27. Gotcha!
30. Trumpet mute effect
32. "Me and My ___"
33. Nightfall
35. "The ___ Vanishes"
37. A dark one has a silver lining
41. Tops near Xmastime
43. Amaze
45. Pool table stone
46. Luau dance
48. Beef-rating gp.
49. Cook's qty.
51. Salon job
53. Stocking stuffer
54. Howdy Doody intro
57. Map makers
59. Peter Schickele's P.D.Q.
60. Singer of "Moonshadow" and "Peace Train"
65. Ready to pour
67. Defense gp.
68. Rash treatment
69. Puts away
70. Cliff projection
71. Anteing words
72. Folgers rival
73. Erupter of 1669 and 2002, among others
74. "The ___ of the Rings"

DOWN

1. Stare stupidly
2. 40 Down turned it
3. Opposite of Greeley's direction
4. Russian refusals
5. Doofus
6. "___, not again!"
7. Hopper's spot
8. Holmes' creator
9. Oohs and ___
10. Title role for Jane Fonda
11. "12 Angry Men" event
12. Unseals
13. Seamstress Betsy
21. "That smarts!"
22. Chang's twin
26. Warsaw ___
27. Inserts
28. Toss
29. Sailing
31. Launder
34. Historic flight site
36. University or lock company
38. Evict
39. Put back the way it was

Feline Foibles

Solution on Page 345

1	2	3	4	■	5	6	7	8	■	9	10	11	12	13
14				■	15				■	16				
17				■	18				■	19				
20				21					22	■	23			
■	■	■	24			■	25			26				■
27	28	29	■	30		31		■	32			■	■	■
33			34	■	35			36	■	37		38	39	40
41				42			■	43	44					
45					■	46	47			■	48			
■	■	■	49		50	■	51			52	■	53		
■	54	55				56		■	57		58	■	■	■
59				■	60			61				62	63	64
65				66	■	67				■	68			
69					■	70				■	71			
72					■	73				■	74			

40. 6/6/1944
42. Hepburn/Tracy film "___Set"
44. Jean Harlow's last film
47. Brash newbie
50. Film
52. West of Brooklyn
54. Jolly sack man
55. ___ impulse (go by whim)
56. Cut a rug
58. Be of use
59. Foreman
61. Ollie's pal
62. Sailor's saint
63. "The Big Clock" film style
64. Transmit
66. Free ad

ACROSS

1. Opera site
8. Way to fire
14. Was one's peer
15. Sung-about river
16. "For entrées, I'll have the ___"
18. Sushi suck-down
19. Agreements
20. *Ad ___ per aspera* (Kansas motto)
22. Push a boat
25. . . . and the beef with ___ . . .
31. League member in a Holmes tale
32. Climber clamp
33. Steve's singing partner
34. Alaskan native
36. . . . and an appetizer of ___ . . .
39. "Better Off ___"
40. Alex Haley miniseries
41. Great one?
43. Throws in
47. . . . and a cup of ___
52. High point
53. Circuit City, now
54. Brown ermines
55. Like sardines

DOWN

1. Tirana bucks
2. Sea color
3. At Davy Jones's locker
4. "Adaptation" star
5. Matterhorn, e.g.
6. Thompson of "Back to the Future"
7. Taken in
8. Trash barrel
9. Podcast network
10. GI Janes
11. Sign
12. "Do the Right Thing" director
13. Author Deighton
17. "Fame" actress
20. "Coming to America" prince
21. Start-up assn.
22. Expense
23. Flip ___
24. Lets
25. "Scent of a Woman" director
26. WWII island fight site
27. Combined
28. Fad "pet"
29. Revolves
30. "Say it ___ so, Joe"
34. Like some sloths
35. Raffle ticket
37. Wears down
38. Kids connect them
41. The ___ continues
42. Tech info source
43. Used sale condition
44. Norm Macdonald "SNL" role
45. Early Spielberg flick
46. Agile
47. Possesses
48. Elect
49. As well
50. Soccer mom mobile
51. Sought office

Chinese Food

Solution on Page 346

1	2	3	4	5	6	7	■	8	9	10	11	12	13
14							■	15					
16							17						
18				■	■	19					■	■	■
■	■	■	■	20	21				■	■	22	23	24
25	26	27	28						29	30			
31							■	■	32				
33					■	■	34	35					
36					37	38							
39			■	■	40					■	■	■	■
■	■	■	41	42				■	■	43	44	45	46
47	48	49						50	51				
52						■	53						
54						■	55						

ACROSS

1. Cook fast
6. Notion
10. Chew
14. Judge Judy portrayer
15. Market pyramid
16. Scrubbed mission
17. Steal a noodle?
19. Stink
20. Arincini site
21. Pixar film on sportsmanship
22. Yeah, right!
26. Innocent or guilty
27. Showy splash
28. High-energy
30. Fun-loving
32. Overindulgers
34. Lured in
38. Snuggle
39. Changing place
40. Concerning part of the eye
42. Feast master
43. Do away with
45. Tidal flood
46. TA's help them
49. Tiny opening
51. Aussie hoppers
52. Loan deal
53. Baby bed
55. Stats
56. Noodles to see by?
61. ___-do-well
62. Sailing
63. Alfa ___
64. Sidra portrayer
65. Jiggy dance?
66. Black

DOWN

1. Dandy
2. 66, e.g.
3. Lust
4. Coffee pot
5. Slapstick missiles
6. They're all about eave
7. Elton John hit
8. Lesotho, to South Africa
9. Pale
10. Noodle animal?
11. To the point?
12. Greek market
13. Least good
18. Gladys Knight backup
22. Maytag rival
23. Sword
24. Like some restrooms
25. Noodle handful?
27. Will stuff
29. Big strings
31. Cuzco type
33. Bring up, or what might be brought up
35. Freight
36. Año starter
37. Parts of some Madonna games
41. Role again
42. Friendly
44. Graffiti addition

Using Your Noodle

Solution on Page 346

1	2	3	4	5	■	6	7	8	9	■	10	11	12	13
14					■	15				■	16			
17					18					■	19			
■	■	■	■	20						■	21			
22	23	24	25	■	26				■	27				
28				29	■	30			31			■	■	■
32					33		■	34				35	36	37
38						■	■	■	39					
40						41	■	42						
■	■	■	43				44		■	45				
46	47	48			■	49			50	■	51			
52				■	53					54	■	■	■	■
55				■	56						57	58	59	60
61				■	62				■	63				
64				■	65				■	66				

46. Director's word
47. Bridget portrayer
48. Sales proposal
50. Building afterthought
53. Guru
54. Cork site
57. Lump
58. Dr. plan
59. Commandment count
60. Tofu fiber

ACROSS

1. DeMille genre
5. Acknowledge
10. Gabs
14. Cher's ex
15. "Moody River" singer
16. Actress Best
17. Billboard advertiser
19. Takes to court
20. Pittsburgh product
21. Offensive time?
22. Corrida cries
23. Stench
26. Soon
28. Table finery decision
32. Feedbag fill
33. In the past
34. "Thrilla in Manila" and others
38. CIA forerunner
39. Mice and men
42. Poe's "The ___ and the Pendulum"
43. Form
45. "Don't know yet" TV airing
46. Welk lead-in
47. Bunker Hill general
51. Modernizes
54. Fringe
55. Drudge
56. Cipher org.
58. New York Public Library statues
62. Trailer truck
63. Ragtime dance
66. Nights before
67. Bandleader Shaw
68. Beef stamp initials
69. Midterm, say
70. MacArthur victory site
71. "Saturday Evening ___"

DOWN

1. Recedes
2. "I don't wanna!" look
3. About, legally
4. Inducements
5. Tummy muscles
6. "You can make it with Play-___"
7. Ring around the cellar
8. Be a bull
9. Suffer eruptions
10. Like some questions
11. Like some movies
12. Genuflect
13. Impudent
18. Joe Tynan portrayer
24. Fiery gem
25. Prego alternative
27. Balls
28. Pigeon sounds
29. Leftover dish
30. "___ Long Way to Tipperary"
31. Rich cake
35. Tale's second word
36. Ike's ex
37. Plant part
39. Nuisance
40. Not just willing

National Leaders

Solution on Page 346

41. "Dragnet" org.
44. Sam, in "Casablanca"
46. Swallowed without question
48. Tux, often
49. Allay one's fears
50. "The ___ Duckling"
51. ___ the applecart
52. Tick off
53. Igloo shapes
57. Showy
59. -ish
60. Assents
61. Now, in the ER
64. Scout Carson
65. Shoebox letters

ACROSS

1. Sternward
6. An H might signify it
9. Lettuce type
13. Type of panel
14. It's no ___!
15. CB comment ender
16. Voodoo land
17. Fit for market
19. Mental exercise?
21. Bearlike
24. Math theorist
25. Dress on "Gilligan's Island"?
28. Hosp. pay plan
29. "Star Wars" kid
30. Stonehenge worshiper
34. "Just Shoot Me" actor
37. Mad Hatter's drink
39. Nut. fig.
40. Password re-generator
44. Batted at
46. Attacks
47. Midas wine?
50. With a smile
51. Shrek and the like
55. Small rail
56. Chop
57. '60s jacket
58. It is often charged
59. Uh-huh
60. Pun response

DOWN

1. Tree or burnt remains of one
2. Phyllis Diller wrap
3. Rope-a-dope guy
4. Market buy in a nursery rhyme
5. Three-fer
6. Shrub
7. Hairy twin
8. Oracle site
9. Rent payer
10. Hospital hangup
11. Prove wrong
12. ___ Mawr
18. Debt offering
20. Doris Day's "will be"
21. Cries of disgust
22. "The ___ of the Ancient Mariner"
23. Kiss at Hogwarts
26. One opposed
27. Lender's claim
31. WWW destinations
32. Thought
33. Scurry
35. Charlie Parker's instrument
36. Singer Lenya
38. Jason's ship
41. Generous
42. 37 Across type
43. Bookkeeper's book
44. Cheeky TV cry

The In Crowd

Solution on Page 346

1	2	3	4	5	■	6	7	8	■	9	10	11	12
13					■	14			■	15			
16					■	17			18				
■	■	■	19		20								
21	22	23				■	■	24					■
25						26	27				■	■	■
28			■	■	29			■	30		31	32	33
34			35	36	■	37		38	■	■	39		
■	■	■	40		41				42	43			
■	44	45				■	■	46					
47						48	49				■	■	■
50								■	51		52	53	54
55				■	56			■	57				
58				■	59			■	60				

45. Get used to it
47. *Que* ___?
48. Polar boat risk
49. Swindles
52. Plato's P
53. Good Feelings, e.g.
54. Cause of Icarus's downfall

ACROSS

1. Celt
5. Word in many Hope/Crosby film titles
9. Standoffish
14. "___ La Douce"
15. Shower-wall piece
16. Ship's lower hull
17. Revue of '46 with Gene Kelly
20. High IQ gp.
21. Barbecue site
22. Former soldier
23. Aged
24. Rhoda's mom
26. Balcony section
28. Uses a mortar and pestle
31. Of a manner
34. Kind of rhododendron
37. ___ carte
39. French cheese
40. Gene Kelly musical comedy with Skelton and Ball
43. Astronaut Shepard
44. Hankering
45. The 12 ___ of Israel
46. Chomp
48. Designate
50. Salesman's offer
52. Bawl
53. Lawyers' gp.
56. This means trouble
58. Overbearing
61. Corporate symbols
63. Easily his standout film
66. Lamebrained
67. NYC or London section
68. Church alcove
69. Jerk's drinks
70. Skeptic's comment
71. Villain's look

DOWN

1. Thingamabob
2. The Little Mermaid
3. Revise
4. Needs to catch up
5. Hwy. crosser
6. Crankcase bottom
7. "M*A*S*H" star
8. Skillful
9. Flowering
10. ___ Abner
11. Army color
12. S-shaped molding
13. Gala
18. Less fixed
19. Banana ___
25. Anne Frank had one
27. Scary elf
28. Quick look
29. Daybreaks
30. Hearst's takers
32. ___-de-camp
33. Romanian coins
34. First man
35. Bantu language
36. Like a ghost town
38. Moving

Gene Kelly

Solution on Page 347

41. Pro vote
42. Sock design
47. Nuns and OCD people have them
49. Reaper's weapon
51. Actor Chaney
53. Open wide
54. Idaho city
55. TV's Mr. Grant
56. Like you see it
57. Producer De Laurentiis
59. Yes!
60. Holier-than-thou sort
62. ___-B
64. Student's concern
65. "Some Like It ___"

ACROSS

1. Gets bigger
6. Skye cap
9. Saw wood
14. Otherworldly
15. Skating on thin ___
16. Sank, as a putt
17. Ben's acting mom
18. Ed. gp.
19. Goodnight girl
20. Sinatra song
23. A very long time
24. In the style of
25. Far from friendly
30. Peculiarity
34. Storage area
35. Make a choice
36. It makes MADD mad
37. Hemingway opus
42. Extra-wide shoe
43. Holiday night
44. Sectors
45. She's her children's mother
48. Type of box or kick
50. Rock channel on cable
51. EarthLink rival
52. Palm Beach locale
60. Grammarian's concern
61. Tin Man's request
62. Revered ones
64. Style of a room
65. It needs refinement
66. Alabama march site
67. Attire
68. "A Few Good ___"
69. Aggravate

DOWN

1. Jewel
2. The Great Barrier ___
3. Spoken
4. Lean
5. Sewer line
6. Tiny Tim verb
7. ___ impulse
8. Carnivore's meal
9. "Star Trek" defense
10. Actor Fell
11. It's spread on bread instead
12. Gambling town
13. "I Dream of Jeannie" actress
21. Electric ___
22. Was required
25. Despised
26. "The ___ Woman"
27. Bethlehem product
28. Carol starter
29. Hosp. ward
30. HQ
31. Car introduced on 9/4/57 and dropped on 11/19/59
32. Perspiration
33. Chicken
35. Corrida cry
38. "Why, you've got a lot of ___!"
39. Mickey's ex
40. Was CEO of
41. "Mad About You" role

Astronomy 101

Solution on Page 347

1	2	3	4	5	■	6	7	8	■	9	10	11	12	13
14					■	15			■	16				
17					■	18			■	19				
■	20				21				22					
■	■	■	■	■	23			■	24			■	■	■
25	26	27	28	29			■	30				31	32	33
34					■	■	35			■	■	36		
37					38	39				40	41			
42			■	■	43			■	■	44				
45			46	47			■	48	49					
■	■	■	50			■	51			■	■	■	■	■
52	53	54				55				56	57	58	59	■
60					■	61			■	62				63
64					■	65			■	66				
67					■	68			■	69				

46. Barrio buddies
47. Says
48. It's something to sneeze at
49. Jeff Lynne's rock gp.
51. Blazing
52. Actor Hirsch
53. Man with a mouse
54. Eagerly await
55. "Make ___ for Daddy"
56. Stand up
57. Cartoon light bulb
58. Moron
59. Diva Gluck
63. Used the divan

ACROSS

1. Memorable event
6. Come or go
10. Closed
14. Purple bloom
15. Blunt blade
16. It has a slowly slanting tower
17. Build
18. Emeraldish
20. Indian takeout joint?
22. Gloomy guy?
23. It looks like a stile
24. Like some gov. bonds
27. Hi or bye
31. LA neighborhood
33. Chinese takeout joint?
37. Them, in "Them!"
38. Leaves out
39. But is it ___?
40. Gush
41. Deep cut
42. Japanese takeout joint?
44. Intl. relief org.
46. Madman
47. Wii ancestor
48. Assist
50. One ___ kind
51. Greek takeout joint?
57. Lube tool
60. Farm refrain
61. First man
62. Leprechaun's land
63. Carrier until '97
64. Old and gray one?
65. Psychic
66. Field lark

DOWN

1. Obi-Wan portrayer
2. Trevi Fountain coin
3. Pub orders
4. SST unit
5. Domino's pizza boxes
6. African grasslands
7. Grand pic
8. Brer Rabbit teller
9. It might be tapped
10. Nimble
11. Hurry
12. Function
13. Old M&M color
19. Smile
21. Unfeeling
24. Regal dance done in ¾ time
25. False
26. Pater ___
27. Clavell miniseries
28. Compassionate
29. Licorice flavors
30. Strips
32. Out of commission
34. ___ de cologne
35. Taxing people
36. Utmost
40. Reimburse
42. Galas
43. Data
45. Islets

Takeout Food

Solution on Page 347

49. Range rover
50. Possessor
51. It isn't over 'til it's over
52. Certain
53. Definitely, Diego!
54. Pile
55. Sundial number
56. Storm safety
57. Pinup's leg
58. Nut. info
59. Dumbo feature

ACROSS

1. Follow
5. "Are not!" reply
9. Mud bath spot
12. Boulevard
13. "Diff'rent Strokes" actor
14. Knowledge
15. Ginger ale maker
17. Complete
18. Like some funds
20. Treated with goos and gahs
24. The Silver State
27. "Born Free" author
29. Entrée accompaniments
30. Hitchhiker's desire
31. Pen point
33. Aussie howdy
34. Blue-green ducks
36. "Those Were the Days" car
38. Gridiron conference
40. Least wacky
41. Ungrounded one
43. The Greatest
45. Florida county
50. WWII woman
51. Skin hole
52. Marty Feldman role
53. Soap ingredient
54. Laurel, not Hardy
55. Jury member, they say

DOWN

1. RN's skill
2. Showe or battery
3. B&B
4. Meadow
5. Leave alone
6. Sober-minded gp.
7. Ambulance blarer
8. Black stones
9. Am-scray
10. Author
11. What happened next?
16. Molds
19. "My Two Dads" actor
20. "End of the Road" author
21. Ta-ta, Toulouse
22. Bum steer
23. Shoe lady
25. Distributes cards
26. So far
28. Nothing
32. Diamond heads?
35. Slow patches
37. Rani wear
39. Cats inspirer
42. "GWTW" locale
43. Leather-working tool
44. Now I ___ me down to sleep . . .
46. Small pothole
47. Census question
48. A deer, a female deer
49. Flub

Father's Day

Solution on Page 347

1	2	3	4	■	5	6	7	8	■	9	10	11
12				■	13				■	14		
15				16					■	17		
■	■	■	■	18					19		■	■
20	21	22	23			■	24				25	26
27						28	■	29				
30				■	31		32	■	33			
34				35	■	36		37				
38					39	■	40					
■	■	41				42			■	■	■	■
43	44		■	45					46	47	48	49
50			■	51				■	52			
53			■	54				■	55			

ACROSS

1. "GoodFellas" star
6. "Miss Saigon" setting
9. Six-Day War general
14. Cuzco resident
15. Vigoda who was Fish
16. Dunne of "Cimarron"
17. Standards
18. Football line
20. Whitney who invented the cotton gin
21. Clean air org.
23. Caviar base
24. Comic Caesar
25. Beaver barrier
26. Cafe ___
28. Soapy Jones portrayer
29. Drainage pit
31. Tiny
33. Jim Bakker's downfall
35. Church section
37. First Greek letter
41. One who makes it happen
43. "'Twas nothing"
45. Sinatra classic
46. Division word
48. Gaelic
49. Paper amounts
51. Tubes for dinner
53. The first summer blockbuster, some say
56. Like an abacus
58. PC rival
61. ___ before beauty
62. Crackpot
63. "___ to Joy"
64. Rod Hull's bird
65. Crude
68. Juilliard grad
70. Moral man
71. Former Russian orbiter
72. Legal claims
73. Bird berths
74. Ambulance letters
75. Beetle Bailey superior

DOWN

1. Hankered
2. ___ Gay
3. Carving medium
4. Rotating disk
5. Tailor's concern
6. Like Fran Drescher's voice
7. "Donna Reed Show" network
8. Joy
9. Stop spot?
10. Slot machine part
11. Baker's need
12. Actress Dickinson
13. Essentials
19. Barely anything
22. Larvas' elders
27. Pompous sort
28. Full of it
30. Removes blockages
32. Vegas lead-in
33. Tailor's concern
34. ___ takers?
36. Watchful hours?
38. Edge

Around the Rim

Solution on Page 348

1	2	3	4	5	■	6	7	8	■	9	10	11	12	13
14					■	15			■	16				
17					■	18			19					
20			■	21	22		■	23			■	24		
25			■	26			27			■	28			
■	■	29	30			■	31			32		■	■	■
33	34			■	35	36			■	37		38	39	40
41				42			■	43	44					
45					■	46	47			■	48			
■	■	■	49		50			■	51	52			■	■
53	54	55		■	56			57			■	58	59	60
61			■	62			■	63			■	64		
65			66				67		■	68	69			
70					■	71			■	72				
73					■	74			■	75				

39. ___-been
40. Swallowed
42. Drain cleaner
44. Seeped
47. Covert org.
50. Neighbor
52. Ethics
53. Land of the Rising Sun
54. See eye to eye
55. Houdini's last name
57. Go-getters
59. You are ___ friends
60. "___ you, Red Baron!"
62. They go with tucks
66. Bon ___
67. Vigor
69. "The Company"

ACROSS

1. Coin toss call
6. FDR follower
9. Gloomy guy
12. Arm bones
13. JFK init.
14. Genetic strand
15. Got a golf shot?
17. Toothpaste tube letters
18. Outperform
19. Lah-di-dah type
20. Sandy's cry
23. Waned
25. Brno's locale
28. Cheech of Cheech and Chong
31. Eye or can follower
32. Spanish dessert wine
33. NPR's Montagne
34. Sawbuck
35. Auto's maximum load
37. Packed house
38. Oz lion portrayer
40. Hello or goodbye
43. Sphere
44. Guy trying to get a date?
48. Paddle
49. Brew holder
50. Bikini type
51. Sched. slot abbr.
52. "___ of the Tiger"
53. Sells

DOWN

1. March start
2. Building wing
3. Santa ___ winds
4. Refrain from "The Banana Boat Song"
5. As ___ on TV
6. Priam's wife
7. Dome-shaped Buddhist shrine
8. Beer keg need
9. Regal seance sounds?
10. Word processor button
11. 9–5 maker
16. Empty, like an inflatable pool
19. Welds
20. Son of Venus
21. Catch at the rodeo
22. Parisian lingerie item?
24. Mint worker
26. Close by
27. Careen
29. Lab hunchback
30. Alliance since 1949
32. Fruit served in balls
34. Green Wave's school
36. Old sprite
38. Heisted money
39. Part of UAE
41. RCA product
42. Anagrammed stadium near Shea
44. ___ and cry
45. Big time
46. Completion
47. Metric wts.

ID Theft

Solution on Page 348

1	2	3	4	5	■	6	7	8	■	9	10	11
12					■	13			■	14		
15					16				■	17		
■	■	■	18					■	19			
20	21	22	■	■	23			24			■	■
25			26	27			■	28			29	30
31						■	32					
33					■	34						
■	■	35			36			■	■	37		
38	39			■	40			41	42	■	■	■
43			■	44						45	46	47
48			■	49			■	50				
51			■	52			■	53				

ACROSS

1. In fashion
5. Spinning letters
8. Oil bigwigs
12. Tea type
14. Gambler's game
15. Nonkosher breakfast option
16. Shed item
17. Elbow's site
18. Prayed-for Meany
19. D-Day craft
20. Naval frosh
22. Litigate
24. Downwind
25. Father
26. A fifth, less-known brother
28. Steep slope
30. Dawg
31. ___ Khan
32. Check again
35. Man with a plan
39. Sugar source
41. Seep
42. Swedish flyer
43. Green Gables girl
44. CEO deg.
45. Hwys.
48. A Bobbsey twin
49. Galway's land
51. Soon . . .
53. Lodge members
54. Behemoth battle
55. ___ *la vie*
56. Roadie gear
57. Lah-di-dah

DOWN

1. Willy Wonka kid
2. Wallops
3. Netizen's conditional
4. ___ *esta usted*?
5. Piques
6. Full assembly
7. Collided
8. Frequent
9. Seafood dish
10. Schwarzenegger film
11. Cerebral ___
12. Cowboy gear
13. Cat call
21. Turned into
23. Fire glower
24. One who divides to multiply
26. Lab amounts
27. Scrap
29. Improve wine
32. Add postage
33. Keystone Kops creator
34. Lease terms
35. High school class
36. Hanging art
37. Missouri mountains
38. Circus guy
40. Extra inning
46. Comic Philips
47. "Brave New World" brew
50. Superlative ending
51. This ___ test . . .
52. Besmirch

Mommie Dearest

Solution on Page 348

■	1	2	3	4	■	5	6	7	■	8	9	10	11
12					13				■	14			
15									■	16			
17			■	18				■	■	■	19		
20			21	■	■	22		23	■	24			
25				■	26				27				
■	28			29			■	30			■	■	■
■	■	■	31			■	32				33	34	■
35	36	37				38			■	39			40
41				■	42			■	■	43			
44			■	■	■	45		46	47	■	48		
49			50	■	51					52			
53				■	54								
55				■	56			■	57				■

ACROSS

1. Jack of "Rio Lobo"
5. Pound, e.g.
9. Shadowbox
13. Green salsa need
15. Gaelic tongue
16. Electric 'eel clicking comment?
18. Very, musically
19. Genie home
20. "Jurassic Park" concern
22. Old Faithful and others
25. Political shocking action?
29. Allow
30. Rash treatment
31. Comedian Philips
32. Kal Kan rival
33. Greek Ts
34. 007's Fleming
36. Roz in "Frasier"
37. Goal
38. Shocking toon words?
41. Forces in
43. GI addr.
44. Yours and mine
45. Rice ___
49. Shocking "Romancing the Stone" sequel?
54. Bid
55. CBN founder
56. Noted Niels
57. Donkey sound
58. Tater

DOWN

1. Lab burner
2. Flat parts
3. Roadie gear
4. Illnesses
5. Snapshot
6. Flamenco cry
7. Pipe joint
8. Head
9. Appears
10. Moved along
11. Campfire leftover
12. "Losing My Religion" band
14. Ruin
17. Jay followers
21. Maria's lead-in
22. Be a sore winner
23. Copy dept.
24. Unemotional
25. Self-stuffer
26. First intent
27. Big talker
28. Leaves out
32. Assigns
35. Hush-hush gp.
38. Had on
39. Soak up
40. Topmost
42. Head honcho
46. Talk like Winthrop Paroo
47. Outfielder brother
48. ___ for oneself
49. Boxing blow

Shocking!

Solution on Page 348

1	2	3	4	■	5	6	7	8	■	9	10	11	12
13				14					■	15			
16									17				
18					■	■	■	19				■	■
■	■	■	20		21	■	22					23	24
25	26	27				28				■	29		
30				■	31			■	■	32			
33				■	■	34		35	■	36			
37			■	38	39				40				
41			42				■	43			■	■	■
■	■	44				■	■	■	45		46	47	48
49	50					51	52	53					
54				■	55								
56				■	57				■	58			

50. The Plastic ___ Band
51. Not opposed
52. Fill-in letters
53. "You there!"

ACROSS

1. "That hurts!"
5. Flat hats
9. It might cause sticker shock
14. Art preceder
15. Away from the wind
16. French sauce
17. Go to the side
18. Auel's "The ___ of the Cave Bear"
19. Mollycoddles
20. Ray Charles hit
23. Bat wood
24. Zorro sergeant
25. "Wurst" humor
27. Likeable Prez
29. Rocks at the bar
30. Gave food to
33. ___ Doria (fated ship)
35. Had food
36. The Stooges, e.g.
37. Bogart/Hepburn classic
40. Cover
41. Picnic pest
42. Watch!
43. "___ Howdy Doody time!"
44. Mazel ___
45. Made in ___
46. Frequent Powell costar
47. Reporters, often
49. IRS employee
51. "A Brief History of Time" author
56. ___ dish (lab vessel)
57. Like some food orders
58. It turns litmus red
60. Wayne or Flynn
61. First garden
62. Detective Wolfe
63. Trainyard verb
64. City ___ (newspaper area)
65. Jimmy the Greek's forte

DOWN

1. Giant Giant
2. Nope
3. Spice rack items
4. Pursues
5. Dashboard gauge
6. Suggest
7. Stiller's partner
8. Miss in Majorca
9. Villain
10. Spanish wine
11. Smidge
12. Novelist Waugh
13. Insurance concern
21. Taker
22. Henry Higgins's specialty
25. Singer Page
26. Doff
28. Sing to the music
30. Did a gig
31. Farm refrain
32. Marie Osmond's brother
34. Knock lightly
35. Respond
36. Wine cask
38. Made up

Face Cards

Solution on Page 349

1	2	3	4	■	5	6	7	8	■	9	10	11	12	13
14				■	15				■	16				
17				■	18				■	19				
■	20			21					22					
■	■	23			■	24						■	■	■
25	26		■	27	28		■	29			■	30	31	32
33		34				■	35			■	36			
37						38				39				
40				■	41			■	42					
43			■	44			■	45			■	46		
■	■	■	47				48		■	49	50		■	■
51	52	53							54				55	■
56					■	57				■	58			59
60					■	61				■	62			
63					■	64				■	65			

39. Doc who is a lemon
44. Casualwear
45. Grammarian's concerns
47. Kitchenwear
48. ___ Island (U.S. state)
50. It has 88 keys
51. Relaxing spots
52. Part of MIT
53. "___, Brute?"
54. News nerd
55. Fence in
59. ___ and don'ts

ACROSS

1. Comedians
7. Fish hook
11. EPA concern
14. King Arthur's resting place
15. Milky gem
16. Cannes water
17. Heart-healthy Japanese lunch?
19. Washboard ___
20. Gab
21. Come about
22. Deli sausage
24. Anti-poetry rant?
26. Fought, as a war
29. They might grind
30. "Chocolat" actress
31. "Tell ___ About It"
32. Less distant
36. Hide ___ hair
37. Faux ___
38. "Your point?"
39. Before, before
40. Runoff spot
42. Boil in oil
43. Bridge unit
44. Consecrate
46. Stood up
47. Trying to find a space?
51. Refrain from farming?
52. Let
53. 007's Fleming
56. Part of IPA
57. Sculpture shed?
60. MLK Jr., e.g.
61. ___ fixe
62. Subatomic particle
63. Cleaning compound
64. Singing Mama
65. Siesta

DOWN

1. Elusive
2. Iris layer
3. Die at the box office
4. Last in a seq.
5. Pierogi place
6. Bergen's dummy
7. Tries to get
8. Snore-concerned
9. Jack Sprat's no-no
10. Like Rose Bowl parade floats
11. Stiller's partner
12. Blue Ribbon maker
13. Pizzazz
18. Similar environments
23. Sky bear
24. Night
25. TV's Fine, e.g.
26. "The World of Suzie ___"
27. Baseball bro
28. Lass
31. "The Creation" creator
33. Take back
34. Memorable times
35. He played Odo
37. Chem table
38. The Governator
41. Mischievous deity

Because I Have To

Solution on Page 349

1	2	3	4	5	6		7	8	9	10		11	12	13
14							15					16		
17						18						19		
20				21						22	23			
			24						25					
26	27	28			29									
30					31				32			33	34	35
36				37				38				39		
40			41				42				43			
			44			45				46				
47	48	49							50					
51						52						53	54	55
56				57	58						59			
60				61					62					
63				64					65					

42. Stable females
43. "Sold out" letters
45. Century plants
46. Betwixt
47. Buck of books
48. Alvin of dance
49. Kidder costar
50. Hemingway title ender
53. Divisive word
54. The whole shebang
55. Agatha Christie title ender
58. Nabokov novel
59. GI's addr.

ACROSS

1. Lead in the book that begins "Call me Ishmael"
5. Beatles tune "Back in the ___"
9. "Baby Jane" portrayer
14. Brussels-based org.
15. Falafel bread
16. Gumbo veggies
17. Fed head through 1/31/06
19. Bird bills
20. Dick's Veep
21. Sales ___
23. "How about that!"
24. Like a ___ of bricks
25. "The Giving Tree" author
30. Lamp liver
31. Between
32. Like raw linen
35. ___ and don'ts
36. Pick-me-ups
39. Make wet
41. Knitted blankets
42. Sentence structure
43. Place for a massage
44. Raggedy ___ (dolls)
45. It's afoot, to Holmes
46. Map dot
48. Tonto portrayer
51. British bar
54. Manning of the Giants
55. Poitier title role
56. Smut
58. ___ and repeat
61. Hall-of-Famer Hank
64. Nonspecific
65. Gleason guffaws
66. Mayberry lad
67. Ford flop
68. Go berserk
69. Notice

DOWN

1. Foreboding feeling
2. A Marx brother
3. Didn't dine out
4. Afrikaner
5. FedEx foe
6. Thimbleful
7. Goes on a hunger strike
8. Saree wearer
9. Comic Newhart
10. ___ out a living
11. Loman portrayer, say
12. He played Sulu
13. Krupp Works site
18. "Sleeper" hostage
22. Physical comic's staple
26. Directory makers
27. Elsa, in "Born Free"
28. Air apparent?
29. Construction worker's headgear
30. Artist Klimt
32. CPR givers
33. Demure
34. Circus brothers
37. Channel identified by James Earl Jones
38. Draft initials

Christmas Colors

Solution on Page 349

1	2	3	4	■	5	6	7	8	■	9	10	11	12	13
14				■	15				■	16				
17				18					■	19				
20					■	■	21		22	■	■	23		
24			■	25	26	27				28	29			
■	■	■	30					■	31				■	■
32	33	34		■	35			■	36				37	38
39				40			■	41						
42						■	43			■	44			
■	■	45				■	46			47	■	■	■	■
48	49					50					■	51	52	53
54			■	■	55			■	■	56	57			
58		59	60		■	61		62	63					
64					■	65				■	66			
67					■	68				■	69			

40. Like a busted bronco
41. Church alcove
43. Green group's paper
47. Channel owned by Disney
48. Damon Knight's "To ___ Man"
49. Homer epic
50. They're on weather maps
51. Gets ready
52. Cut open
53. One over par
57. Mitch Miller's instrument
59. Mystery author Grafton
60. Wiggly one
62. Proposal defeated in 1982
63. Psychic's sense

ACROSS

1. Score, in part
6. Bobby Pickett's nickname
11. Bond
13. It may be Roman
15. Keep to one tree?
16. Pizza sauce spice
17. Where potato chips were born
19. Black cat, say
20. Mojito needs
21. Title of respect
22. Depressed
23. Brief competitor
24. Part of a flight
25. Pretend
26. "Maria ___"
27. Parts of computer chips
29. Alla ___
30. Poi plants
31. Like some eyes
32. Prep for a test run
33. Peculiar
36. Poet Lazarus
37. Senses
38. Peel
39. It's made with chocolate chips
42. They make clothing lines
43. Tried
44. Most popular Mouseketeer
45. Sneaky shooters
46. Word with horse or common
47. Remains

DOWN

1. Bahrain capital
2. Virginal
3. It's a wrap
4. Rapper-turned-actor
5. "Bidin' My Time" singer
6. Pats on the back
7. Post-Passover period
8. Clicks
9. Qom comers
10. Fruity drink
11. Some soups
12. Trim
13. Honkers
14. Beck hit
18. Pleasantries
23. Villain
24. America's Cup vessel
25. Jack Benny feuder
26. Old Italians
27. The London Underground, say
28. Sticking out straight
29. Grumbles
31. Solitary fish
32. Eco-friendly verb
33. "Annie Get Your Gun" role
34. Laundromat items
35. Scouts do good ones
37. Specialty
38. Old man
40. Lust
41. Leave out

Let the Chips Fall Where They May

Solution on Page 349

ACROSS

1. Pilot
6. Veggie fare
11. Depressed
14. Wrangler's show
15. Ease up
16. Farm tool
17. Beatle song
20. One who had a little lamb
21. Case or pilot leader
22. "Cry Me a ___"
23. Like Rudolph's nose
24. ___ of Fundy
25. Ache
27. Animal holder
28. Turncoat or deserter
32. Camping treat
35. ___ squad
36. Insult
37. Beatle song
40. Oater actor
41. Pigtail liquids
42. Darlings
43. Luxurious food
45. Top flyboy
46. When all ___ fails
47. Where Ipanema is
48. Formerly Beta item
51. Hubert's successor
54. Brass metal
55. Wrath
56. Beatle song
60. Chicken ___ king
61. Stand
62. Rub out
63. Chess pieces (even queens)
64. Casino lineups
65. Flavor

DOWN

1. Poultry purchase
2. Lerner's partner
3. Ran in neutral
4. Slippery fish
5. Soda choice
6. Brash
7. Neighbor
8. Jekyll's workshop
9. PIN getter
10. Honey
11. Hood's knife
12. First-rate
13. Fawn or stag
18. Detach gradually
19. Like some seats
25. Li'l kisses
26. Freshly
27. First showing
28. Desi role
29. Sax type
30. Burr brouhaha
31. Goes off course
32. Raced
33. Gander or drake
34. Fiery stone
35. She played Mrs. Mertz
38. Favoritism
39. Bounce

Beatles Music

Solution on Page 350

1	2	3	4	5		6	7	8	9	10		11	12	13
14						15						16		
17					18						19			
20				21						22				
23				24				25	26					
			27				28					29	30	31
32	33	34				35					36			
37					38					39				
40					41					42				
43				44					45					
			46					47				48	49	50
51	52	53					54					55		
56					57	58					59			
60				61						62				
63				64						65				

44. They might have cuckoos
45. "___ Misbehavin'"
47. Insurance concerns
48. Travel documents
49. Pie periphery
50. '66 tune "Walk Away ___"
51. Counterfeit
52. Soccer great
53. Seuss's "If ___ the Zoo"
54. Rind or peel
57. ___ of Olay
58. Cow call
59. Pitching stat

ACROSS

1. Tiny
6. Check out again
12. Slowly discontinue
15. First name in mystery writing
16. Not weighed down
18. Fancy holder
19. Type of drum
20. MADD target
21. Pip
23. Apparel
25. Shed
28. Batter or golfer position
31. Massage
33. Princess perturber
34. Abandoned space station
35. Fiery fiddler
36. Not Rep. or Dem.
37. Beethoven classic
42. Financing letters
43. Yadda-yadda
44. Swallowed
45. Jr.'s jr.
46. Pose for a portrait
47. Gumbel of "Today"
50. Bottomless
52. Sear
54. Slave away
56. Updated
58. Banish
61. '60s sporty car
62. Genesis evocation
66. Cook who says "Bam!"
67. Bequests
68. Movie rating influencer
69. Premonitions

DOWN

1. Localities in Robin Hood's day
2. Freebie for a fridge
3. Volcanic dust
4. Answer to "Shall we?"
5. Borrowed sum
6. Funny Charlotte
7. "Great googly-moogly!"
8. Ryan's daughter
9. Addis Ababa's land
10. "Ain't ___ Sweet?"
11. ___ and feather
12. And
13. Grammarian's concern
14. Skater Lipinski
17. Playful polecat
22. $5K word in "GWTW"
24. Finance veep on campus
26. Time to be without
27. Fake fanfare cry
29. Frasier's brother
30. Ebert or Roeper
32. Ill-gotten gains
35. Gretzky's gp.
37. Old ___ (card game)
38. Andy's boy
39. Acclimatized
40. Assemble or flock
41. Like Felix Unger
47. Oil a palm
48. Noodle

Illuminating

Solution on Page 350

■	1	2	3	4	5	■	■	■	6	7	8	9	10	11
12						13	14	■	15					
16								17						
18			■	19					■	20			■	■
21			22	■	■	23			24	■	25		26	27
■	28		29	30			■	31		32	■	33		
■	■	■	34			■	35				■	36		
37	38	39				40					41			
42			■	43				■	44			■	■	■
45			■	46			■	47				48	49	■
50			51	■	52		53		■	■	54			55
■	■	56		57	■	58			59	60	■	61		
62	63				64						65			
66						■	67							
68						■	■	■	69					■

49. Charitable fractions
51. ___ dish (lab container)
53. Skater's jump
55. They're drawn when deciding
57. "I don't care one ___"
59. Kid's block
60. "Rio Lobo" actor
62. Outfielder Dykstra
63. Rod Hull's bird
64. TV Tarzan
65. Arctic sight

ACROSS

1. "Ugly Betty" victim
5. Sales stat.
8. Where one's slip is showing
12. War god
13. Red tape escape
15. Ad hoc structure
16. Replacing
17. Seedy character?
19. Out
20. Drank
24. Guessing game
27. "Take on Me" band
30. Dawn goddess
31. Mature
32. Middle
37. Rainbow fish
38. Sparkly attire
42. Dairy drink
45. One way in
48. "Africa" band
49. Icelandic port/air base
50. Open a tad
51. Marries
52. Animal pouch
53. Kwik-E-____

DOWN

1. Islamic decree
2. Zones
3. Streisand title role
4. Revere
5. Eyewitness, briefly
6. "And Then There Were ___"
7. Survey
8. Wunderkind
9. Marker
10. "Strange Magic" band
11. Sports judge
14. First name of "The Great"
18. "Citizen X" star
21. Actress Zadora
22. He was at Chang's side
23. 46 Down's initials
25. Sawyer or Swift
26. Obscure
27. Do something
28. That girl
29. A year in Yucatan
33. Underground starches
34. Chopin work
35. ___ or madam
36. Gong, or kosher cracker
39. Spanish wine
40. Union site
41. Hybrid attire
43. Santa's stuff
44. ⅓ of a film
45. Musical tool
46. 23 Down's nickname
47. Flop

Midterms

Solution on Page 350

1	2	3	4	■	5	6	7	■	8	9	10	11
12				■	13			14				
15				■	16							
17			18							■	■	■
19						■	■	20		21	22	23
■	■	■	24			25	26					
27	28	29	■	■	30			■	■	31		
32			33	34				35	36	■	■	■
37					■	■	38			39	40	41
■	■	■	42		43	44						
45	46	47						■	48			
49								■	50			
51				■	52			■	53			

ACROSS

1. Not quite right
4. U.K. Inc.
7. 32-card game
11. "Ten Stupid Things . . ." author
13. "Bloom County" boy
14. The buck stops here
16. "More to Love" host
17. Clothing line
18. 5th word of "American Pie"
19. Organic compound
20. Strange
23. Ignition preceder
24. A poet gets sick
26. Like some umps
28. Fib tellers
29. Help wipe out construction
33. Homer's neighbor
34. Santana hit song of '99
35. Roscoe of Westerns
37. Hockey great
38. Waffle maker
42. Ripped
43. No notes here!
45. Time, e.g.
46. Fusion pros
47. Was a passenger
48. "Monsters, ___"
49. Moist

DOWN

1. Jimmy the Greek's specialty
2. Pro bono
3. Kind of market or circus
4. Belg. neighbor
5. Some chords
6. Mild swear
7. Hook crook
8. "Vertigo" star
9. Charity worker
10. Like a sandal
12. Mailman?
15. Great googly moogly!
21. Idiots
22. Spartan slave
24. Inflamed
25. Space cadet
26. Heartbreaker singer
27. "Almost done!"
30. Love
31. Kale
32. Go downhill
36. Bone dry
39. Got bigger
40. "Pretty Woman" star
41. Brew cooker
44. Jon and Kate's network

Road Rules

Solution on Page 350

1	2	3	■	4	5	6	■	■	7	8	9	10
11			12				■	■	13			
14							15	■	16			
17				■	18			■	19			
■	■	■	20	21				22	■	23		
■	■	24							25			
26	27				■	■	■	28				
29					30	31	32				■	■
33			■	34						■	■	■
35			36	■	37			■	38	39	40	41
42				■	43			44				
45				■	■	46						
47				■	■	48			■	49		

ACROSS

1. Salon jobs
6. Pageant wear
12. Sleep issues
14. Chop
15. Luna's counterpart
16. Slanty sort
17. Like some snow
18. Incite
19. Teenage spots
20. Tea house wear
22. Gas co.
23. Doris Day title start
25. 4-time Indy champ
26. Some nobles
28. This group
32. Whazzup, Juan?
37. Tough fiber
38. Recipe amt.
39. Neighbor
40. It's near Binghamton
42. Like a mudblood
44. "Turn Turn Turn" writer
45. Upcoming experience?
46. From A to Z
47. Little hooters
48. Six-line stanza
49. Salon alteration

DOWN

1. OTC exchange
2. Glimpse
3. Like some skates
4. "Frasier" actress
5. In one's right mind
6. "Star Wars" and "Star Trek," e.g.
7. Bass topper
8. Sailor
9. Ones who greet (var.)
10. Prove
11. Region
13. Mexican missus
21. Root beer brand
24. Big foot?
25. Employ
27. "Road House" actress
28. Postulate
29. First name in hair care
30. Ants
31. Tap
33. Skin bump
34. Mistreated
35. Type of bond
36. Military de-stresser
38. Seer's deck
41. Neural network
43. Bryn ___

Q&A

Solution on Page 351

1	2	3	4	5	■	■	6	7	8	9	10	11
12					13	■	14					
15						■	16					
17						■	18					
19				■	20	21		■	22			
23				24			■	25				
■	■	■	■	26			27		■	■	■	■
28	29	30	31		■	32			33	34	35	36
37				■	38			■	39			
40				41		■	42	43				
44						■	45					
46						■	47					
48						■	■	49				

ACROSS

1. Like the game, to Holmes
6. Hobo
9. Healing ointment
14. Ipanema or Omaha
15. "I've got you now!"
16. Thicknesses
17. Cartoon flapper
19. On the ready
20. One way to make yourself
21. Color
23. "Born Free" lioness
24. One in similar shoes as you
26. Proceed
28. Indian drink
31. Douglas ___
33. Look through
34. OPEC liquid
35. Chrysler car from '29 to '60
37. Newspaper page
39. Magazine bill request
40. Ice cream purchase
44. Loan shark
46. "I'll ___ your ten and raise you . . ."
47. Shabby homes
50. Ike's command
52. Horde head
53. More kitsch
55. Autobahn auto
57. Army members
58. Where to find ernes
60. He was dis-tressed
64. Immigrant's stumbling block
66. GI amusers
68. Song and dance show
69. Sample a substance
70. Cove
71. Caught forty winks
72. Chow down
73. People, places or things

DOWN

1. "Mamma Mia" group
2. Levee measure
3. It's sworn or minced
4. Squid kin
5. "Scarborough Fair" herb
6. Ghost's gotcha
7. Tot's trouble claim
8. Tie up loose ends
9. Relaxing place
10. Comics caveman
11. Not bring undue attention
12. Against
13. Heir's concern
18. Complaint
22. Plumber's L
25. "Easy" or "Pale" follower in the cinema
27. Comic Carney
28. Lovebird call
29. Cheer starter
30. Ginger ___
32. Taylor of "The Nanny"
36. Sealy rival
38. Marx Brothers flick
39. Red herrings
41. ___ Kabibble
42. PBS grantor

Oops!

Solution on Page 351

1	2	3	4	5	■	6	7	8	■	9	10	11	12	13
14					■	15			■	16				
17					18				■	19				
20						■	21		22	■	23			
■	■	■	24			25	■	26		27				
28	29	30		■	31		32	■	33					
34			■	■	■	35		36				■	■	■
37			38	■	39					■	40	41	42	43
■	■	■	44	45					■	■	■	46		
47	48	49				■	50		51	■	52			
53						54	■	55		56		■	■	■
57				■	58		59	■	60			61	62	63
64			65		■	66		67						
68					■	69			■	70				
71					■	72			■	73				

43. Commandment count
45. Go downhill
47. Landing connection
48. "Messiah" man
49. On the go
51. Eject
52. Kobe robe
54. Earth Day verb
56. "Mack the Knife" singer
59. Biggest continent
61. Enterprise helmsman
62. ___ for business
63. Pulls down
65. Opera site
67. Choose

ACROSS

1. Dr. Casey
4. "___ Wonderful Life"
8. Following behind
13. ". . . and to ___ goodnight!"
14. Any time now
15. Common retirement locale
16. What happened
19. Loosen
20. Bilko's rank
21. Had some grub
22. Unruly crowd
25. Luau loop
26. Peanuts blanket-holder
28. Captivate
33. Concerning
36. Stuff into the suitcase
38. Rush off to marry
39. The central figure
42. Student
43. Ripped
44. Put back as was
45. Abscam, etc.
47. Fruit of one's labors
49. GI address
51. Trouble
52. '60s car of song
55. Blah
60. Enjoyed
62. His predecessor's shocking wrong answer
65. Kite catchers
66. Smith who sang "God Bless America"
67. Tributes
68. Wigwam
69. On
70. Newsman Koppel

DOWN

1. To the point, or without a point
2. Upper crust
3. Pruneface or the Brow, in "Dick Tracy"
4. Merwyn Bogue, to Kay
5. As well
6. Farm females
7. Shootist Adams
8. Dreamed of
9. This clue
10. "Impressive, huh?"
11. Mideast gulf
12. ___ the Stilt
13. Ocean hue
17. Big rig
18. Algonquin Indian
23. ___ upon a time . . .
24. Exploded
26. '60s sex symbol
27. "Stompin' at the ___"
29. So all can hear
30. Daybreak
31. Newspaper page
32. Divorce center
33. Play parts
34. Close
35. "Mon Oncle" star
37. Ahnold's wife
40. Contract mumbo-jumbo
41. Shortage

Notorious

Solution on Page 351

	1	2	3		4	5	6	7		8	9	10	11	12
13					14					15				
16				17					18					
19							20							
21				22	23	24		25						
			26				27		28		29	30	31	32
33	34	35			36			37		38				
39				40					41					
42						43					44			
45					46		47			48				
				49		50		51				52	53	54
55	56	57	58				59			60	61			
62								63	64					
65						66					67			
68						69					70			

46. Rant
48. Be a goldbrick
50. Expo '70 site
52. Crystal encloser
53. Stay ___ (keep listening)
54. Chooses
55. Onetime Senate majority leader
56. Concerning
57. Mother May I? noun
58. Quaker's pronoun
59. ERA or RBI
61. Pony pace
63. DDE arena
64. Sales ___

ACROSS

1. The long ___ of the law
4. Jules Verne genre
9. Switches to telephoto
14. The ___ is cast
15. Actress Burstyn
16. Tony musical for LuPone
17. Went up
19. At ease, to civilians
20. Fictional slob
22. Actor Connery
23. "Quiet on the ___!"
24. Where stakes are laid: abbr.
27. Story
31. Some
34. Monty Python opener
37. Go through mail
39. Entertain
40. Jazz/blues singer
43. Rushed to wed
44. Game with water or horses
45. Termination
46. It's sprayed
48. Beauts
50. D-Day transport
51. Moist
53. Radar's grape drink
57. She plays Miranda Hobbes in "Sex and the City"
62. Word before a flash
65. Type of comedy
66. Fourteen ___ gold
67. Oneness
68. This gal
69. The Shah, for one
70. Mexican moolah
71. ___ and feather

DOWN

1. Ciao, Chico!
2. ___ and repeat
3. Islamic holy city
4. Crystal ball gazer
5. Money or seafood word (not "fin")
6. Ingrid, in "Casablanca"
7. Bite the hand that ___ you
8. West or East islands
9. "___ Hour" (movie spoofed in "Airplane!")
10. A bun in the ___
11. Tin Man's request
12. From where Charlie never returned
13. What Getz got
18. Verb for Howard Dean
21. Hospital-clean
24. Use a soapbox
25. Bird of prey claw
26. Mix
28. "Ring Around the Rosie" word
29. Woody Allen's "Sweet and ___"
30. Feminist letters
32. Snake's poison
33. Faberge item
34. Perfect
35. Bathroom cover
36. Rude laugh
38. Cooking qty.
41. GI's addr.

Presidential Pretenders

Solution on Page 351

1	2	3	#	4	5	6	7	8	#	9	10	11	12	13
14			#	15					#	16				
17			18						#	19				
20									21			#	#	#
22				#	#	#	23			#	#	24	25	26
#	#	#	27	28	29	30	#	31		32	33			
34	35	36	#	37			38	#	39					
40			41					42						
43						#	44				#	45		
46						47	#	48			49	#	#	#
50			#	#	51		52	#	#	#	53	54	55	56
#	#	#	57	58				59	60	61				
62	63	64			#	65								
66					#	67					#	68		
69					#	70					#	71		

42. 36 Down maker
47. Abates
49. Tiff
52. "To ___ own self be true"
54. Be
55. Foofaraw
56. Ear or beauty preceder
57. Hatfields or McCoys
58. Abominable Snowman
59. Disease ending
60. Type of insurance
61. Refusals
62. Try the bunny slope
63. Blemish
64. George's lyrical brother

ACROSS

1. Out
6. ___ dash
10. Fill
14. Wore
15. Top cutter
17. Black shades
18. Bullish trend
19. Patient
21. Back-talker
22. Large lizard
26. Like some counters
30. Land-rich
33. Stitch's pal
34. "I" focus
35. Add weight
36. Mass tongue
37. Brynner's costar as "I"
38. Sandy's bark
39. Work watchdog
40. Orange ___
41. Native language
45. Preposterous
46. Somewhat
50. Heart material
54. Wastes away
57. ___ kitchen
58. Detours
59. Summer team
60. Beer need
61. Cozumel coin
62. Succinct

DOWN

1. Clearings?
2. Liplike parts
3. Revered ones
4. Servants
5. Alternately
6. Lowlife
7. Norseman
8. Chip in
9. Go all out
10. Parody
11. Singer DiFranco
12. Bo's number
13. Bit of work
16. Ragu rival
20. Muff up
23. Sneak ___
24. Not blanco
25. Cherish
27. TNT event
28. Art print
29. Cuban boy
30. Bright lizard
31. Choco-crock
32. Fissures
36. Arbiter
37. Memento
40. Least strong
42. Goes along with
43. Burst forth
44. Amscray!
47. Moving
48. Old digs

MT–Headed

Solution on Page 352

1	2	3	4	5	■	6	7	8	9	■	10	11	12	13
14					■	15				16				
17					■	18								
19					20							■	■	■
21						■	■	■	22			23	24	25
■	■	■	26			27	28	29						
30	31	32			■	33				■	■	34		
35				■	36					■	37			
38			■	■	39				■	40				
41			42	43					44			■	■	■
45						■	■	■	46			47	48	49
■	■	■	50			51	52	53						
54	55	56							■	57				
58									■	59				
60				■	61				■	62				

49. Nervous
51. French film
52. Staying power
53. Old U.S. gas co.
54. Bat wood
55. Ring finish
56. Shred

ACROSS

1. Torme forte
5. Author Puzo
10. ___ for questioning
14. Forearm bone
15. Old toothpaste
16. Sub in a tub
17. Berlin song of '29
20. "___ Street" (kid show)
21. "This is an ___!" (angry call)
22. They know what they're doing
25. They're taboo
26. Prep for a picture
30. Fold a page
33. Fine-tuned
34. Magician Henning
35. Bard's brouhaha
38. Berlin musical of '46
42. Had been
43. Working condition watchdog: abbr.
44. Della or Pee Wee
45. Ill-___ gains
47. Takes great pleasure (in)
48. Amassed
51. Info
53. Resolute
56. ___ band (person strapped with traps)
61. Berlin song introduced by Kate Smith
64. Famous New York canal
65. Alfredo or Tabasco
66. Silver-tongued
67. ___ of approval
68. Forest members
69. Jimmy the Greek's forte

DOWN

1. Dines
2. Game where Mustard might have done it
3. ___ in one's pants
4. Ciao
5. Vein doctor?
6. Mil. addr.
7. Bled
8. "___ the Woods"
9. 29 Down land
10. Film genre
11. Name in millennial news
12. Release
13. Naps
18. Get in the way of
19. Sicilian spouter
23. Least normal
24. Calmed
26. "Pygmalion" playwright
27. She had a Gioconda smile
28. B&Bs
29. Circle of life
31. Brazil neighbor
32. Tripper?
35. "Rock of ___"
36. Sunset
37. Till fill
39. "I ___ Rhythm"
40. Suave

Irving Berlin

Solution on Page 352

1	2	3	4		5	6	7	8	9		10	11	12	13
14					15						16			
17				18						19				
20								21						
				22		23	24			25				
26	27	28	29			30		31	32					
33						34						35	36	37
38					39					40	41			
42					43					44				
			45	46						47				
48	49	50					51		52					
53					54	55			56		57	58	59	60
61							62	63						
64					65						66			
67					68						69			

41. "Crying Game" star
45. Former "Today" guy
46. Fiery stone
48. Fashion fads
49. Love love LOVE
50. Gymnast with a song
52. Big books
54. Empty ___
55. Russian ruler
57. *Cogito, ___ sum*
58. Minor
59. Litmus affector
60. Apprehends
62. Take to court
63. One-spot

ACROSS

1. Carlos's coin
5. Grateful Dead T-shirter
9. Arrow mate
12. Brainstorm
13. Energy unit
14. Likeable Prez
15. Select sandwich?
17. Fail a polygraph
18. Small sofa
19. Worked hard
21. Bronx cheer
24. Wise men
27. Security temp
30. Slalom hazard
31. Tears
32. Net giggle
33. IRS mo.
34. ___ Bill
35. Corleone creator
36. Arcade finale
38. Judgelike?
39. Superheroes often have them
41. Scribe
43. Heir's gain
47. Wide spaces
48. Soapy sandwich?
51. Rod Hull's bird
52. Whistleblowers
53. British candy bar
54. Igor's hangout
55. Teresa's those
56. Pied Piper's parade

DOWN

1. Dice spots
2. Actress Falco
3. Splinter group
4. Yellow ribbon spot
5. A Dwarf
6. Half-hearted laugh
7. Table items?
8. Comebacks
9. Sandwich with goat cheese?
10. "Grapes of Wrath" extra
11. Garden pest
13. Smokey ___ Cafe
16. Pod members
20. Simple ___
22. Sticker sticker
23. Not after
24. Party person?
25. La Scala instrument
26. Wurst sandwich?
28. Seep
29. Trudge
31. Money in
34. Beverage
35. Reconstructionist
37. Freddy's street
38. "Titanic" heroine
40. Comes together
41. Rind
42. Mrs. Peel
44. L x W
45. Sour
46. Heroic verse

Sandwich Orders

Solution on Page 352

49. Lea plea
50. Lib. items

ACROSS

1. "___ Yankee Doodle Dandy"
4. Ore doors
9. Charlie's song
12. Deut. preceder
13. Bridget portrayer
14. What kneading removes
15. Ovine holiday
18. Concurs
19. Lucrezia's bro
20. Gave it a shot
21. Monkey deity
22. Mental picture?
23. Ricardo's landlord
24. Ovine tenet
29. Wee pies
30. Doofus
32. Multiplexes
35. Etch
37. Dotes upon
38. Blackbeard's town
39. Ovine actress
41. Butterfly/bee guy
42. Skidoo
43. Links concern
44. ___ as dirt
45. TV's Mr. Grant
46. Moping

DOWN

1. Do you believe ___?
2. She played Capt. Janeway
3. Mapmaker whose name got adapted
4. Rainbow-shaped
5. "Disco Duck" guy
6. Lodger's rest
7. 4 o'clock crafts
8. The ___ inning stretch
9. Palindromic lady
10. Princess headgear
11. "Our Miss Brooks" star
16. Big foot?
17. Axiom maker
21. Tests weightwise
23. Quagmires
25. Barbara Walters portrayer
26. Structural plate
27. Smidgens
28. Oktoberfest site
31. Fought
32. Chocolate base
33. Pastoral verse
34. Contract type
35. Pickled bud
36. Tray type
38. Actress Campbell
40. ___ Solo

I See Ewe

Solution on Page 352

1	2	3	■	4	5	6	7	8	■	9	10	11
12			■	13					■	14		
15			16						17			
18						■	19					
20					■	21						
22			■	■	23					■	■	■
■	24		25	26						27	28	■
■	■	■	29					■	■	30		31
32	33	34					■	35	36			
37						■	38					
39						40						
41			■	42					■	43		
44			■	45					■	46		

ACROSS

1. Blacksmith's need
6. Duplicate response
10. Does in, mob-style
14. Ebbets Field great
15. Lion's den
16. Employ
17. The Magi
19. Roulette bet
20. Gulag land
21. Large wasps
23. Kin of Vesuvius
25. Rub out
26. ___ on a true story
30. Tandy's hubby
33. Landed
34. Tiny
36. ETO's CIC
39. 12, on dice
41. Galas
43. Aye
44. Bats an eye, say
46. Judges
47. Cable man's job
49. Scout's rider
50. Messy ones
52. Woody's son
55. Envelop
58. Made of clay
63. Assess
64. Kids' ball game on a paved surface
66. Spy Aldrich ___
67. Herr's gal
68. "Wait ___ Dark"
69. The Red Planet
70. Show boredom
71. Painter's tripod

DOWN

1. They may be martial
2. Radar's drink
3. Action word
4. Understanding words
5. Gave a sideways glance
6. Newsworthy refugee
7. "Yan ___ Cook"
8. Toward the top
9. -ish
10. "The Gift of the Magi" author
11. Old-time emporium
12. Guitar ridges
13. Sight or smell
18. ___ and caboodle
22. Actress Adoree
24. Shtick
26. Labor outcome
27. Hand cream ingredient
28. Revolver
29. Catchall abbr.
31. Fissure
32. Mayberry sot
34. Montessori, say
35. Jacob's twin
37. Batty
38. U.S. map giver of old
40. Cropped up
42. Box-office sign

3 to 6

Solution on Page 353

1	2	3	4	5	■	6	7	8	9	■	10	11	12	13
14					■	15				■	16			
17					18					■	19			
20							■	21		22				
■	■	■	■	23			24	■	■	25				
26	27	28	29		■	■	30	31	32				■	■
33				■	34	35					■	36	37	38
39				40			■	41			42			
43			■	44			45			■	46			
■	■	47	48					■	■	49				
50	51				■	■	52	53	54		■	■	■	■
55					56	57	■	58			59	60	61	62
63				■	64		65							
66				■	67				■	68				
69				■	70				■	71				

45. CFO, often
48. Fixate
49. Wrenching concept
50. Get out of here!
51. Andean animal
53. Latter airing
54. Lots of "Deck the Halls"
56. Indefinite
57. Asta's keeper
59. StarKist product
60. Costello's from Susquehanna got broken
61. Part of HOMES
62. Dickens's "little" girl
65. Detroit union abbr.

ACROSS

1. The 4077th, for short
5. Elvis's "Don't Be ___"
10. Simile words
14. Queen of scat
15. Must
16. Barge
17. Skeet target
19. Like some excuses
20. Befuddled
21. Looked at angrily
23. Wardrobe
24. Embarrassment
25. Skinny fish
26. "___ Geste"
27. "Evita" role
30. Sprain locale
33. Flavorless
34. Blushing
35. Null and ___
36. "What good ___ it do?"
37. Far from, in hide-and-seek
38. Select
39. Bandage
40. Spirited
41. Moistened
42. It's sworn
43. Homework unit?
44. Tales that are spun
46. Have more staff than your rival
50. Sore
52. Leave to another country
54. Bigotry
55. Top lawyer
57. Wail
58. Elicit
59. Bar in the bathroom
60. It locks the ox
61. Bowling button
62. Hurl

DOWN

1. Pilgrimage destination
2. Divvy up
3. Angle
4. Place to bale
5. Sculptor's tool
6. Anger
7. Like some cars
8. U.S. WWII campaign, not in the U.S.
9. Opposite of steno script
10. Koran reader's faith
11. Friend from Oz
12. Big book
13. Was in hock
18. Blender setting
22. Praise
24. Easter animals?
26. Wine type
28. Kept
29. Whirlpool
30. Swear
31. Uh-uh
32. Wright site
33. Boxing matches
36. Rodeo performer
37. Differ

Frequent Flyers

Solution on Page 353

1	2	3	4	■	5	6	7	8	9	■	10	11	12	13
14				■	15					■	16			
17				18						■	19			
20								■	21	22				
23						■	■	24					■	■
■	■	■	25			■	26				■	27	28	29
30	31	32			■	33					■	34		
35				■	36					■	37			
38			■	39					■	40				
41			■	42				■	43			■	■	■
■	■	44	45				■	■	46			47	48	49
50	51					■	52	53						
54				■	55	56								
57				■	58					■	59			
60				■	61					■	62			

39. Ripped
40. "Moulin ___"
43. "All in the Family" sound effect
45. "And save us the ___ seats"
47. Myopic cartoon character
48. World holder
49. Veggies often served with haggis
50. Ann's twin
51. See ya!
52. Bruised items
53. Create
56. First lady

ACROSS

1. Ripoff
5. Street ___
9. Florida destination
13. Focal points
14. Doorbell
15. Snake eyes
16. So be it!
17. Shield
18. Hirschfeld hider
19. Joey Scarbury hit
22. Stumble spitting out
23. "Casablanca" composer
25. "Green ___"
27. Black Sea resort
28. LAX watchdog
31. Invest
33. "SNL" segment
34. Jerry Mungo hit
38. Baptism or bar mitzvah
39. "Where's ___?"
40. Fall asleep
41. 007 enemy
44. Brief job
46. Some machine guns
48. Bone used when you sit
52. Norman Greenbaum hit
54. Musican Puente
55. "Bolero" composer
56. Pierce
57. Old machine gun
58. Remove signs of
59. Rick's love
60. Big blaze
61. Cub Scout packs
62. Ranked player

DOWN

1. Thick slices
2. Sky streaker
3. Fast train
4. Low points
5. Elated
6. Swiss alp
7. Gives off
8. Chrysler of '28
9. Least ugly
10. Light paper
11. Pisan penny
12. ___ rule . . .
14. Spelunking sites
20. Host
21. Sunburnt
24. Like some films
26. Big fighters
28. Initial
29. Hatred
30. One who tries
32. Void
35. Harry Potter pal
36. Religious writing
37. Type of dressing
42. Poitier title role
43. Like some property
45. Statement to prove
47. Gawk
49. Basket fiber
50. Tsar's edict

One-Hit Wonders

Solution on Page 353

1	2	3	4	■	■	5	6	7	8	■	9	10	11	12
13				■	14					■	15			
16				■	17					■	18			
19				20						21				■
22							■	23						24
■	■	■	25				26	■	27					
28	29	30	■	31				32	■	■	33			
34			35						36	37				
38				■	■	39					■	40		
41				42	43	■	44				45	■	■	■
46						47	■	48				49	50	51
■	52						53							
54				■	55					■	56			
57				■	58					■	59			
60				■	61				■	■	62			

51. Oopsy!
53. Lendl of tennis
54. Cooking qty.

ACROSS

1. Plumbing problems
6. Israel's Eban
10. Stink
14. Wall Street rally
15. Idiot
16. Usher's destination
17. Microwave maker
18. Impolite
19. Create
20. Event where the U.S. showed it off
23. "We ___ not amused!"
24. Went for home plate
25. Feeling of dread
29. What it was
32. Census question
34. Autumn tool
35. Repair
36. It's at no extra cost
40. Meal ender, often
42. Not at home
43. Capable
45. Peeve
46. The rest of his name
51. Joplin's "___ Leaf Rag"
52. Legal claim
53. Take a chair
56. His specialty
60. Big rig
63. Vesuvius overflow
64. Church instrument
65. Lute-shaped fruit
66. Completed
67. College VIPs
68. Rash treatment
69. Readers' retreats
70. Spooky

DOWN

1. Movie genre
2. Grapevine item
3. Silly
4. Football play
5. Meager
6. Scared
7. Huge rock
8. "It doesn't ___ well with me"
9. "Family Ties" lead role
10. Mormon singing family
11. Narc org.
12. Acorn's aspiration
13. 66, notably: abbr.
21. "Don't Bring Me Down" gp.
22. Waits impatiently
26. Errand runner
27. "I told you so!" look
28. Prose
29. Golly!
30. Down in the dumps
31. Mamie's man
32. Isle near Curacao
33. Costume
36. Gel
37. One of three men in a tub
38. Big Blue
39. Yalie
41. Knight's title

Fuller Experience

Solution on Page 353

44. Animate
47. Star in "Ninotchka" and "Claudia"
48. Indian instruments
49. Golf stick
50. Make hard to read
53. Honey bun
54. Tabriz native
55. On edge
57. Divot
58. "To ___ and to Hold"
59. Kite catcher
60. Place to be in hot water
61. Slippery fish
62. "Little Red Book" man

ACROSS

1. Former baseball bigwig
6. Past time
10. Caller's declaration
14. Stag
15. Graphic
16. Nope
17. Big brothers?
19. Fiery fiddler
20. DeFazio's pal
21. What Tai and Randy do
22. Growing matters
25. Like a radio personality
27. Discussion platform
28. "TV Guide" topic
31. "Chant" chanters
32. Like some families
33. DDT restrainers
34. The ones over there
35. Patriotic org.
36. Dean terms
39. Model's skill
41. Nicotrol devices
42. Bounces
43. Spiritually lift up
44. Tropical fruits
45. Pace
47. GI stow
49. "Othello" heavy
50. Tumbler's problem?
54. Satan's work
55. Ball catcher
56. Susan's eventual Emmy-winning role
57. Actress Russo
58. My word!
59. U-Haul rival

DOWN

1. Took a pew
2. Actor Wallach
3. Park place?
4. Depressed
5. Starts
6. New York Library guards
7. Trouble spots?
8. Axis voice
9. Pulver, e.g.
10. Pivotal port city in WWII
11. Kvetcher's motto?
12. Batman's Ward
13. 86's phone spot
18. Connect
21. Seasoning or adviser
22. Funny bones
23. Tennis event
24. Israeli alcohol?
26. Cyrano standout
28. Story movers
29. Vile vapor
30. It makes Missouri misery
32. Sea monster of Greek myth
34. Not kosher
37. Froglet
38. Mishmash
39. Sandwich man, often
40. Speech
42. Math class, for short

Begone

Solution on Page 354

1	2	3	4	5	■	6	7	8	9	■	10	11	12	13
14					■	15				■	16			
17					18					■	19			
■	■	■	20						■	21				
22	23	24					■	25	26				■	■
27						■	28						29	30
31					■	32								
33			■	■	34					■	■	35		
36			37	38					■	39	40			
41								■	42					
■	■	43					■	44						
45	46				■	47	48					■	■	■
49				■	50							51	52	53
54				■	55				■	56				
57				■	58				■	59				

44. Like a stegosaurus
45. Level
46. Gutter spot
48. Smidgen
50. Horner's last words
51. Auction action
52. "Alrighty then" guy
53. Feather go-with

ACROSS

1. Baby announcement starter
5. Lost
10. "Ain't She Sweet" composer
14. Beverage from India
15. Fight
16. Actress Campbell
17. '40s trumpeter/bandleader
19. Huckster's wad
20. Like some swimsuits
21. Part of a title of a Poirot mystery
23. Incumbent's campaign verb
24. April Fools' trick
25. Computer key by the spacebar
26. Tommyrot
29. Unflavorful
32. Nanas
33. Spoon-bender Geller
34. Fisherman's need
35. Crazy birds?
36. De Mille's style
37. New age movement popular in the '70s
38. Islamic proclamation
39. Racetrack shapes
40. "Willow Weep for Me" bandleader
42. Half a dance?
43. Worry
44. Utopian, to a dove
48. Utility worker
50. "If I Loved You" R&H musical
51. Tennis great
52. Jazz pianist/composer/ bandleader
54. Hitchcock's "___ Window"
55. Genghis Khan's Golden group
56. Cultivate
57. Swerves
58. In front
59. Frank and Ava

DOWN

1. A god's lifeblood
2. Macbeth's title
3. Ranee's wear
4. Nielsen/Hays/Hagerty laughfest
5. ___ misery
6. Land area
7. Identical
8. She-sheep
9. Viers who didn't win
10. Consecrate
11. Jazz drummer/bandleader
12. Fairly matched
13. Non-note music symbol
18. Stock concern
22. Shoots the breeze
24. What we'll try first
26. Royal topper
27. Seed cover
28. Movies, for short
29. Huffed and puffed
30. Sot
31. Jazz clarinetist/bandleader
32. Suggested
35. Man's place?

Bandleaders of Yesteryear

Solution on Page 354

1	2	3	4	■	5	6	7	8	9	■	10	11	12	13
14				■	15					■	16			
17					18					■	19			
20								■	21	22				
23							■	24					■	■
■	■	■	25			■	26						27	28
29	30	31			■	32					■	33		
34				■	35					■	36			
37			■	38					■	39				
40			41					■	42			■	■	■
■	■	43					■	44				45	46	47
48	49					■	50							
51				■	52	53								
54				■	55					■	56			
57				■	58					■	59			

36. Rate
38. Greek cheese
39. Frequent line for Mary Tyler Moore
41. Circus people
42. Hauled
44. Doogie Howser's girlfriend
45. Classic car
46. Fishing net
47. "Citizen Kane" and "It's a Wonderful Life" props
48. Actor Cooper who said "Nope"
49. Sailing
50. Preserve, as meat
53. ___ la la

ACROSS

1. Duds
6. 50%
10. Expense
14. Evil one
15. Lake or canal
16. She was with the King
17. Silly
18. Yes or no follower
19. Peachy-keen
20. Liberace prop
22. Mil. weapon, casually
23. Buddhist sect
24. Futuristic Woody Allen film
26. Does well
31. Slippery fish
32. Factory watchdog: abbr.
33. Punched-out chant
35. Oaf
39. Slender
40. Chaos
42. Andy's boy
43. Beverage
45. End of a Gleason line
46. Nick's wife
47. Tank or tanker fill
49. Guard
51. "___ hope all ye who enter here"
55. A long time ___
56. Mary had a little one
57. Fleshy orange fruit
63. Israeli Eban
64. Eager
65. Blew it
66. Shopping plaza
67. Big-chinned comic
68. 51 Across quoter
69. Pitcher Hershiser
70. Ore refuse
71. Coworker of Kent and Lane

DOWN

1. Bank guaranteer
2. Actress Olin
3. Mideast gulf
4. Lilypad place
5. Use a hanky
6. Stall
7. Sheik or such
8. Tall-tale tellers
9. Hen or sow
10. Stuffed pasta
11. Best
12. Eve tempter
13. Spud
21. Sponge
25. Mouseward cry
26. Realty sign
27. Chatroom person
28. Indian beverage
29. Human ___ (circus performer)
30. Socks it away
34. Dangerous
36. Once ___ a time
37. Grow weary
38. Enthusiasm
41. Dance line

Can-Can

Solution on Page 354

44. Tease
48. Ones from around here
50. Holy city?
51. Memorable car renter?
52. Elephant king
53. Mosey
54. Type of orange
58. Simone of jazz
59. Spoken
60. Vases
61. For ___'s sake
62. TV's Jeannie

ACROSS

1. Pocket bread
5. Goad
9. Coolidge's VP
14. Red-rind cheese
15. Spiffy
16. Dodge
17. H.H. Munro
18. Endure
19. "The Mysterious Island" writer
20. Ice cream truck driver, sometimes
23. Wine valley
24. Not at home
25. Meese, to Reagan
29. Boxing letters
32. Pizzazz
36. Iraqi neighbor
37. Active one
38. Matthau movie
41. B&Bs
42. Monopoly payment
43. Vamp
44. Divot's daddy?
45. Lack a common advantage
47. Lovebird sound
48. Subway ___
53. Arrogant, title fictional role
59. New currency
60. Had a mortgage
61. Alliance since 1949
62. Memorable battle site
63. Dunderhead
64. Old West request
65. Title role for Burr
66. Actor Ray
67. Stage decor

DOWN

1. Ants at picnics, say
2. Kind of potato
3. Occupied
4. Pedro's pal
5. Sell like hotcakes
6. ___ the sign
7. Deep cut
8. Words to Brutus
9. Eat heartily
10. Sidestep
11. Somewhat hot
12. Poet St. Vincent Millay
13. Spotted
21. D-Day beach
22. Planet satellites
26. Transit for Tarzan
27. Goodnight girl
28. Took care of
29. Exactly
30. "From Here to Eternity" actress
31. Give or take
32. Porter song "Miss ___ Regrets"
33. Whoops!
34. On the ___ (getting better)
35. "Nova" network
37. Cub scout unit
39. Sign of teething
40. Nail-___ (tense time)
45. Enters via a password

The Good, the Bad and the Ugly

Solution on Page 354

1	2	3	4	■	5	6	7	8	■	9	10	11	12	13
14				■	15				■	16				
17				■	18				■	19				
20				21					22					
23						■	■	■	24		■	■	■	■
■	■	■	■	25		26	27	28			■	29	30	31
32	33	34	35		■	36				■	37			
38					39					40				
41				■	42				■	43				
44			■	45					46		■	■	■	■
■	■	■	47			■	■	■	48		49	50	51	52
53	54	55				56	57	58						
59					■	60				■	61			
62					■	63				■	64			
65					■	66				■	67			

46. Did
47. Pataki's predecessor
49. They're peeled
50. Concerned words
51. Erode
52. Kilimanjaro weather
53. Jazz or Magic
54. Hoof it in Hilo
55. Ages in history
56. "Star Wars" mystic
57. M.P.'s concern
58. Canasta play

ACROSS

1. School gp.
4. Circle segments
8. Classic Hitchcock film
12. Performance place
13. Gangster's gal
14. Son of Seth
15. Derisive cry
16. Part 1 of quote
18. Noughts and ___
20. Bob and Ray's medium
21. Soil component
22. DDE's initials
24. Bus. no.
25. "The Mikado" or "Naughty Marietta"
27. Cribbage counters
28. Tokyo, once
29. TV slot for later
31. Whirring sound
34. Part 2 of quote
39. Genetic letters
40. MADD target
41. He played Major Strasser in "Casablanca"
42. Adios
44. Bill and Hillary's kid
46. Part 3 of quote
48. Impair
49. Impair
50. War, to Sherman
51. Ginger ___
52. I, in "The King and I"
53. Glimpse
54. Leary dropped it

DOWN

1. Movie with the quotation
2. Shred
3. Make yourself ___
4. Accumulated
5. Kimono
6. Cedar ___ (storage area)
7. Conniving
8. Singer McEntire
9. Nervous
10. Freezing for the camera
11. Bars, legally
17. Like a boffo B'way show
19. More certain
23. France's Chaplin
26. Soy product
27. Jury or wall unit
30. ___ Hills, CA
31. The Creator, in Hinduism
32. Hopi or Incan
33. Dried grape
35. Wealth
36. Dreary
37. Ethics
38. Gawked
40. Pair
43. Mrs. Peel
45. Beatles film
47. "___ Big Clock" ('48 noir film remade as "No Way Out")

One of Hitchcock's Classics

Solution on Page 355

1	2	3	■	4	5	6	7	■	8	9	10	11
12			■	13				■	14			
15			■	16				17				
18			19				■	20				
21					■	22	23		■	24		
25					26			■	27			
■	■	■	28			■	29	30		■	■	■
31	32	33		■	34	35				36	37	38
39			■	40			■	41				
42			43		■	44	45					
46					47				■	48		
49				■	50				■	51		
52				■	53				■	54		

ACROSS

1. Spray can gas
8. Leads a panel
10. Bad apples
12. Stint
13. Explosive stuff
14. Tina's ex
16. Guy's lady
17. "Matrix" hero
18. Alicia of "Falcon Crest"
20. Dogleg shape
21. Security passes
22. Security monitors
23. "A Touch of ___"
25. You and me
26. "___ apple a day . . ."
28. Spots
29. Clomp, Jabberwock-style
31. Infamous
33. "Bolt" or "Mulan," e.g.
35. Wag
36. Toto tower
37. Fitting
38. British ender
40. You ___ here
41. One way to stand
44. Fixes
46. Know-it-all
50. One can be over 1,000 years old
51. Mama's boy

DOWN

1. Time Warner merger
2. Hagman sitcom costar
3. One who strips and stuffs
4. Spoke
5. Teflon
6. Bart's bus driver
7. Motivator Buscaglia
8. Us or O
9. ___ Lanka
10. Lab units
11. They can be used for kickflips
12. Enliven
15. Mailers
16. Trinket
19. Approval
24. Abner's radio pal
25. I've had it ___ here!
27. Wyle of "ER"
28. Took a load off
30. Upset
32. Give it a shot
34. Try
39. Mock-up
40. Stay in
42. Terse one
43. Vacay
44. She had a little lamb
45. Austin to D.C., say
47. Hydroelectric letters
48. Craving
49. You get 6 for a TD

Be of Good Cheer

Solution on Page 355

ACROSS

1. Endures
6. Gloomy
9. Gives a darn
14. Presumptuous intro
15. Greek letter
16. Comment to the audience
17. ___ bear
18. Sleep signal
19. Biblical gift
20. He was on "The Dick Van Dyke Show"
23. "___ Mommy Kissing Santa Claus"
24. Debt
25. Tony Orlando's partners
28. Primary strategy
31. Very weak, like a plan
35. Thoughts
37. Exchanged
39. Patty Hearst kidnap gp.
40. It tripped Dick up, sometimes
43. Our lang.
44. Mined quantity
46. Exchange
48. Almodovar's agreement
49. Gloom
52. Bloc that's broken up
53. Kin of the FBI and CIA
55. Tie together
57. She was on "The Dick Van Dyke Show"
64. Angry
65. Doc flock
66. Pamphlet
68. Comic ___
69. Concealed
70. Submit a resume
71. Appears
72. Hwy.
73. The ones here

DOWN

1. Golf hole edge
2. Mighty mite
3. Grain or missile holder
4. Lady of old Russia
5. Fathers
6. Write badly
7. "Excuse me"
8. Darkens
9. Bit part
10. Generally
11. Peel
12. Author Ferber
13. Clothing line
21. Dog's sassy comment
22. Princess headwear
25. Frisbees
26. Ike's two-time opponent
27. Is adorned in
29. Home sweet home
30. Vet's tour place, for some
32. Locations
33. Fixes
34. Garden tool
36. La preceder
38. Explosive letters

The Dick Van Dyke Show

Solution on Page 355

41. Now
42. Paving goo
45. Carson was at his wedding
47. Actor Valentino
50. Rub the wrong way
51. Edge
54. "The 39 ___"
56. Like some milk
57. Avoid
58. Funny Johnson
59. Steak request
60. The Cowardly Lion
61. Give off
62. Like some fruit
63. Slippery swimmers
67. Bread type

ACROSS

1. They come out of a comedian's mouth
5. IRS employee, often
8. Daytime TV award
12. A Four Corners corner
13. What's-___-name
14. Sonic sound
15. "Jabberwocky" critter
17. Coll. VIP
18. Secret agent
19. Lake or canal
20. Bat stat
21. Rebuilt city on the Elbe
24. Snuggles
28. They go low
31. Log-in need
32. Fluffy clouds
33. Writer Knight
34. Polymer part
35. It gets rewarded
37. Big Blue
39. Chip in
40. Relaxing spot
43. Messy one
45. Pungent spice
47. Naked
48. Mind expander?
49. Air
50. Kite catcher
51. Dover's st.
52. Roe

DOWN

1. Gingivitis spot
2. Upon
3. Like wild meat
4. This girl
5. Like Cajun cuisine
6. Feels sorry for
7. Cinders
8. Slacken
9. Impetus
10. Othello, by birth
11. Village People classic
16. Mark out
22. Beaten
23. Ticklish guy
24. Elsie's chew
25. "Monk" airer
26. For display only
27. Rain unit
29. Corrida cry
30. Mister
32. Smart's org.
34. Lead
36. Hurried
37. Ain't behaving?
38. Smudge
40. Lah-di-dah
41. First vid game
42. "Rag Mop" brothers
44. Bonnet buzzer
46. Consumed

Mother's Day

Solution on Page 355

1	2	3	4	■	5	6	7	■	8	9	10	11
12				■	13			■	14			
15				16				■	17			
18			■	19				■	■	20		
■	■	■	■	21				22	23		■	■
24	25	26	27				■	28			29	30
31						■	32					
33					■	34						
■	■	35			36				■	■	■	■
37	38		■	■	39				■	40	41	42
43			44	■	45				46			
47				■	48			■	49			
50				■	51			■	52			

ACROSS

1. Retreat spot
4. Indian buck
9. Tote
10. Field that is now Minute Maid
11. Chats
13. Does poorly
14. Fitting
15. Boot attachment
16. Don't ___ on me
18. Check in or out
22. "Telltale Heart" concern
23. Elton's John
24. Hwy. crosser
25. Dud
26. Study
30. Titillate
31. Swiss mountains
32. Pan go-with
33. Spots

DOWN

1. Baby tree
2. "___ in Boots"
3. Ginger ___
4. Aretha hit
5. Identity multiplicator
6. Guru
7. Long wait
8. Small spaces
9. Short poem
11. File type
12. No one does it like her
16. Away from here
17. Thick drops
19. Sign of 4 Down
20. Kitchen folk
21. The Keystone ___
25. Bail at poker
26. Possesses
27. "___ Believer"
28. Steve Martin song honoree
29. Meadow call

Wallop

Solution on Page 356

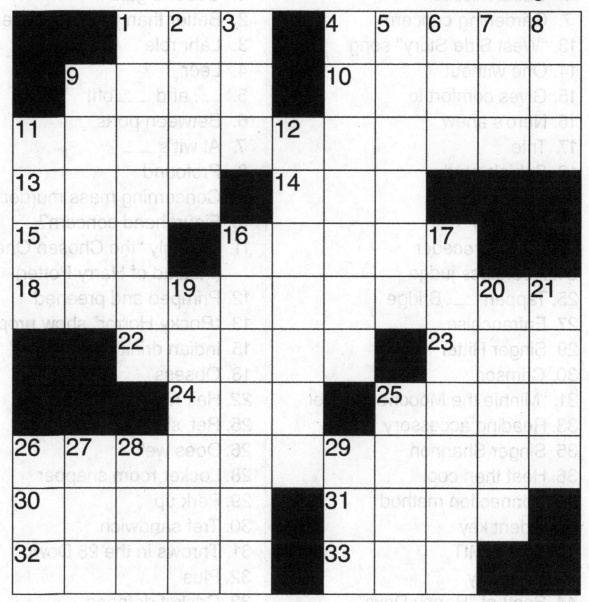

■	■	1	2	3	■	4	5	6	7	8
■	9				■	10				
11					12					
13				■	14			■	■	■
15			■	16				17	■	■
18			19						20	21
■	■	22					■	23		
■	■	■	24			■	25			
26	27	28				29				
30					■	31				■
32					■	33			■	■

ACROSS

1. Cesta missile
7. Gardening concern
13. "West Side Story" song
14. One without
15. Gives comfort to
16. Nero's anew
17. Trite
19. Sabin's study
20. Pale grey
21. Newbies
23. Storm preceder
24. Hourglass judge
25. Tappan ___ Bridge
27. Enfranchise
29. Singer Ritter
30. Crimson
31. "Minnie the Moocher" singer
33. Reading accessory
35. Singer Shannon
36. Heat then cool
37. Connection method
38. Indent key
41. Part of MIT
42. Bone-dry
44. Scott of "Happy Days"
45. Dutch painter Jan
47. Stuffy study?
50. Where acrobats meet
52. Sashayed
53. Punish by fine
54. Built
55. Like Russian dolls
56. List

DOWN

1. Gaucho garb
2. Better than put on a pedestal
3. Lahr role
4. Leer
5. . . . and ___ off!
6. Between ports
7. At wit's ___
8. Profound
9. Concerning mass murder
10. Figurehead concern?
11. Possibly "the Chosen One" (instead of Harry Potter)
12. Primped and preened
13. "Rocky Horror" show prop
15. Indian drink
18. Obsess
22. Hair nets
25. Ref, slangily
26. Does well
28. Locker room snapper
29. Perk up
30. Tref sandwich
31. Throws in the 28 Down
32. Plus
33. Cricket defence
34. Former
37. Part of DM
38. Less sweet
39. Readied to fire
40. Woody's "Cheers" surname
43. Demolisher
44. Singer Midler
46. Pleasant

Let It Ride

Solution on Page 356

■	■	1	2	3	4	5	6	■	7	8	9	10	11	12
■	13							■	14					
15								■	16					
17								18	■	19				
20				■	■	21			22	■	23			
24			■	25	26		■	27		28				
■	■	■	29			■	30							
■	■	31				32							■	■
33	34							■	35			■	■	■
36							■	37			■	38	39	40
41				■	42		43		■	■	44			
45				46	■	47			48	49				
50					51	■	52							
53						■	54							■
55						■	56						■	■

48. Angers
49. Conduit
51. Alert color

ACROSS

1. Idiot
6. On the level
11. Strong cleaner
14. Beelike
15. The Donald's ex
16. Q-Tip target
17. Voila, veggies!
19. Hatchet
20. Blanket
21. Actor Tayback
22. Ticket dispenser
25. Most nasty
27. Zone-related
29. Desperate's Susan
30. ___ finance
31. Smelly
33. Copter part
36. Breather
38. Some stadiums
40. French spread
41. Unkind words
43. Flat flattener
45. Churchill signal
46. Enjoy a book
48. Flathead users
50. Endanger
53. Dream
54. Fish ___ fowl
55. Goodman's instrument
57. Darth Vader, at first
58. "The car hurt an insect"
62. Scoreboard fig.
63. Comic Martin or Carell
64. Clockwork, mostly
65. Title starter, often
66. French moms
67. Rims

DOWN

1. Tree juice
2. EMT skill
3. Hurry
4. The San Diego Chicken, e.g.
5. ___ spaghetti . . .
6. Free agent?
7. At any time
8. Iona athletes
9. It may be malicious
10. More flavorful
11. Let things go wrong
12. Vertical graph line
13. Build
18. Vaulted, like a horse
22. Ivan and Nicholas
23. Ward off
24. Scanning error
26. Cut a class
28. Some beans
32. Details
34. "SNL" alum
35. Shortstop Pee Wee
37. Kite catcher
39. Peaceful
42. Wry humor
44. Payback
47. Water down
49. Moistened

To Be or Not to Be

Solution on Page 356

1	2	3	4	5	■	6	7	8	9	10	■	11	12	13
14					■	15					■	16		
17					18						■	19		
■	■	■	20								■	21		
22	23	24					■	25			26			
27							28	■	29				■	■
30			■	31				32	■	33			34	35
36			37	■	38				39	■	40			
41				42	■	43				44	■	45		
■	■	46			47	■	48				49			
50	51					52	■	53						
54			■	55			56					■	■	■
57			■	58								59	60	61
62			■	63					■	64				
65			■	66					■	67				

50. Ill-suited
51. Bill cycle
52. See ya
56. Wander
59. Paper or plastic item
60. Before
61. Slalom shape

ACROSS

1. Wander
5. Household animals
9. Enjoyment
14. You're something ___!
15. Jack, of oaters
16. Ike's two-time opponent
17. Fisherman's concern
18. Actress Raines
19. Brewed beverages
20. Hemingway novel
23. Writing on the wall
24. John, to Ringo
25. Bandleader Kyser
26. Chicken ___ (meal in one place)
29. Mighty mites
31. Hilarious
32. Mesh
33. Boat front
37. Rustic cry of amazement
40. Little Red Hen's cry
41. Let up on
42. Bert's TV pal
43. ___-four-dollar question
45. Bear witness
46. 911 abbr.
49. Salinger title word
50. Broadcasts
51. "A Clockwork Orange" star
57. It has many layers
58. Workmate of Ruth and Lily
59. Cleveland Indian?
60. Speed
61. Snide look
62. "Rock of ___"
63. Big Bertha's birthplace
64. Increases
65. Dowels

DOWN

1. Singer McEntire
2. Norse king
3. Cambodia's continent
4. Superman's city
5. Baseballer Reese
6. Columnist Goodman
7. Lanky
8. Woody Allen's "___ Crooks"
9. Bomb sound
10. Concept
11. Mini-mart worker
12. Kismet
13. Fraidy-cat
21. Radiates
22. "Car 54" officer
26. Short chessman
27. Sandwich cookie
28. Pinball no-no
29. Pretentious
30. Sneakers, e.g.
32. Honduras neighbor
34. Ancient letter
35. Elevator company
36. Sharpen
38. Having paraffin, chemically
39. D.C. subway
44. Like some patches

Well, Well, Well

Solution on Page 356

1	2	3	4	■	5	6	7	8	■	9	10	11	12	13
14				■	15				■	16				
17				■	18				■	19				
20				21					22					
■	■	■	23				■	24			■	25		
26	27	28				■	29				30	■	■	■
31					■	32				■	33	34	35	36
37					38					39				
40				■	41				■	42				
■	■	■	43	44				■	45					
46	47	48	■	49			■	50				■	■	■
51			52				53					54	55	56
57					■	58				■	59			
60					■	61				■	62			
63					■	64				■	65			

45. Helpful ones
46. Show feelings
47. Lion's ruffs
48. Diets, with "down"
50. Was in the cast
52. Make do
53. Wilbur's whinnier
54. Consequently
55. Told a fib
56. Minus

ACROSS

1. Veggie burger brand
5. Salami town
10. Miser Marner
11. Camel kin
12. On-call gizmos
13. More frequently
14. Pear type
15. "Uncle!"
16. Nut. letters
17. Leaf pore
19. Nail above my tool bench
21. Plato's porch
25. Dare word
26. Bessie kicked the can
28. Kept in check
30. Giant #4
31. Floods
34. More clever
36. Mystery film of '44
37. Capital south of Bismarck
38. Acoustic
39. Paquin and Pavlova
40. "Our Town" and "Hamlet"
41. Nasty

DOWN

1. . . . with nasty teeth
2. Bread spread
3. Early tenor
4. Biblical jawboned animal
5. Blue mood
6. Tolkien costume part
7. U.S.-European alliance
8. Leviticus says to count it
9. Bern's river
10. Footwear with a tunic
12. Make sense of
15. Motorola rival
18. Pyramids, e.g.
20. Sci-fi weapon
22. HSM hero burned off some steam
23. Westerns
24. Cave, in poetry
27. An amino acid
29. Some ducks
31. Zsa Zsa verb
32. Beatle McCartney
33. X factor
35. Actress Olin
37. "The Office" role

Double Features

Solution on Page 357

ACROSS

1. Kept watch, say
8. Turkish VIP
12. Spot on the board
13. Cackle
15. Presidential birthplace, sometimes
16. Count in French
17. Sworn words
18. Came in first
19. Elevate
20. Alliance since 1949
22. Give it a shot
24. Linden of "Barney Miller"
25. Panache
26. Hot rum drinks
27. Hwy. crosser
28. Fizzy drink
30. Nice thing to say
31. Old always
32. "Sold out" letters
34. Pulver, e.g.
36. "Full Monty" star
38. Loki's daughter
39. Pun response
41. Black
44. ARC code
45. Casual greeting
46. "Your Show of Shows" comedienne
47. Call forth
49. Dam org.
51. Clickable comp. system
52. Rome's river
53. Mt. Waialeale has a lot of it
55. Sigourney Weaver sci-fi flick
56. Bright night light
57. Makes lace
58. Casual wear

DOWN

1. Polar
2. South American capital
3. And so on
4. Defrost
5. It goes downhill fast
6. Poet Wylie
7. Thieves' place
8. Horrible
9. Latch
10. Sam Spade portrayer
11. Set in motion
12. "Dave" actor
14. Big name in astronomy
19. "Last Picture Show" writer/director
21. John Lennon's middle name
23. Egg ___ yung
29. Some chickens
32. California peak
33. Like some engines
35. Pine ___
37. Compaq bought them in 1998
40. Knot-tying spots
42. Latin eye
43. They're done in salons
48. Bump into
50. One opposed

Bogged Down

Solution on Page 357

■	1	2	3	4	5	6	7	■	8	9	10	11	■
12								■	13				14
15								■	16				
17			■	18			■	19					
20		21	■	22		23				■	24		
25			■	26						■	27		
■	■	28		29		■	30			■	31		
32	33		■	34		35	■	36		37		■	■
38			■	39			40		■	41		42	43
44			■	45					■	46			
47			48			■	49		50	■	51		
52					■	53				54			
55					■	56							
■	57				■	58							■

53. Turncoat
54. PETA concern

ACROSS

1. Object
5. "One" alternative?
8. Lola's love
12. "Flo" role
13. ___ the lights
14. Restaurant handout
15. Spar parts
17. It might be split
18. Needed back
19. Not crazy
21. Communion offering
24. Orange and black butterfly
27. Actress Massey
28. It might be bitter or split
29. West of Brooklyn
30. Mekong country
31. Possesses
32. Go out to sea
33. "Rocky III" costar
34. Coal or corn holder
35. Backbone
36. UMass site
38. "Our Miss Brooks" star
39. "If ___ the Zoo"
40. U.S. code crackers
41. Capital near Lillehammer
43. Baby moth
48. Iron bond
49. Woolly word
50. Past time
51. "___ on Down the Road"
52. Place to be a stick-in-the-mud?
53. Thick soup

DOWN

1. Campus crawler
2. Mad Hatter's drink
3. Foul up
4. Infuriates
5. Plot size
6. Abner's radio pal
7. You might learn yours
8. Maytag rival
9. Lovely Rita, e.g.
10. John Lennon's middle name
11. Yo-ho-ho bottle
16. Kirlian photo goal
20. Plus
21. Fred's wife
22. It may be false or tripped
23. Large gradual slopes
24. What I ___ to say . . .
25. "Cider House Rules" actor
26. Trojan woman
31. Petty tyrant
32. Spreads way out
34. '60s burner
35. Pageant wrap
37. Slowly break down
40. March Madness gp.
41. Be outstanding
42. "The Old Man and the ___"
44. Catch some Zs
45. Cheerio base
46. 66, e.g.
47. Cat call

How Long Has It Been?

Solution on Page 357

1	2	3	4	■	5	6	7	■	8	9	10	11
12				■	13			■	14			
15				16				■	17			
■	■	■	18			■	19	20			■	■
21	22	23			■	24					25	26
27					■	28			■	29		
30				■	31			■	32			
33			■	34			■	35				
36			37				■	38				
■	■	39				■	40			■	■	■
41	42			■	43	44				45	46	47
48				■	49			■	50			
51				■	52			■	53			

ACROSS

1. '60s TV lad
5. DJ job
10. "That's Italian!" brand
14. "Recount" actress
15. Ruby's husband
16. Nights afore
17. Queen type
18. What I ___ to say
19. Kinks classic
20. Perot's party
23. Banish
24. Car spot
25. Has faith
34. Coach Parseghian and others
35. Text
36. "Where Eagles Dare" actress
37. Mover's wheels
38. Action sequence
39. Card-game ending cry
40. Andean tuber
41. Sale spot
42. Bond type
43. Classic question
47. Billboard charter
48. 90s CD-ROM mailer
49. Stones' 47 Across
56. Tricky one
57. Fool
58. Russian John
60. Luke's acting brother
61. Like 56 Across
62. Sub head
63. Part of REO
64. Actress Garson
65. Swelled

DOWN

1. Eccentric
2. Lima's place
3. Bush's "Axis of Evil" member
4. Outflanks
5. "Better get ready / ___ the rock steady"
6. I feel so ___
7. "___ Mommy Kissing Santa Claus"
8. Cloud number
9. Scrams
10. Empathize
11. Common caller
12. Neuter
13. Olympic chant
21. Carol starter
22. Bend the elbow
25. Devastation
26. Spinach-like plant
27. Porch for poi
28. Writer Sinclair
29. Cape Cod town
30. Pefectionist
31. Bach work
32. Round gasket
33. Reverse (var.)
38. Keeping as was
41. Foot attachments
42. Becoming one
44. "Monster Mash" sound prop

You're So Vain

Solution on Page 357

45. Less saggy
46. TV knob
49. Cereal server
50. Got by
51. Stench
52. "Aim" follower
53. Speaker company
54. . . . happily ____ after
55. Handle
56. Head of London
59. This instant

ACROSS

1. Letter opener
5. Fly
9. Hoover's chicken holder
12. Wide river valley
13. Leprechaun's land
14. Miss the mark
15. Production producer
17. Canadian capital?
18. Rod Hull's bird
19. Alaskans call it "oomingmak"
21. Beseech
25. Poli ___
26. Headwaiters
28. Opposing one
31. Shaker Lee
32. Tres cliche
34. Hook's nemesis
35. Suffragist Carrie
37. Film phenom of 1977
39. Comic caveman
41. Snob
42. Rubble
45. Sushi dots
46. Take advantage of
47. Like some chicken
52. A word to Bo-Peep
53. Offbeat in Aberdeen
54. "Greed" star Pitts
55. It's worshiped at the beach
56. Scraped by
57. It looks like a white Wookie

DOWN

1. Medium with an aspect ratio
2. Carol Burnett tuggee
3. ___ carte
4. Unfreeze again
5. Loan getters, say
6. Texas tea
7. Calla lily, e.g.
8. Iconic puzzle
9. "Wild Bunch" director
10. Twistable cookie
11. Jurassic carnivore
16. Raising payment abbr.
20. Renaissance festival pros
21. Colorful computer
22. Give that ___ cigar!
23. Chili protein, often
24. Archie's wife
27. Flight bar
29. Mrs. Peel's replacement
30. Part of MIT
33. Rye malady
36. Craggy hill
38. Breathless?
40. Amuse
42. Edits, in other words
43. Jacob's twin
44. Hit bottom
48. "Alrighty then" guy
49. ___ Dawn Chong
50. Extreme ending
51. Initials shared by Dubya and Cheney

Measure for Measure

Solution on Page 358

1	2	3	4	■	5	6	7	8	■	9	10	11
12				■	13				■	14		
15				16					■	17		
■	■	■	18			■	19		20			
21	22	23				24	■	25			■	■
26							27	■	28		29	30
31			■	32				33	■	34		
35			36	■	37				38			
■	■	39		40	■	41						
42	43				44	■	45			■	■	■
46			■	47		48				49	50	51
52			■	53				■	54			
55			■	56				■	57			

ACROSS

1. Archie's command
7. Punched perf
12. Higlighted
13. Amass
14. Square meter
15. Judge's request
16. Film role for Harrison, 4 times
17. Drink with tequila and triple sec
19. Swedish superstore
21. Most twisty
22. Infectious bacteria
24. Grand saga
25. Secret cover?
27. Trap
31. "Shane" star
33. Wee one
34. Skin soother
38. Blunted sword
39. It uses Scotch and Drambuie
41. Story ___
42. Those opposed
43. High muckamuck
45. "Cider House Rules" actor
46. "Fantasticks" lead role
47. Deadly Asian snake
48. Tried to lose

DOWN

1. Address
2. Roll-up top
3. Hairy cousin
4. "The Flim-___ Man"
5. Former Turkish money
6. E'er
7. What frogs are doing
8. Fruity rum drink
9. Actress MacDowell
10. Pair parts
11. Either of a dietary couple
12. Quartz ___
18. Spaces
20. Vodka cocktail
23. Big-boned
26. Forbidden fruit place
28. Like a dogie
29. Oz city hue
30. Bounce yet again
32. Closed, in a way
34. Middle Eastern drink
35. Like the Hebrew calendar
36. Old Roman port
37. Spicy sauce
40. Mezzanine section
44. Bowler, e.g.

Drinks at 9

Solution on Page 358

■	1	2	3	4	5	6	■	7	8	9	10	11
12							■	13				
14							■	15				
16			■	17			18					
19		20		■	21							
22				23	■	24				■	■	■
25					26	■	27			28	29	30
■	■	■	31			32	■	33				
34	35	36					37	■	38			
39								40	■	41		
42					■	43			44			
45					■	46						
47					■	48						■

ACROSS

1. Fills in
6. "My Friend ___"
10. Ella's queendom
14. Ciao
15. Bath bar
16. Camera or eye part
17. Benny Goodman hit
20. Chair-stander's cry
21. Raveis rival
22. Talk a blue streak
23. Chicken choice
25. Reveille opposite
26. Urban eyesore
28. Gov't dept.
30. ___-been
33. Tarzan, for one
35. Veggie ___
36. Deficiency
37. Anne Boleyn's daughter
40. Dram or dyne
41. "G.I. Jane"
42. Fake diamond source
43. Wanted poster letters
44. Musician Jones
46. London area
47. Snug
49. Fertile
51. Its slip is showing
52. Fitness place
53. Tribute
56. Handyman
61. Tale starter
62. Soft cheese
63. Necklace fastener
64. Magic purchase thing for Jack
65. News bit
66. Do data entry

DOWN

1. Steal
2. Ernie's widow
3. "That Touch of ___"
4. Coat hanger
5. Seinfeld fixation
6. It had 12 tribes
7. Balderdash
8. West of Brooklyn
9. ___ financing
10. Exercise unit
11. Fill in diagonally
12. Draws a bead
13. Kerr's qty.
18. Kid of jazz
19. Partially-healed part
23. Cooking stock, frequently fishy
24. Anarchist, perhaps
25. Hitchcock flick
26. Mary had it, to Mr. Grant
27. Chrysler mogul
29. That's show ___!
31. Explosive sound
32. Beauty's depth
33. Blue-green
34. Like a town crier
36. Croce's bad boy
38. Well ___-di-dah
39. Memorable ship

Top Cards

Solution on Page 358

1	2	3	4	5	■	6	7	8	9	■	10	11	12	13
14					■	15				■	16			
17					18					19				
20			■	21			■	■	■	22				■
■	■	■	23				24	■	25				■	■
■	26	27			■	28		29			■	30	31	32
33					34	■	35			■	36			
37					38					39				
40				■	41			■	42					
43			■	44				45	■	46				■
■	■	47	48			■	49		50			■	■	■
■	51				■	■	■	52			■	53	54	55
56					57	58	59				60			
61				■	62				■	63				
64				■	65				■	66				

44. Simile words
45. Imam or emir
48. Like some wine barrels
50. Fitting
51. Scourge
53. She sang with Krupa
54. Lucy's costar
55. "SportsCenter" home
56. Burdened biblical one
57. Hoover headed it
58. . . . but is it ___?
59. Fib
60. Saloon order

ACROSS

1. Hardly thrilled
6. Henhouses
11. Mission control, for short
14. Airline hub in Chicago
15. Data fed to a computer
16. Actress Ruby or Sandra
17. Finger or toe
18. Like day-old bread
19. Tribute in verse
20. Start of Bill Saluga's bit
23. What reapers reap
24. Classic scatter
25. Queen of Soul
29. Bit of snow
32. Ice cream holder invented at a World's Fair
33. Ta-ta
35. Health hangout
38. End of Bill Saluga's bit
42. Actor Erwin
43. Spicy French sauce
44. Thanks ___!
45. Arty nonet
47. Golf sock design
49. Israel's Eban
51. The Emerald ___
53. End of several lines in "The Court Jester"
61. Boat blade
62. Sound portion
63. O. Henry forte
64. Compete
65. Singer/dancer Cara
66. "If You Knew ___"
67. Discontinue
68. Items in an Olympic parade
69. Exams

DOWN

1. Miss Marple discovery
2. The Buckeye State
3. Prego rival
4. Red explorer?
5. Clip off
6. Pancho's kid?
7. Readily available
8. Milky gem
9. Influence
10. Morticia Addams's favorite rose part
11. Without a smell
12. Power a bike
13. Later!
21. 2nd Amendment gp.
22. Rodent reaction
25. They have scenes
26. Cheer
27. Overloaded
28. 4 o'clock drink
29. Samoa neighbor
30. Wellington W.C.
31. ___ Wednesday
33. Cookie man
34. Marina ___ Rey, CA
36. Gene or swimming follower
37. Toss into the pot
39. Vegas leader

Old Lines

Solution on Page 358

1	2	3	4	5	■	6	7	8	9	10	■	11	12	13
14					■	15					■	16		
17					■	18					■	19		
20					21						22			
■	■	■	■	23				■	■	■	24			
25	26	27	28			■	■	29	30	31			■	■
32				■	■	33	34				■	35	36	37
38				39	40						41			
42			■	43					■	■	44			
■	■	45	46				■	■	47	48				
49	50			■	■	■	51	52			■	■	■	■
53				54	55	56					57	58	59	60
61			■	62					■	63				
64			■	65					■	66				
67			■	68					■	69				

40. Golfer's concern
41. Henpeck
46. Car bloc
47. Manila thrilla
48. Just say no
49. On top of
50. Scarecrow's need
51. Cake topper
52. Pumps and clogs
54. The Little Match Girl, say
55. Toss
56. Concept
57. One of two answers
58. Politician Perot
59. Segment
60. Banjo ___ (Eddie Cantor)

ACROSS

1. Joe's serving
6. Fuel concern
12. Robin portrayer of film
13. Einstein-haired reviewer
14. Tactic type
15. Sony rival
17. Sushi fish
19. The Common Mkt.
20. Meet
21. #7 of the Yanks
24. Dallas-Phil. dir.
25. Title film role for Danny DeVito
27. Release from a post
29. He played Uncle Felix in the "Spy Kids" movies
30. She played Maude
33. Got a birdie, e.g.
35. Boss
38. Ex of Artie, Frank, and Mickey
39. Greet
40. Do without
44. "Splish Splash" singer
45. Ponder
46. Become accustomed
47. Shoe doc
48. Purple People ___

DOWN

1. Lucrezia's bro
2. Ragamuffin
3. Give kudos to
4. ___-cochere
5. Native Alaskan
6. Workplace watchdog
7. Tai ___
8. Embroider
9. King head
10. Pleasantry
11. Lucy's landlady
16. Drink cube
18. Had a snack
21. Godzilla foe
22. Bath path
23. Utmost
26. Sot sound
27. Weird Al flick
28. Born
29. Painter Monet
30. Lebanese capital
31. Whole
32. Scrooge, eventually
33. Eel-shaped fish
34. Eggy?
36. Steve's wife
37. Accra land
39. WWII rapid-fire gun
41. Powell or Grant, e.g.
42. Derby, e.g.
43. He played Quincy's aide

Hit Parade

Solution on Page 359

1	2	3	4	5	■	6	7	8	9	10	11	■
12					■	13						■
14					■	15						16
17					18		■	■	■	19		
20						■	21	22	23			
24			■	■	25	26					■	■
■	■	■	27	28						■	■	■
■	■	29						■	■	30	31	32
33	34					■	35	36	37			
38			■	■	■	39						
40			41	42	43		■	44				
■	45						■	46				
■	47						■	48				

ACROSS

1. Friar's Club event
6. "Mr. Holland's ___"
10. He had a whale of a tale
14. Moslem Almighty
15. Actress Pitts
16. Just eh
17. Replaced
20. Yo-yo or Slinky
21. Ratted out
22. Holy pictures
23. Zany Martha
24. Ziti kin
25. Farewells
28. Female fight gp.
29. Catch red-handed
32. Hermit
33. Subfaction
34. ___ mia!
35. Fidgetiness
38. Steak order
39. Gambler's concern
40. Little red-haired girl
41. Charlie's downfall
42. Donkey call
43. Talked to God
44. Fakes
46. Big Ben, e.g.
47. Hun hero
49. "Please leave your message at the ___"
50. Greek cross
53. Being a jack-of-all-trades
56. Tardy
57. "___ John" letter
58. Jazzman Blake
59. It goes downhill fast
60. Desires
61. Musical hiatuses

DOWN

1. Actor who flipped a coin
2. Mishmash
3. True friend
4. "My Gal ___"
5. Similar-word books
6. UFO smell
7. Desire
8. It's of no ___!
9. "Round up the usual ___"
10. Pale
11. Folk-song fest
12. On the briny
13. Connecticut Yankee's knighted name
18. "Those Were the ___"
19. Wicked acts
23. "Chico and the Man" actress
24. Waits impatiently
25. Fire ___
26. He played Mr. Chips
27. Like some highways
28. "Peter Pan" girl
30. Bandleader Shaw
31. ___ on a true story
33. Fizzy drinks
34. Panama ___
36. Battle site

Wear ’em on the End

Solution on Page 359

1	2	3	4	5	■	6	7	8	9	■	10	11	12	13
14					■	15				■	16			
17					18					19				
20			■	21				■	22					
■	■	■	23				■	24					■	■
25	26	27				■	28				■	29	30	31
32					■	33				■	34			
35					36					37				
38				■	39				■	40				
41			■	42				■	43					
■	■	44	45				■	46				■	■	■
47	48					■	49				■	50	51	52
53						54					55			
56				■	57				■	58				
59				■	60				■	61				

37. Conference attendee
42. South Pacific song “___ Ha’i”
43. “Bonnie and Clyde” director
45. ___ gun (mercenary)
46. Hog wild ones?
47. The hole things
48. Duck or color
49. Mint mister
50. Keep ___ on (follow)
51. Working
52. Over 1,001 ___!
54. Gosh!
55. Color

ACROSS

1. Used the phone
7. Bovary or Curie
13. Moral bases
14. Like a clock with hands
15. I spilled my beer bottle and it's leaking out!
17. Bread spread
18. Proceed
19. Springsteen's birthplace
22. Process
24. III, to II
25. It keeps the sand from stinging you!
30. Potemkin Steps city
31. Patronize a diner
34. Wait, why not return to land and get on with my life?
36. Banish
38. "The Puzzle Palace" topic
39. Pyramid topper
40. Weird musician?
41. Mexican shell
44. There's just one of me—the rest will be couples
52. Military approach
53. Gentlemen's place?
54. Mother not to be fooled
55. Back to where I was . . .

DOWN

1. 38 Across counterpart
2. They might be personal
3. Meadow
4. ___-di-dah!
5. ___ Lilly
6. One way to the Net
7. Poet Angelou
8. Commentator Rooney
9. Belafonte refrain
10. ___ Baba
11. Vast, in slang
12. Goad
16. Hemsley sitcom
19. Troupe gp.
20. Moping
21. In front
22. Sky bear
23. Swedish auto
24. Bike wheel part
26. Cinder
27. Spider-Man's supply
28. ___ avis
29. One ___ time
32. 180-degree turn
33. Half a fly?
35. Chilly powder
36. Caught a perp
37. Actress Massey
41. Cool G
42. Way off
43. Surrender
45. But is it ___?
46. Little singer
47. Dog whose voice sounds like Peter Lorre
48. Undertake

Open Wide and Say "Ah"

Solution on Page 359

1	2	3	4	5	6	■	7	8	9	10	11	12
13						■	14					
15						16						
■	■	■	■	■	■	17				■	18	
19	20	21	■	22	23		■	■	■	24		
25			26				27	28	29		■	■
30						■	31				32	33
■	■	34				35						
36	37		■	■	■	38			■	39		
40		■	41	42	43		■	■	■	■	■	■
44		45					46	47	48	49	50	51
52						■	53					
54						■	55					

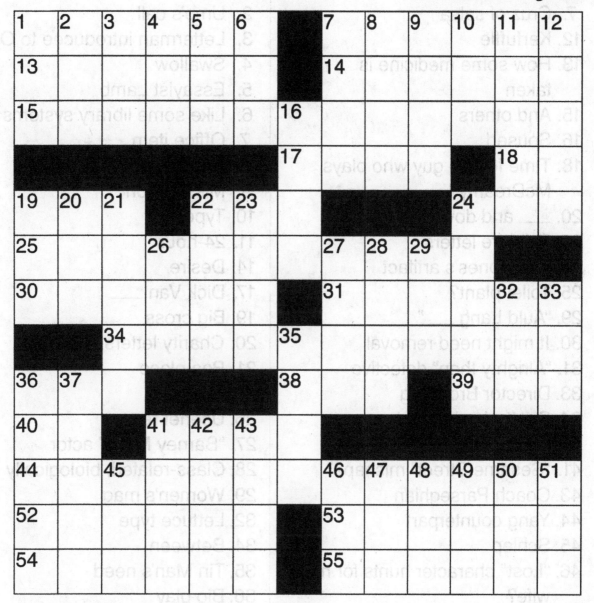

49. "___ to Boil Water"
50. Santa ___ winds
51. It pokes an aye out

ACROSS

1. Some cosmetics
7. Cruz of salsa
12. Kerfuffle
13. How some medicine is taken
15. And others
16. Soused
18. Time for the guy who plays McDreamy?
20. ___ and downs
23. Fair-hire letters
24. Indy Jones's artifact
25. Toilet plant?
29. "Auld Lang ___"
30. It might need removal
31. "Alrighty then" detective
33. Director Browning
34. Spotted salamander
38. Stare
41. "Sesame Street" mishap?
43. Coach Parseghian
44. Yang counterpart
45. Schlep
46. "Lost" character hunts for his wife?
52. "SNL" role for Belushi
53. Vile vapor
57. "Breaking Up Is Hard to Do" singer
58. Gold bars
59. Write anew
60. Clash song site

DOWN

1. 66, e.g.
2. Ump's call
3. Letterman introducee to Oprah
4. Swallow
5. Essayist Lamb
6. Like some library systems
7. Office item
8. Red one?
9. Miss out on
10. Types
11. 24-hour
14. Desire
17. Dick Van ___
19. Big cross
20. Charity letters
21. Pea place
22. This gal
26. Usenet req.
27. "Barney Miller" actor
28. Class-related, biologically
29. Women's mag
32. Lettuce type
34. Between
35. Tin Man's need
36. Bio play
37. KFC choice
38. Chats it up
39. Zones
40. Hide and seek clue
42. Old Turk
47. Sculpture type
48. ___ on the knuckles

Losing My Religion

Solution on Page 359

1	2	3	4	5	6	■	7	8	9	10	11	■	■
12						■	13					14	■
15						■	16						17
■	■	■	18			19							
20	21	22	■	■	23			■	■	■	24		
25			26	27				28	■	29			
30							■	31	32		■	■	■
■	■	■	33			■	34				35	36	37
38	39	40		■	41	42							
43			■	■	■	44			■	■	45		
46			47	48	49				50	51	■	■	■
52							■	53			54	55	56
■	57						■	58					
■	■	59					■	60					

49. Autumn item
50. Actress Lollobrigida
51. Droops
54. Blake Edwards film
55. Kingston Trio hit
56. Fireplace remains

ACROSS

1. Piglike animal
6. "Star Wars" letters
9. Holding back
12. Mistake
13. Lobby gp., often
14. Pekoe or Earl Grey
15. Suit type
17. Eddie Murphy flick
18. Skilled
19. ___ been meaning to tell you something . . .
20. Quick cut through a diamond
24. Got by, barely
25. Greek leader?
26. Set starter
28. Suggest
30. Bring to the pier
33. Tell-all movie title start
35. Become accustomed
36. Camp beds
38. Home of the first auto race track in the USA
40. He played TV's Fish
41. Genie holders
42. Toon chihuahua
43. Trunk item
48. Michael Jackson hit
49. Bo's no.
50. Be a fink
51. Surprised gasps
52. Reagan-era mil. plan
53. Telethon gifts

DOWN

1. Recipe amt.
2. Darth Vader, earlier
3. Hook's nemesis
4. Some questions
5. Large turnip
6. Huckster's rants
7. Spatters with paint
8. "Law & Order: SVU" actor
9. No-hit, no-walk result
10. Ho preceder
11. Went off course
16. Cereal box acronym
20. Tin-pushing org.
21. ___ for one, and . . .
22. Hair problem
23. Brute force
24. Roulette bet
27. Stick it in again
29. Like the killer bees
31. Not to
32. Marsh
34. Suit maker
36. Runner's load type
37. "Live and Let Die" concept
39. ___ finance
41. D-Day crafts
44. "The ___ of Pooh"
45. Hairy cousin
46. Wade opponent
47. Pulver, e.g.

Bowl-a-Rama

Solution on Page 360

1	2	3	4	5	■	6	7	8	■	9	10	11
12					■	13			■	14		
15					16				■	17		
■	■	■	■	18					■	19		
20	21	22	23					■	24			
25				■	26		27			■	■	
28				29	■	30					31	32
■	■	33				34	■	35				
36	37			■	38		39					
40			■	41					■	■	■	■
42			■	43					44	45	46	47
48			■	49			■	50				
51			■	52			■	53				

ACROSS

1. Maude portrayer
4. Sea color
8. Fills suitcases
13. Sleep phase
14. Feature of America's Sweetheart
15. Potatoes style
17. "Dog Day Afternoon" actor
19. Had
20. Chess pieces
21. Barnyard biddy
23. Remove a colon, perhaps
24. Leaning
27. Chicago mobster
29. Ballroom dance
31. Fetch
32. Filming locales
33. God with a hammer
35. '70s style
40. Consumed
42. Hwy. crosser
43. Furnishings
44. Came up
45. Early lit. learning
47. Dweeb
48. Owns
50. Before the audience
52. Pitcher recently returned to the Yankees
57. First game of the season
58. Fly high
59. Poet's work
60. This means trouble
61. ___ on one's territory
63. "Mammy" singer
68. Choo-choo part
69. Lukewarm
70. Mapmaker
71. They're sown
72. Busy airports
73. Attempt

DOWN

1. Bikini part
2. Snakelike fish
3. Ten-___ fuse
4. Ricky Ricardo had one
5. Fivesome
6. Large coffee brewer
7. Hawaii hi
8. Leap
9. Washboard ___
10. Nixon's gp.
11. Fella
12. ___ stone (permanent)
16. Memo
18. Accumulates
22. Spanish painter
24. Sailing
25. Curse
26. Gambling game
28. Somewhat
30. Spoken
34. Gambler's letters
36. Refined
37. Sinatra title role
38. Attraction near Cornell

You Can Call Me Al

Solution on Page 360

1	2	3	■	4	5	6	7	■	8	9	10	11	12	■
13			■	14				■	15					16
17			18					■	19					
■	■	■	20			■	21	22		■	23			
24	25	26				■	27			28				
29					30	■	31				■	■	■	■
32				■	33		34		■	35	36	37	38	39
40				41	■	42			■	43				
44					■	45			46	■	47			
■	■	■	■	48	49		■	50		51				
52	53	54	55				56	■	57					
58				■	59			■	60			■	■	■
61				62		■	63	64				65	66	67
68						■	69				■	70		
■	71					■	72				■	73		

39. Tell the waiter what you want
41. Radar's drink
46. Deceptive talk
49. Makes amends
51. Sewer's supplies
52. Tennis great
53. Crazy birds
54. Big
55. "My Three Sons" son
56. Arrive at
62. Not Dem. or Rep.
64. Bud's portly pal
65. Used a stool
66. "Concentration" conjunction
67. House of Lords disapproval

ACROSS

1. Wild pigs
6. Rod
9. Rip-off
13. Taxing month
14. A nice thing to say
15. Tribal council member
17. Cartoon flapper
19. Ralph ___ Emerson
20. Diva's ditty
21. Nile biter
22. Rooftop rod
23. U.K. airmen
24. WWII pin-up girl
26. From the U.S.
28. Corn servings
29. Hot chocolate
31. Word on a mall map
32. Newspaper page
36. The Waldorf-___
38. Cul-de-sac
40. "Hey, buddy . . ."
41. First claim
43. Carol leapers
44. Candle holder
45. "M*A*S*H" star
46. The Blonde Bombshell
51. However
54. Fermi or Caruso
55. Triumphed
56. Farm unit
57. Immobile
58. Presidential wife
60. Wigwam
61. Big foot?
62. ___ to the teeth
63. Beatty flick
64. "What happened next?"
65. Temperamental

DOWN

1. Kid's elephant
2. "Aida" or "Carmen"
3. Relics
4. Actress Hayworth
5. Clever
6. Leg up
7. Orphan-no-more
8. Sales ___
9. Workplaces for Ed Norton
10. Bow of film
11. Veer from the script
12. Army award
16. Patton, for Scott
18. '30s heavyweight champ
22. Concur
24. Withstand
25. Football distances
27. Debatable
29. Spending ___
30. CIA forerunner
31. Japanese poem
32. Smell
33. "It's Impossible" singer
34. Termination
35. Driller's deg.
37. Boise's state
39. Actor Bates

Same Name

Solution on Page 360

1	2	3	4	5	■	6	7	8	■	9	10	11	12	■
13					■	14			■	15				16
17					18				■	19				
20				■	21			■	22					
23			■	24				25						
■	■	26	27			■	28				■	■	■	■
29	30				■	31				■	32	33	34	35
36					37		■	38		39				
40				■	41		42		■	43				
■	■	■	■	44				■	45				■	■
46	47	48	49					50			■	51	52	53
54						■	55			■	56			
57					■	58				59				
60					■	61			■	62				
■	63				■	64			■	65				

42. Among
44. Rides a bike
45. Baptismal bowl
46. Topnotch
47. Go in
48. Balderdash
49. Like some bathrooms
50. Lugged
52. Goofed up
53. Kennedy or Roosevelt
56. Bushy do
58. "God'll get you for that" actress Arthur
59. Sweet potato

ACROSS

1. Place to be in hot water?
4. Couches
9. Light brown
14. "___ drink to that!"
15. Motto
16. Knightwear
17. ___ water
18. Boca ___
19. Less mature
20. Marx Brothers movie
23. Make fresh again
24. El Cid or Audie Murphy
25. Beatle spouse
27. Stanley's cry
29. Finale
32. Way or booth preceder
36. Plays accomplice
37. Marx Brothers movie
42. She played Mrs. Mertz
43. Abe Vigoda role
44. Spouse's kinfolk
46. Alcatraz attempt
52. Problem for the Bard
53. Meadow moms
57. Forumwear
58. Marx Brothers movie
62. Nabbed
63. Aesop's lesson
64. Cipher-cracking org.
65. Jane Eyre's charge
66. Wide-___ lens
67. Actress in "L.A. Law" and "The Partridge Family"
68. Actress Oberon or singer Haggard
69. Vladimir's vetoes
70. News hole shrinkers

DOWN

1. Indian instruments
2. "The Daily ___" (Clark Kent's employer)
3. Like edelweiss
4. Write crudely
5. ___-B (dental brand)
6. Command to Fido
7. Put on a pedestal
8. Sub finder
9. Word associated with trees and dogs
10. New York canal
11. Not suitable
12. Freaks out
13. To ___ is human
21. He ran Alice's restaurant
22. How now, brown ___
26. HQ
28. Had sustenance
30. The old college cheer
31. Politician Ribicoff
33. "___ with their 'eads!"
34. Luau keepsake
35. Vegas intro
37. Not produced by machine
38. Witness
39. ___ Victor
40. Darn

Marx Brothers Movies

Solution on Page 360

1	2	3	■	4	5	6	7	8	■	9	10	11	12	13
14			■	15					■	16				
17			■	18					■	19				
20			21						22					■
23					■	24				■	■	25		26
27					28	■	■	■	29	30	31			
■	■	■	■	■	32	33	34	35	■	36				
■	37	38	39	40					41					■
42					■	43				■	■	■	■	■
44					45	■	■	■	46	47	48	49	50	51
52			■	■	53	54	55	56	■	57				
■	58		59	60					61					
62					■	63					■	64		
65					■	66					■	67		
68					■	69					■	70		

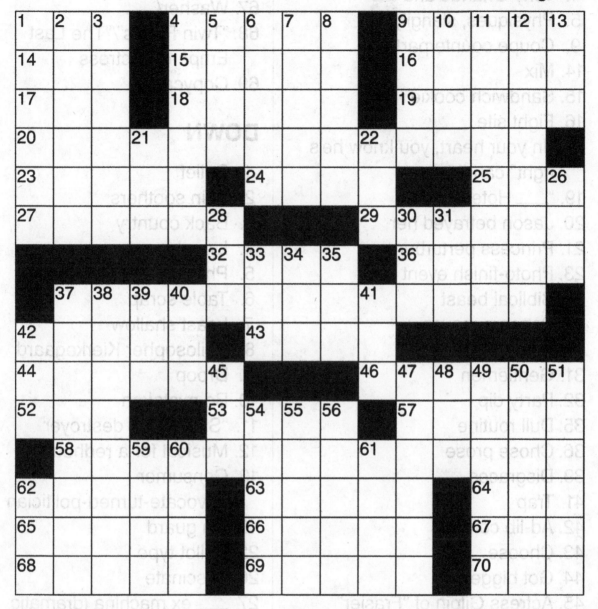

41. ___ Company (C.I.A.)
42. By way of
45. Date frequently
47. Subway gates
48. Swindle
49. Roster
50. Elapsed
51. Term papers

54. "Fireside Theatre" hostess
55. Black
56. ___ protector
59. Little Dickens lass
60. Seat for Charlie or Mortimer
61. Soup additive
62. Flat hat

ACROSS

1. Tony Orlando and ___
5. Physiques, slangily
9. Coupe counterpart
14. Mix
15. Sandwich cookie
16. Fight site
17. "In your heart, you know he's right" candidate
19. "___ Hotel"
20. Jason betrayed her
21. Princess perturber
23. Photo-finish event
24. Biblical beast
25. Popcorn maven
30. Force units
31. Gentlemen
32. Party dip
35. Dull routine
36. Chose prose
39. Disgraces
41. Trap
42. Ad-lib comedy
43. Choose
44. Got bigger
45. Actress Gilpin of "Frasier"
46. Silly birds
48. Frequent Lorre costar
51. IRS employee
54. Publicize
55. Garden tool
56. ___ truly
58. Bible bit
61. Hammett's one-time employer
64. Macabre
65. Gotcha
66. Rubik's ___
67. Washer/___
68. "Twin Peaks"/"The Last Emperor" actress
69. Copycat

DOWN

1. Belief
2. Skin soothers
3. Back country
4. Lymph ___
5. Phyllis Diller accessory
6. Table scrap
7. Least shallow
8. Philosopher Kierkegaard
9. Droop
10. Be mistaken
11. "Star Wars" destroyer
12. Musical for a redhead
13. Consumer advocate-turned-politician
18. On guard
22. Ballot type
26. Fascinate
27. ___ ex machina (dramatic device)
28. Lends a hand
29. Cower
30. Grad's gift
32. Tire initials
33. Bank robot
34. Distant song place
37. Before
38. Drops in the grass

Colorful People

Solution on Page 361

1	2	3	4	■	5	6	7	8	■	9	10	11	12	13
14				■	15				■	16				
17				18					■	19				
20					■	■	21		22	■	■	23		
24			■	25	26	27				28	29			
■	■	■	30					■	31				■	■
32	33	34		■	35			■	36				37	38
39				40			■	41						
42						■	43				■	44		
■	■	45				■	46			47		■	■	■
48	49					50					■	51	52	53
54			■	■	55			■	■	56	57			
58			59	60	■	61		62	63					
64					■	65				■	66			
67					■	68				■	69			

40. Eve's opposite
41. Fencing foil
43. Beastly
47. Eye sore
48. Stared in wonder
49. Stair part
50. ___ of discussion
51. Laugh-a-minute sort
52. Investigation
53. Lou Grant portrayer
57. Killer whale
59. Golfer's concern
60. Mal de ___
62. Originally named
63. Barbie's longtime beau

ACROSS

1. Corporate symbols
6. Ump's call
10. Wrestling surfaces
14. That is to say
15. Monotonous
16. Golden Calf, e.g.
17. Pianist in Louis Armstrong's Hot Five
19. Fisherman's fly
20. Make certain
21. Boston Harbor flotsam/jetsam
22. Anything ___?
23. Hammerstein creation
25. Camera setting
26. Leave out
30. ___ appropriate
32. Waltzer of song
35. Grassy plain
39. Childish retort
40. Expose
41. Gets rid of
43. ___ and saves
44. ___ the thought!
46. Not great, not terrible
47. Fake
50. Take a stab in the dark
53. Realty unit
54. Picnic pest
55. Chowing down
60. Yoko's son
61. Jazz royal pianist who made "One O'Clock Jump"
63. He often played coin-flipping gangsters
64. New money?
65. '50s toothpaste
66. Feed the kitty
67. Mulligan ___
68. More fresh

DOWN

1. A cereal or magazine
2. Gulf in 1991 news
3. Receives
4. Honolulu's isle
5. Tangle
6. Reagan's plan: abbr.
7. Em, to Dorothy
8. Swindles
9. "Born Free" lioness
10. "Kind of Blue" and "Bitches Brew" artist
11. Grownup
12. Trunk
13. Slumber
18. The Say ___ Kid (Willie Mays)
24. Cereal-box initials
25. Peggy Lee hit
26. Poet Khayyam
27. Mama with a mane
28. Thing
29. Latin jazz great
31. Artist Chagall
33. Adores
34. Active one
36. Verne captain
37. Siestas
38. "The Sun ___ Rises"
42. Borrow with a signature

Men of Jazz

Solution on Page 361

1	2	3	4	5	■	6	7	8	9	■	10	11	12	13
14					■	15				■	16			
17					18					■	19			
20						■	21			■	22			
■	■	■	■	23		24			■	25				
26	27	28	29	■	■	30			31			■	■	■
32				33	34		■	35				36	37	38
39						■	■	■	40					
41						42	■	43						
■	■	■	44				45		■	■	46			
47	48	49			■	50			51	52	■	■	■	■
53				■	54			■	55		56	57	58	59
60				■	61			62						
63				■	64				■	65				
66				■	67				■	68				

43. "Murder, ___ Wrote"
45. Stitch
47. Iraq's second-largest city
48. Any one of Earth's four
49. Extortion
51. Ready, ___, go!
52. Polio fighter
54. Pro pilots
56. Gift-wrap fastener
57. "___ Mommy Kissing Santa Claus"
58. Heavenly cloud
59. Equipment
62. Right this second

ACROSS

1. Ghostly pale
6. Tamable one
11. Monitor
14. Replay style
15. Influencer
16. Author Tolstoy
17. Fruit turned to stone
19. Yang's counter
20. Psychic
21. Monopoly piece
22. Jittery
23. Actress turned to stone
27. Nimbly
29. Work
30. Links aide
31. Later editions
35. Tell a whopper
36. Alumni
38. ___ Speedwagon
39. Closed
42. Leader of 11
44. Jazz home
45. Shrill
47. Place turned to stone
51. Horse food
52. Em, to Dorothy
53. Driver's seat
56. Peach stone
57. Media turned to stone
60. Consume
61. Iraqi port
62. Trial partner
63. To a
64. Gloss
65. TV Major

DOWN

1. Nile nippers
2. Blackthorn fruit
3. YouTube candidate
4. Oz city color
5. Xmas drink
6. Kid-lit author
7. Hilton of film
8. Destroyed
9. NY zone
10. Li'l
11. Bonnie's mate
12. Rule
13. Notorious Harding
18. Cambodian cash
22. Scatting Fitzgerald
24. Space author Willy
25. "The ___ Must Be Crazy"
26. Balloon fill
27. Rights org.
28. Increase
31. To the max
32. Preserve
33. Flooring wood
34. Walkman maker
36. Pesky flyer
37. Practice
40. Brewhouses
41. JFK stat
42. Hockey great

Turning to Stone

Solution on Page 361

1	2	3	4	5	■	6	7	8	9	10	■	11	12	13
14					■	15					■	16		
17					18						■	19		
20				■	21				■	■	22			
■	■	23		24					25	26				
27	28						■	29				■	■	■
30					■	■	31					32	33	34
35			■	■	36	37				■	■	38		
39			40	41			■	■		42	43			
■	■	■	44				■	45	46					
47	48	49					50						■	■
51				■	■	52				■	53		54	55
56			■	57	58					59				
60			■	61					■	62				
63			■	64					■	65				

43. 8-stringer on which a Z instrument is named
45. Beach color
46. Loathe
47. Ad type
48. Salary bump
49. Playful animal
50. Ream part
54. Coward in Oz
55. Another
57. "Nova" airer
58. Move it!
59. Sales ___

ACROSS

1. Salad green
6. Dishevel
12. Staff anew
13. Hostile invasion
14. Like some bands
16. Walking in the wind, e.g.
17. Like some fruit
18. It might hold a candle
19. Winged horse
21. River frolicker
22. Morticia's cut rose
23. Scotch drink
25. Presidential home of old
26. Title film heroine of 2001
28. Met numbers
32. Dovetail piece
34. Flyin' lion
36. Yellow-red food dye
38. Island croc?
39. Try the number again
40. Online brokerage firm
41. Sneak peek
42. Avid
43. "Three's Company" star
44. They go downhill fast

DOWN

1. Some pediatrics cases
2. Milk curdler
3. Come out
4. Seussian profferer
5. Crispy cookies
6. Wheel parts
7. Pure prancer?
8. Peter Lorre role
9. Like a meat tenderizer
10. Opposite of a boilmaker?
11. Gardener's tool
15. Mental
20. I once caught a fish ____ . . .
24. "Devil's Dictionary" author
25. Horseman?
26. Garland
27. Detective quarry
28. Slinky's shape
29. Resistance concern
30. Mega-rich
31. Soccer positions
32. Throw sheets
33. *Año* starter
35. "Breaking Away" director
37. Flamenco cries

Mythical Critters

Solution on Page 361

1	2	3	4	5	■	■	6	7	8	9	10	11
12					■	■	13					
14					15	■	16					
17						■	18					
19						20	■	21				
22				■	23		24				■	■
■	■	■	■	25					■	■	■	■
■	■	26	27					■	28	29	30	31
32	33				■	34		35				
36					37	■	38					
39						■	40					
41						■	■	42				
43						■	■	44				

ACROSS

1. Ward off
6. Eightball ball
11. ___ trip
14. Soda unit
15. Emmy role for Susan, finally
16. ___ mitzvah
17. Bookkeeper's concern
20. Saturn or Mercury, e.g.
21. Berle's network in the '50s
22. Utilize
26. First Homeland Security head
30. Glorifies
31. Yelped
34. Snaky swimmers
35. Sulu shipmate
36. John ___ Lennon
37. Reagan Chief of Staff
41. Bus. VIP
43. Comedian Schreiber
44. Dim bloke
47. With child
49. Dennis, to Mr. Wilson
51. Man-made fiber
52. Ceased at sea
53. Took the forefront
55. Stinging insect
56. Fun-loving fellow
64. Noticed
65. Emcee's assignment
66. Simon's "California ___"
67. Brunched
68. Cauldron collective
69. Having lots to lose

DOWN

1. ___ carte
2. Radio's "___ and Sade"
3. And so forth: abbr.
4. '20s auto
5. AWOL student
6. Donnybrook
7. Approximately
8. Golf hole edge
9. Little engine's thought
10. Dawn
11. ___ and flow
12. "A ___ in Calico"
13. Tram filler
18. Off one's rocker
19. Litmus colorer
22. Driving aid
23. Hatchet
24. Rodgers musical comedy
25. Ingrid's famous role
27. Portal
28. "Annie Get Your ___"
29. WWII area
31. Scorches
32. JFK's killer's killer
33. Novelist Levin
35. Chatroom person
38. Like some personalities
39. First lady
40. Sicilian spouter
41. EMT's forte
42. The end of an ___
45. Bartender's question
46. WJM anchor

Military ABCs

Solution on Page 362

1	2	3	4	5	■	6	7	8	9	10	■	11	12	13
14					■	15					■	16		
17					18						19			
■	■	■	■	20				■	21			■	■	■
22	23	24	25				■	■	■	26		27	28	29
30						■	31	32	33					
34				■	■	35					■	36		
■	■	37		38	39						40		■	■
41	42		■	43					■	■	44		45	46
47			48					■	49	50				
51					■	■	■	52						
■	■	■	53		54	■	55				■	■	■	■
56	57	58				59					60	61	62	63
64			■	65					■	66				
67			■	68					■	69				

48. Olympic prize
49. Fine netting
50. 1959 Marty Robbins hit
52. Part of a BLT
54. Rat Pack name
55. "The Way We ___"
56. J. Low gp.
57. Trigger tidbit
58. Be in debt
59. Cable rock station
60. "Ay, there's the ___"
61. Let sleeping dogs ___
62. "___ beginning to look a lot like Christmas"
63. Big foot?

ACROSS

1. Rasher item
6. One way to feel
10. Like some food orders
14. Do penance
15. New currency
16. 1 Down, e.g.
17. They might be loaded
18. Scanned thing at the store
19. Moolah
20. Let in
21. He sang the title song
23. Pal of Stanley or Fran and Kukla
25. Used sale sign
26. Rover
28. Bathroom squares
32. That girl
33. Do a little of this and a little of that
38. Inning count
39. Ike's command
40. Powerful chess piece
41. Right this minute
42. Puts blades to blades
44. Biblical prophet
46. Ginger ___
47. Ping producer
49. Ring site
51. Droopy watch painter
54. Sailing
55. She played 29 Down
59. Domesticates
62. Loafing about
63. Shutter part
64. Totally LOVE
65. "Hot ___" Houlihan
66. Ripped
67. Aladdin's lamp-dweller
68. Dick Tracy's Trueheart
69. Auction ender
70. Go in

DOWN

1. Ali ___
2. Somewhat
3. Donald O'Connor role
4. "The Iceman Cometh" playwright
5. Got comfy
6. Ecru kin
7. Lyre cousin
8. Amphitheater
9. Places to hang your hat
10. Adopts, as a stray
11. ___ hygiene
12. Chutzpah
13. Follow
22. Model airplane, say
24. "Three Kings" extra
26. Throat-clearing utterances
27. Bandwagon cry
29. Shrill-voiced role
30. ___ Gay
31. Ed Norton's workplace
34. Ralph Kramden's workplace
35. Actress who said, "God'll get you for that, Walter"

Singin' in the Rain

Solution on Page 362

1	2	3	4	5	■	6	7	8	9	■	10	11	12	13
14					■	15				■	16			
17					■	18				■	19			
20					■	21				22				
■	■	23			24		■	25				■	■	■
26	27					■	■	■	■	28		29	30	31
32			■	33		34	35	36	37	■	38			
39			■	■	40					■	■	41		
42			43	■	44					45	■	46		
47				48	■	■	■	■	49		50			
■	■	■	51		52	53	■	54					■	■
55	56	57					58		■	59			60	61
62				■	63				■	64				
65				■	66				■	67				
68				■	69				■	70				

36. O in Oahu
37. Legislate
43. Sorrow
45. "Dog Day Afternoon" extra
48. Football cry
50. Weighed down
52. Endures
53. Nome dome home
54. Put into the pot
55. Undo a beau
56. McClurg or Adams
57. Swiss peaks
58. ___ "Fatha" Hines
60. Canal or lake
61. Sixth sense specialist

ACROSS

1. Sacrifice table
6. Voila!
10. Radioman's "A"
14. Ethiopia's Selassie
15. Get off ___-free
16. Happy
17. Mae West's first film as a lead actress
20. Estimator's words
21. "A Yank at ___"
22. Therefore
23. Japanese soup
24. Obeyed
25. Tiny Tim's instrument: var.
29. Calculate
30. Western productions
31. Toupee
32. "Who killed me?" film
35. It won 10 Oscars and a Pulitzer
39. Clean-air gp.
40. Cattle call
41. Put aside
42. Attest
44. Horse gear
45. "When You're ___" (song)
48. ___ and pans
49. Nikon rival
50. Green fruit
51. Comment to Yorick
55. "I coulda been a contender" film
58. Author Ephron
59. Racetrack shape
60. Actress Massey
61. Greek Cupid
62. Simple
63. Marc Antony addressee

DOWN

1. Chan comment
2. Cowardly Lion portrayer
3. Father's Day faves
4. Actor Ray
5. '20s auto
6. Dangerous fly
7. "Gesundheit!" preceder
8. Bump off
9. PIN requester
10. Concurred
11. Fair-haired
12. Jouster's weapon
13. Double-___ sword
18. "Odd Couple" writer
19. At what time?
23. Cat call
24. Come hell or ___
25. Egg on
26. Reagan's Surgeon General
27. Author Ferber
28. Kathie ___ Gifford
29. Tailor's concern
31. Which person?
32. Sub command
33. Till fill
34. Throws in
36. Lug
37. Corn units

Top Films

Solution on Page 362

38. ". . . and ___ one for the Gipper"
42. Island greetings
43. Hollywood and ___
44. Unattractive
45. Teacake
46. "To the ___ Born"
47. Emcee's speech
48. Hummus dippers
50. Volcano spillage
51. Alice's chronicler
52. Suspend
53. O'Neill's "___ Christie"
54. Baseball's Musial
56. O ___ is me!
57. Douglas ___ (tree type)

ACROSS

1. Sailor
4. Meadows
8. "War of the Worlds" world
12. Rage
13. Like Charlie Parker's sax
14. Pitch black
15. Passageway for Indiana Jones
17. Accurate
18. Steak choice
19. Imagine
21. Thanks ___!
22. Helpful samaritan
24. Anoa home
26. Long lock
27. Make into law
29. Imprison
33. Paddle person
38. Logoed rubber accessory
40. Pet peeve
41. As was found
42. Grading concern
43. Mountain monk
44. Wiggle in the rear
47. Optimist's assertion
48. Lady of the haus
49. Driver's stand
50. Lots of time
51. The bright side?
52. Foul up

DOWN

1. Certs rival
2. Like fertile ground
3. Industrially update
4. Chantilly, e.g.
5. "Xanadu" band
6. 24-hr. banker
7. I once caught a fish ___ . . .
8. Shower item
9. Rub the wrong way
10. Pathways
11. Snapelike looks
16. Go to pot?
20. Funny in the head
22. Lion's lair
23. City near Kyoto
25. Flat cap
28. Simon Bar Sinister's aide
29. A Dionne sister
30. Grace land?
31. Ralph Kramden, e.g.
32. Most people
34. Neighbor
35. It's known for its chops
36. One who's a little bit green
37. Roving sot
39. Like cumulus clouds
42. Outdrink action
45. Playwright Levin
46. ___ Luis Obispo

Pets

Solution on Page 362

1	2	3	■	4	5	6	7	■	8	9	10	11
12			■	13				■	14			
15			16					■	17			
18					■	■	19	20				
21			■	22	23							
24				25			■	26				
■	■	■	■	27			28		■	■	■	■
29	30	31	32		■	33			34	35	36	37
38					39			■	40			
41						■	■	42				
43				■	44	45	46					
47				■	48				■	49		
50				■	51				■	52		

ACROSS

1. Pegboard needs
6. Roadside accommodation
11. Cook's amt.
14. Bayou
15. Journey path
16. "Now I see!"
17. Close distance
19. Rand McNally item
20. Quick or slow in quick-quick-slow
21. Finale
23. Naked title character
25. "Divine Comedy" author
28. Buckwheat assent
29. Decorate again
31. Glitzy bit
34. Baby beds
36. Actor Howard or Nielsen
37. "___ Boulevard"
39. Commander-in-Chief command
43. Draft-dodging destination
47. "Love Story" author
48. Type of soup
52. Hidden Hirschfeld name
53. A party to
54. Darns
56. ___-o-shanter
57. Owl sound
60. Director Kazan
62. Ignited
63. See red
68. Ike's command
69. Made hay?
70. Schoolgirl dress feature
71. Reader's spot
72. Nader's "Unsafe at Any ___"
73. Exams

DOWN

1. Carol starter
2. Army member
3. ___ on (enveloped)
4. Planet byline
5. Knight's mount
6. He played a Rocky foe
7. ___ and ah
8. Soup holders
9. James Bond's school
10. Like unseemly behavior
11. Staked plant
12. Medicine man
13. Spinach fan
18. Ship rod
22. Balanced the feud
23. Trajectory paths
24. Lima's land
26. Gretzky's gp.
27. Restaurant accessory
30. Vulgar
32. "Boola Boola" singer
33. Reasons for rosaries
35. Rough waters
38. Blasting letters
40. Shakes
41. Actress Delany
42. "Easy Street" actor
44. Garment opening

Nesting Nests

Solution on Page 363

1	2	3	4	5	■	6	7	8	9	10	■	11	12	13
14					■	15					■	16		
17					18						■	19		
■	■	20				■	■	21			22			
23	24		■	25		26	27		■	■	28			
29			30	■	31				32	33				
34				35	■	36						■	■	■
37					38	■	■	■	39			40	41	42
■	■	■	43			44	45	46	■	47				
48	49	50							51	■	52			
53				■	■	54				55	■	56		
57				58	59		■	■	60		61		■	■
62			■	63			64	65					66	67
68			■	69					■	70				
71			■	72					■	73				

45. "Meet John ___"
46. Actress Sothern
48. Deceived
49. Egg on
50. Kramden's TV pal
51. Utopia
55. George Washington ___ here
58. Subsides
59. Thunder sound
61. Crete or Capri
64. Li'l
65. Peculiar
66. Bran source
67. Scoreboard nos.

ACROSS

1. Untouchable serves
5. Choir member
9. Crisp cookie
14. Venetian-blind part
15. Part of S&L
16. Adept
17. It makes a roar
19. Direct contract type
20. The Shah, for one
21. Swashbuckling actor
23. Pad
24. The hunted
26. Dinner guests
31. ___ out one's welcome
32. Desi song
33. Avow
36. Defeat
37. Rugged rock
38. ___ it on the line
39. Catcher's glove
40. Trouble
43. Like a Dallas knoll
45. Manors
46. Oil gp.
47. "Little Rascals" rascal
48. Regular food
49. June, to the Beaver
52. Sleep soundly
54. Black wood
56. They can be raised or stormed
60. "In your heart, you know he's right" candidate
62. Mil. mistake
63. Misplace
64. Pinto or kidney
65. Fred's sis
66. "Harper Valley PTA" actress
67. Politician Grasso

DOWN

1. ___ in cash (very well off)
2. The It Girl
3. Aggravate
4. "Nana" actress
5. FDR rival Landon
6. Lazybones
7. Sum
8. "I ___ Have Eyes for You"
9. Pretender
10. A long time ___ . . .
11. Lie
12. Yalie
13. Communist
18. Less green
22. Like a pin
25. Dodge product meaning "to hit"
27. Plane place
28. Immigrant island
29. Haley epic
30. Like a chimney sweep
31. Teepee
32. Dock's place, in a Redding song
33. Pains
34. BBC interviewer
35. Roscoe Arbuckle's nickname
36. Card game
38. French article
41. In disagreement

Desert Cry

Solution on Page 363

1	2	3	4	■	5	6	7	8	■	9	10	11	12	13
14				■	15				■	16				
17				18					■	19				
20					■	21			22		■	■	■	■
23			■	24	25			■	26		27	28	29	30
■	■	■	31				■	32						
33	34	35				■	36							
37				■	■	38			■	■	39			
40				41	42			■	43	44				
45							■	46			■	■	■	■
47						■	48				■	49	50	51
■	■	■	■	52		53			■	54	55			
56	57	58	59		■	60			61					
62					■	63				■	64			
65					■	66				■	67			

42. High-schooler
43. Student's stat
44. Extend a contract
46. Darer's words
48. Sulk
49. "Psycho" setting
50. "What's Up, Doc?" actor
51. Actress Loy
53. Rude look
55. Sonny and Cher song title word
56. Merit badge org.
57. "Me ___ My Shadow"
58. "The Facts of Life" actress
59. Super Bowl org.
61. ___ of iniquity

ACROSS

1. WWII craft
4. Card maker
9. Jam ingredient
13. Give two thumbs up
15. Look forward to
16. All over again
17. Clown at a picnic?
19. Lab heater
20. Geronimo or Cochise
21. Namby-pamby
23. Like this clue
25. "Is that your ___ answer?"
26. Blow one's top
28. Mesmerized
31. Brain or ear part
34. The magic word
36. Casper's cry
37. "Holly Jolly Christmas" singer
38. Ill. neighbor
39. Big scoop on a chain, for short
40. Dracula portrayer of yore
41. Awakens
44. Goo-goo-googly things
45. Besieged
47. Upper crust
49. Sovereign or straightedge
51. "We hold these ___ to be self-evident . . ."
54. Like stag, moose or elk
57. Patronized a pizzeria
59. Nostalgic soft-drink name
60. Rebellious insect?
62. 50-50 exam answer
63. Creepy
64. Baking ___
65. Ilk
66. Oozes
67. Dream letters

DOWN

1. Innocent or guilty
2. Home to the Bucs
3. Poison ___
4. Rehems, say
5. I ___ you a debt of gratitude
6. Lines are sometimes read there
7. Rice ___
8. Throws for a loop
9. Pol who had his salad days?
10. Carson character on a farm?
11. Casino town in Nevada
12. Influence
14. Edicts
18. Hammer-wielding god
22. Actress Bancroft
24. Divorced
27. Grammarian's concern
29. Sit for a picture
30. Bests
31. ___ Marlene
32. Place where you'll need a mitt
33. Comedienne who uses a comb?
35. Insect stage
39. ___ on the brink
41. Baum's Dorothy's last name
42. Comes into view

Buggy People

Solution on Page 363

1	2	3	■	■	4	5	6	7	8	■	9	10	11	12
13			14	■	15					■	16			
17				18						■	19			
20						■	21			22				
■	23					24	■	25					■	■
■	■	■	26				27	■	28				29	30
31	32	33		■	34			35			■	36		
37				■	■	38			■	■	39			
40			■	41	42				43	■	44			
45			46			■	47			48		■	■	■
■	■	49				50	■	51				52	53	■
54	55						56	■	57					58
59				■	60			61						
62				■	63						64			
65				■	66					■	■	67		

43. "Peter Pan" extras
46. Romeo's love
48. Ballet skirt
50. Richards of tennis
52. ". . . love, ___ and obey"
53. Elvis's "Blue ___ Shoes"
54. Aardvark snack
55. Tec Wolfe
56. Bell the cat
58. Coal car
61. ___ the balance

ACROSS

1. T-bar rider
6. Pointed
12. Tube pasta
13. Like part of the iris
15. Bolt
16. Greek cool sauce
17. Ship cargo gp.
18. Limelight liker
20. Massachusetts cape
21. "Try to Remember" singer
23. Crack
25. Greek dish with a pita
27. Pro ___
28. Family tracer
29. Least crazy
31. Hold back
33. "To be" in Latin
37. Place with a sala
39. Greek eggplant dish
41. Narrow
42. Wee cartoon folk, with "The"
43. The Plastic ___ Band
44. I wish!
47. Offensive time?
48. Greek stuffed grape leaves
50. Band together
52. Crazy times
53. Printer need
54. Copier component
55. XM radio guy

DOWN

1. Most agile
2. "Prairie Home" guy
3. Fashionable
4. Las Vegas-Omaha dir.
5. State again
6. Indy Jones flick extra
7. Funds for the future
8. Improves
9. Dickens pen name
10. Yield
11. Actress Fanning
14. Carnie concern
16. Focused on
19. Half-full/half-empty item
22. Opposed
24. Just out
26. Loafer parts
30. Small holders
32. "Night at the Museum 2" role
34. Cracker type
35. Marsh bug
36. Oriental
37. Dugouts
38. NASA rocket series
40. Pub orders
41. "Sweeney ___"
45. Big-tongued toon dog
46. Bosc or Anjou
49. Former Russian satellite
51. Wayne's word

It's All Greek to Me

Solution on Page 363

1	2	3	4	5	■	■	6	7	8	9	10	11	■
12					■	■	13						14
15					■	16							
17			■	18	19					■	20		
21			22				■	■	23	24			
25							26	■	27				■
28				■	29			30			■	■	■
■	■	■	31	32					■	33	34	35	36
■	37	38			■	39			40				
41					■	■	42						
43			■	44	45	46				■	47		
48			49					■	50	51			
52							■	■	53				
■	54						■	■	55				

ACROSS

1. Freeway on/offs
6. Tiny
10. Slightly
14. The Little Mermaid
15. Stench
16. Actress Hayworth
17. Harlem Globetrotter star
20. My word!
21. Silly
22. Says more
25. Affirmative
27. Wane
28. Pier group
30. Vacuum tubes
33. Mesmerized
35. Dollop
36. Pie ___ mode
39. Bob Hope film
42. Lawn piece
43. Candy ___
44. Harbor locale
45. Children
47. Pole symbol
48. ___ on the brakes
50. This girl
52. Ardent admirers
53. ___ domain
56. Rick's love
58. Certain dessert
63. Den
64. Polly, to Tom Sawyer
65. Actress Winger
66. Part of A&E
67. Queries
68. Black column item

DOWN

1. Aries animal
2. "You ___ There"
3. Woody's ex
4. Admired one's place
5. Trudge
6. Like Jell-O
7. Rhoda's mom
8. Asta's keeper
9. Annoys
10. Gladiator sites
11. Nervous
12. Not just rue
13. Hamlet, for one
18. "My ___" (Sinatra song)
19. Hitchcock single-set film
22. Helps in a heist
23. Hawaiian musician
24. Challenged
26. John Hancock and others
29. Sample
31. ___ Hickory
32. Coed quarters
34. Ness, notably
36. Asian pug
37. Type of closet
38. President #2 or #6
40. The Plastic ___ Band
41. Desecrates
45. Chalets
46. Changes

What Life Hands You

Solution on Page 364

1	2	3	4	5	■	6	7	8	9	■	10	11	12	13
14					■	15				■	16			
17					18					19				
■	■	■	20				■	21						
22	23	24		■	25		26	■	■	27				■
28				29	■	30		31	32			■	■	■
33					34	■	35				■	36	37	38
39						40					41			
42			■	43				■	44					
■	■	■	45					46	■	47				
■	48	49			■	■	50		51	■	52			
53					54	55	■	56		57		■	■	■
58							59					60	61	62
63				■	64				■	65				
66				■	67				■	68				

48. Muckrake
49. Speed ____
51. Keebler employee
53. Governor Grasso
54. Pac-12 overseer
55. Hence
57. ____ jerk
59. Squid weapon
60. "Civil War" airer
61. Enmity
62. Chow down

ACROSS

1. Illinois college town
7. Classic theft film
13. "Later!"
14. Starting place
15. Picnic pests
16. "Star Trek" explores new ones
17. What a band fights?
18. Director Coen
20. Nice words
21. Asian edge range
23. Too long a time
24. Respond to getting spooked
25. Rigging rope
27. They might all be covered
28. Sushi spots
29. Racket
30. Stand for art
33. Enter
37. Luau loops
38. Blockade
39. Payment
40. Rage
41. Command to Fido
43. Doubled and stretched "Star Wars" word
44. Stupidity awards are named for him
46. Things to be discussed
48. Online brokerage firm
49. Maroon, thru maritime
50. Like some fish
51. Quite

DOWN

1. Beneficial
2. Nautical hitchhiker
3. Roll one's eyes, audibly
4. Sea *si*
5. Memo
6. No-frills
7. Martin cohort
8. Monopoly piece
9. Xmas tree
10. Blockhouses?
11. Bluegrass or jig musicmaker
12. Metro blowups
19. Mason's carrier
22. Old strings
24. Canadian town and a park
26. Time Warner lead-in, once
27. Comic's routine
29. Green goddess
30. Leaves out
31. Ventilate
32. "The Treasure of the ___ Madre"
33. Pouch
34. Clumsy
35. Seer
36. Less detailed
38. Ate well
41. Shirts or skins, say
42. "Who's the Boss?" role
45. Card game that's all luck
47. Hole

Final Measures

Solution on Page 364

1	2	3	4	5	6	■	7	8	9	10	11	12
13						■	14					
15						■	16					
17			■	18		19			■	20		
21			22	■	23			■	24			
25				26			■	27				
■	■	■	28			■	29			■	■	■
30	31	32			■	33				34	35	36
37				■	38			■	39			
40			■	41				42	■	43		
44			45			■	46	47				
48						■	49					
50						■	51					

ACROSS

1. Answer, in "Jeopardy!"
4. ___ Alamos
7. Modern encyclopedia, say
12. . . . the ___ from the palace has the brew that is true!
14. U. of Maine town
15. Astronomic event of 1997
17. Jeannie portrayer
18. Not at all
19. Elton John hit
24. Lively dances
27. Politician Morales
28. Op-ed author
29. Takeover type
32. Boat blade
33. Steinbeck's row
34. Sets up
38. Pong maker
39. Simplicity
43. "Lethal Weapon" director
47. Saying
48. Podium
49. Camera concern
50. Mess up
51. Li'l

DOWN

1. Pain
2. Food fish
3. Moolah
4. Mad or ad follower
5. Bunker portrayer
6. Soldiers from India
7. Cuckoo for ___ Puffs
8. ___ one's sorrows
9. CD-___
10. ___ for the road
11. Bon ___
13. Pre-Easter
16. Dr.'s deg.
20. Fury
21. Surrender
22. Penultimate story word
23. Actor Calhoun
24. Cartoon Betty
25. Milky gem
26. Former Capri coin
29. More quickly
30. Vader, as a kid
31. Space in
33. Go bad
35. Google rival
36. Postal purchase
37. See 40 Down
40. "Price Is Right" announcement, with 37 Down
41. Dry
42. Sea eagle
43. Lit. program
44. TSA concerns
45. Op ___
46. Text getter, for short

Polarity

Solution on Page 364

1	2	3	■	4	5	6	■	7	8	9	10	11
12			13				■	14				
15							16					
17				■	18					■	■	■
■	■	■	19	20						21	22	23
24	25	26					■	■	■	27		
28						■	29	30	31			
32			■	■	■	33						
34			35	36	37					■	■	■
■	■	■	38					■	39	40	41	42
43	44	45						46				
47					■	48						
49					■	50			■	51		

ACROSS

1. Represent
7. Towel word
11. Pick apples?
14. Dickens waif
15. Biz boss
16. "Chances ___"
17. Uncle Junior's nephew
19. "Star Wars" prog.
20. Have trouble getting out
21. Our closest star
22. "Good Eats" host Brown
26. Julius or Ethel of spydom
28. Some horses
30. Galas
31. Long times
32. Succinct
35. Icy treat
37. Strike type
40. 180
42. Bond, briefly
43. Part of CSI
45. Portal
47. Puts up with
50. Choice words?
51. Polar cover
52. Olympic no-no
54. Federal URL ending
55. Held by
60. A Stooge
61. "Shall we?" response
62. Book of prophecies
63. Actress Jillian
64. Wise rival
65. Haifa hello

DOWN

1. URL part
2. "Evil Woman" gp.
3. Wrestling hold
4. Wall climber
5. Skyhawk maker
6. Gentle gait
7. L.A. beach
8. Tests
9. Nurse Betty portrayer
10. Bitter
11. Hush Puppies mascot
12. Compost
13. Sentients
18. Cowpoke
22. Boulle film extras
23. Oz coward
24. Almost a dozen
25. Vulgar
27. Victoria "Posh Spice" ___
29. Forgetful actor's request
33. Desmond portrayer
34. Soda jerk offering
36. Hype to the max
38. Scot's odd
39. Rank
41. Cassandra, e.g.
43. Bad mark
44. Pupal protector
46. Red veggie
48. Sailing
49. Short-fused

Singing to the Choir

Solution on Page 364

1	2	3	4	5	6	■	7	8	9	10	■	11	12	13
14						■	15				■	16		
17						18					■	19		
■	■	■	■	20							■	21		
22	23	24	25		■	26					27			
28					29			■	■	30				
31				■	32			33	34				■	■
35				36			■	37					38	39
■	■	40					41			■	42			
43	44				■	■	45			46				
47					48	49			■	50				
51			■	52					53		■	■	■	■
54			■	55							56	57	58	59
60			■	61				■	62					
63			■	64				■	65					

53. Disease ender
56. Popular tower
57. ___ Abner
58. Confucian way
59. Resistance unit

ACROSS

1. Jerk's output
6. Saloon
9. Chaney of monster movies
12. Radium discoverer
13. ___ as directed
14. Gotcha!
15. Sky-blue
16. Joplin's specialty
18. "Rosencrantz and Guildenstern are Dead" playwright
20. A bit of negativity?
21. ___ the knot
24. De Mille flick, say
27. Sunrise direction
30. Wedding page word
31. "Eight Is Enough" star
34. Swallowed
35. Director Kazan
36. Achy
37. En ___ (together)
39. Place to relax
41. "Dragnet" and "M*A*S*H" star
47. It's pricy at the pump
49. Prolonged assault
50. It's under a lid
51. Brokaw's network
52. Come in
53. Take after expenses
54. Federal purchasing org.
55. Thrown for a loop

DOWN

1. Ella's specialty
2. Greek liqueur
3. Buddy Rich instrument
4. Type of bag
5. Take care of
6. Pat baby on the back
7. Stat!
8. Boat event
9. Assailed
10. A little resistance?
11. Dundee denial
17. Give it the old college ___
19. "Paper Moon" star
22. ___-do-well
23. Krupa who plays the 3 Down
24. Cheese in a red rind
25. Hummus dipper
26. Very large glacier
28. "Wheel of Fortune" purchase
29. Writer's cramp, e.g.
32. Swerving
33. Russian royalty
38. "Casablanca" pianist
40. Did more than say "cheese"
42. Massages
43. Village People hit
44. Jazzy tenor sax player
45. "The African Queen" scripter
46. Social misfit
47. Sword beater
48. It might be seeded

Tom, Dick, and Harry

Solution on Page 365

1	2	3	4	5	■	6	7	8	■	9	10	11
12					■	13			■	14		
15					■	16			17			
18				19							■	■
■	■	■	20			■	■	21			22	23
24	25	26		■	27	28	29		■	30		
31				32					33			
34			■	35				■	36			
37		38			■	■	39	40		■	■	■
■	■	41		42	43					44	45	46
47	48						■	49				
50			■	51			■	52				
53			■	54			■	55				

ACROSS

1. Like Dora, in old jokes
5. Inexpensive
10. Before, put before
13. Stern on the bow
15. Get-up-and-go
16. It might be cured
17. Wares
19. Gambler's letters
20. He had a great white hope
21. Student
23. Rugrat
25. They often wear stripes
28. Like a fleabag hotel
29. He played a lion
31. Easily set off
34. Singing group
36. Knife neighbor
37. Contradicts
39. Eye part
43. Birdlike
45. Pirate flag item
47. "Phantom" prop
52. Famous last words
53. There ___ to be a law
54. Author Angelou
56. Greedy taker
57. Of no avail
60. Purina rival
62. Car in a Ronny & the Daytonas song
63. Vague derogatory name
68. Every
69. It's in the dumps
70. Ruby's mate
71. Roulette bet
72. Sealy rival
73. Crew

DOWN

1. Badly lit
2. "___ the Force, Luke"
3. One-day-plus dance event
4. Schickele talks about his son
5. Person often wearing stripes
6. Brick holder
7. Actor Jannings
8. Church section
9. They might be under glass
10. Rang up
11. Films like "Fantasia"
12. One with stem cells
14. Sear
18. Help a heister
22. Cartoon dog with a voice like Peter Lorre
23. RN's forte
24. Diamond Head's site
26. Museum rock
27. Dine
30. Clean out
32. Eye part
33. Farm tool
35. Driving events
38. First lady
40. Likeable President
41. Lunatic asylum
42. High singer

Holding Hands

Solution on Page 365

1	2	3	4	■	■	5	6	7	8	9	■	10	11	12
13				14	■	15					■	16		
17					18						■	19		
■	■	20				■	■	21			22			
23	24		■	25		26	27	■	■	28				
29			30	■	31			32	33					
34				35	■	36					■	■	■	■
■	37				38		■	39			40	41	42	■
■	■	■	■	43			44		■	45				46
47	48	49	50						51	■	52			
53					■	■	54			55	■	56		
57					58	59	■	■	60		61		■	■
62			■	63			64	65					66	67
68			■	69					■	70				
71			■	72					■	■	73			

44. Get in one's sights
46. Haul
47. Wildcat
48. Disco dance
49. Classic
50. Orr's org.
51. Tatum's dad
55. Ray of movies
58. Certain
59. Wound reminder
61. "Hey, buddy"
64. DDE's preceder
65. Eureka
66. Gourmet's school
67. ___ and haw

ACROSS

1. Kindergarten basics
5. . . . but something doesn't quite ___
10. ___ melt sandwich
14. Breakfast, lunch or dinner
15. Bible part
16. Windows rival
17. One of the bad guys
20. Old-fashioned remedy
21. Serious bearing
22. French state
24. ___ a plea
25. Battering ___
28. One of the bad guys
34. And others
36. Fiery gem
37. Teed-off golf stroke
38. ___ Lisa
39. Airline guesstimate: abbr.
40. On an ___ keel
41. Cancel
43. Dole's '96 running mate
45. Ireland's alias
46. Surprise attack site
49. Colorer
50. ___ de vie
51. Love god
53. "We, the People . . .," famously
58. Getting
62. "Big Three" summit
64. "The ___ of the Ancient Mariner"
65. Abacus or snake
66. Shah's country
67. Baseball's Slaughter
68. Bosc and Anjou
69. Like Felix Unger

DOWN

1. Both: pref.
2. Pager's sound
3. Chaplin prop
4. Cake serving
5. Guacamole fruit
6. Not Rep. or Ind.
7. The D in FDA
8. One of the Big Three
9. Passover
10. Its blossoms are way up high
11. Apartment or condo
12. Ship of 1492
13. The bad guys, with "The"
18. See ya!
19. Egg-shaped
23. Kansas city
25. Sketch the minefield again
26. Seek penance
27. Heavenly gift?
29. See you ___!
30. Fiery food
31. Infuriated
32. All
33. She recently played Bridget
35. Poet ___ (Tennyson, Wordsworth, etc.)
42. Andean animal
44. Bar orders or bag handlers

WWII

Solution on Page 365

1	2	3	4	■	5	6	7	8	9	■	10	11	12	13
14				■	15					■	16			
17				18						19				
20						■	21							
■	■	■	22			23	■	■	24			■	■	■
25	26	27	■	28			29	30				31	32	33
34			35	■	36				■	37				
38				■	■	39			■	■	40			
41				42	■	43			44	■	45			
46					47					48	■	49		
■	■	■	50			■	■	51			52	■	■	■
53	54	55				56	57	■	58			59	60	61
62								63						
64				■	65					■	66			
67				■	68					■	69			

47. Frisbee kin
48. Lion's sound
52. Yarn unit
53. Bonfire
54. "Singin' in the ___"
55. "St. ___'s Fire"
56. Ore vein
57. "Never ___ sentence with . . ."
59. About
60. Final Four org.
61. Lady's escort
63. Not "agin"

ACROSS

1. Fancy soapbox
5. Enjoys a book
10. Booth fare
14. Charlie Chan's comment
15. Like some goals
16. Uh-huh
17. Stay tuned
20. Pipe cleaner
21. Over 1,001 ___!
22. ___ havoc (makes problems)
23. Cooking instruction
24. Sousa group
25. Net
28. Church chairs
29. Jigsaw puzzle concern
32. Birdlike
33. One way to go
34. Flay
35. Stay tuned
38. Lends a hand
39. Dryer fuzz
40. It goes in the black column
41. Cereal box initials
42. "Shave and a haircut—two ___"
43. Wanting a lot
44. Guns, like an engine
45. Divot
46. Clever
49. Holier-than-___
50. "___ Pinafore"
53. Stay tuned
56. Top-notch
57. "The Wonder ___"
58. Something about you
59. Sometimes kids connect them
60. Comic Bruce
61. Biker LeMond

DOWN

1. Wonka writer
2. Hi thar, by the spar!
3. Dot in the water
4. Lay down the lawn
5. Impales
6. Return key
7. Famous cookieman
8. "L.A. Law" actress
9. Shipboard Shirley Temple film of '36
10. Weary
11. DOL org.
12. Fuel tank problem
13. "Shall we?" response
18. Excursion
19. Coffee containers
23. Plays usher
24. Sired
25. Col. Potter's aide
26. Steer clear of
27. In a way
28. Half of all chess pieces
29. Test answer
30. Peeved
31. Irritable
33. Speeds
34. Sat for a picture
36. Popeye's love

Stays

Solution on Page 365

1	2	3	4	■	5	6	7	8	9	■	10	11	12	13
14				■	15					■	16			
17				18						19				
20			■	21				■	22					
■	■	■	23				■	24				■	■	■
25	26	27				■	28				■	29	30	31
32					■	33				■	34			
35					36					37				
38				■	39				■	40				
41			■	42				■	43					
■	■	■	44				■	45				■	■	■
46	47	48				■	49				■	50	51	52
53						54					55			
56				■	57					■	58			
59				■	60					■	61			

37. Groovy, man
42. Sister of Jo, Meg, and Amy
43. Like some photos
44. Red herrings
45. Butter tool
46. Somewhat
47. Flee, flea
48. It has flaps
49. Ness, e.g.
50. "The Children's ___"
51. Seconds
52. Plan A ruiner
54. "___ Willie Winkie"
55. Mouth muffler

ACROSS

1. Nonveggie drink
8. Meddlesome ones
13. Legendary box
14. Part of UHF
15. "10" fans?
16. Compass type
17. It's pronounced like a short I
18. Honduran dollar
20. "I ___ Rock"
21. Tale with a 16 Across
23. Gymnast Korbut
24. Atahualpa, e.g.
25. Puerto Rico, e.g.
26. On the morning shift?
28. Since that time
31. Wags
32. H.S. math class
34. Level
35. Watches
39. Waitron, e.g.
43. Hawaiian Don commanding the boat?
45. 10 ccs., e.g.
46. Oh well
47. Horse hue
48. Schnozzes
49. At this time
50. Cookie type
52. Holder that looks like a squeegee
53. Former UN leader
55. Porker taking gym class?
57. Caterpillar rival
58. Stinky critters
59. He played Dr. Kildare
60. Sheathes

DOWN

1. Within limits
2. Boise to Bismarck dir.
3. Fred's sister
4. Bend the elbow
5. Shake
6. Sound barrier
7. ___ least one web transaction
8. Wild cat
9. 10 Down "Magic" band
10. See 9 Down
11. Ore hauler
12. Respectful bows
13. Fertilizer compound
15. Suit nicely
19. ___ the new year
22. Surgical tools
24. Be nosy
27. "Understood"
29. "Fame" actress
30. Mistress of the dark
33. Memorial
35. Anthem in Ottawa
36. Hogwash
37. Egg layer
38. "Rinse and repeat" item
40. Formal dance props
41. Bars in court
42. "The Cloister and the Hearth" author

Not Okay

Solution on Page 366

		1	2	3	4	5	6	7		8	9	10	11	12
	13									14				
15										16				
17				18					19			20		
21		22				23					24			
25						26				27				
28				29	30		31							
			32			33		34						
35	36	37					38		39			40	41	42
43								44			45			
46					47					48				
49				50					51			52		
53			54			55					56			
57						58								
59						60								

44. Tip of the House
48. Golf problem
50. Paperboy's wad
51. Elderly
54. "Chances ___"
56. Like an AA, say

ACROSS

1. Tilt slightly
5. "Heat of the Moment" band
9. Cheat
14. Sandwich cookie
15. Runt-sized
16. Gun or trap type
17. "To Kill a Mocking Frog" author?
19. Candle type
20. Fed the kitty
21. Dick the tec
23. "Caught ya!"
24. Hush-hush gp.
25. "The Wood Hopper's Ball" bandleader?
28. Arturo's agreement
29. Currency started in 2002
30. HO product
34. Made untidy
38. Croquet site
39. Dutton sitcom
41. New Age glow
42. Trumpeter's expanders
45. Deli staple
48. Oldtime?
50. Ali, then
51. Comedienne who'll keep you hopping?
55. Econ. stat
58. Record speed
59. Tenor Mario
60. Mistake
62. Presumptuous intro
64. "Working at the Frog Wash Blues" singer?
66. About a drop
67. Yet again
68. Mayberry lad
69. Range
70. Outbox
71. Shed item

DOWN

1. "Mean Girls" star
2. Von Bulow portrayer
3. They might deviate
4. Guzzle
5. ___ financing
6. More torrid
7. Do-nothing
8. Sea *si*
9. Fondue cheese
10. Kurosawa classic
11. Vernacular
12. Jazzy Hines
13. Have a fit?
18. Reagan's Meese
22. Shark bait
26. Biblical animal
27. Prayer units
28. Singer O'Connor
30. "Trading Spaces" airer
31. Simple cheer
32. Amazement
33. Craggy hill
35. Go to court
36. Picther's stat
37. Pop
40. Flowering plant
43. Pie type

Froggy Mountain High

Solution on Page 366

1	2	3	4	■	5	6	7	8	■	9	10	11	12	13
14				■	15				■	16				
17				18					■	19				
20					■	21			22		■	23		
24			■	25	26						27			
■	■	■	28				■	29				■	■	■
30	31	32					33	■	34			35	36	37
38				■	■	39		40	■	■	41			
42				43	44	■	45		46	47				
■	■	■	48			49	■	50				■	■	■
51	52	53					54				■	55	56	57
58			■	59					■	60	61			
62			63		■	64			65					
66					■	67				■	68			
69					■	70				■	71			

44. Couch
46. Yore
47. More crude
49. Asian assassins
51. Pares down
52. A lot of nerve?
53. Acid type
54. Slate, e.g.
55. Nehi flavor
56. Phone maker
57. Snoop
61. Cheer
63. Sample soup
65. 100 lbs.

ACROSS

1. Climbed a rope
9. Halloween mo.
12. "M*A*S*H" setting
14. Alt. spelling
15. Seuss's "If ___"
17. Squeak by
18. Seraglio (14 Across)
19. "Michael Collins" actor
20. Upsets
22. Glued
24. Burn jasmine, say
25. Patton, e.g.
26. Manager
27. Soak in sauce
28. Important
31. It's for the birds
32. "The Thinker," e.g.
33. Less noisy
35. Monopoly pieces
36. Corrosion-resistant metal
37. Defenseman with the most points in a season
38. Where "Bottle Shock" was filmed
40. School gp.
41. People who go
46. Night
47. Slow cooker
48. Banned poison
49. AOL purchase

DOWN

1. Big foot?
2. TV knob
3. Simple ___
4. Sgt. addressees
5. "Misty" singer
6. Full one's lungs
7. Jugs
8. Stupefy
9. Get jetlag, say
10. One who parties for show
11. Pumps, of a sort
13. Siskel's follower
16. Muscat man
20. Eatery
21. Beginnings
23. 100-member group
24. Bent
25. Guy's mate
26. Moved diagonally
27. More in Mexico
29. Some parking
30. Soak in again
33. Instant
34. Removes weapons from
36. Flick
39. Paratha alternative
42. Bio-bubble
43. Pitcher's stat.
44. Tear
45. Observe

Rant and Rave

Solution on Page 366

1	2	3	4	5	6	7	8	■	■	■	9	10	11
12								13	■	■	14		
15									16	■	17		
■	■	■	■	18						■	19		
■	■	20	21				■	22		23			
■	24					■	25						
26				■	■	27							
28				29	30			■	■	31			
32							■	33	34				■
35						■	36						■
37			■	38		39				■	■	■	■
40			■	41						42	43	44	45
46			■	■	47								
48			■	■	■	49							

ACROSS

1. Markers
6. Slime
9. Doorway part
13. Swallowed easily
14. ___ a bee in one's bonnet
15. Away from the wind, at sea
16. Yet to be studied
18. Family group
19. Loft-y building
20. Zig or zag
21. Sidestep
22. Follow-up comedians
25. Layered dessert
27. Lift maker
28. Like the Andrea Doria, for many hours
29. Soft lob in table tennis
33. First name in old horror
34. Prep tea
36. ___ trip
37. Maternity ward cry
40. No longer fresh
42. Prod
43. Did a tailor's job
45. Get a toaster, perhaps
49. Like anchovies
50. London or NYC area
51. Toreador bravos
54. Sidewalk edge
55. Pretend
57. ___ vera
58. Creme-filled cookie
59. Category
60. "Navy Blues" actress
61. Marks a ballot
62. Make sense

DOWN

1. Smear
2. Sicilian spewer
3. Rustic rugs
4. Mole mazes
5. Mineral spring
6. Rubbernecked
7. Was bossy
8. Brit ref. vols.
9. Animal that brays
10. Dog-tired
11. Stiller's comedy partner
12. Inclinations
14. Serengeti laugher
17. Ukraine city
21. Cut with a scissors
23. The ___'s meow
24. On
25. "___ Ha'i" ("South Pacific" song)
26. Thanks ___!
29. Dover's st.
30. Central part
31. Leer
32. Pigeon-___
34. Aries or Leo
35. "The ___ of the Sierra Madre"
38. Mayberry matron
39. Elephant hue
40. "The ___ Erwin Show"

Where's Nana?

Solution on Page 366

1	2	3	4	5	■	■	6	7	8	■	9	10	11	12
13					■	14				■	15			
16					17					■	18			
19				■	20				■	21				
■	■	22		23					24					
25	26						■	27				■	■	■
28					■	■	29					30	31	32
33			■	■	34	35				■	■	36		
37			38	39				■	■	40	41			
■	■	■	42				■	43	44					
45	46	47					48						■	■
49					■	50				■	51		52	53
54				■	55					56				
57				■	58				■	59				
60				■	61		■	■	■	62				

41. Dovetailed with a tab
43. Allergy-season sound
44. "On Golden Pond" bird
45. Felix's sloppy roommate
46. Journalist Zahn
47. Jetson son
48. Sheep sheds
52. Pale brown
53. ". . . together, ___, kick!"
55. Fowl or bovine disease
56. Turkish title

ACROSS

1. Sear
5. Wise leader
10. RIF ad, e.g.
13. Jam need
15. Green
16. Gambler's mecca
17. Scarer just over par?
19. Plaything
20. Old weavers
21. Bike needs
23. I wish!
25. Cancels out
26. Lost steam
27. Texas border town
28. Apple slag
29. Classic clown
30. Soreness
33. "Happy New Year!" preceder
34. Catherine the Great, e.g.
37. "2001" role
38. Labels
40. Has
41. Cleaners
43. Fluff up
45. Loud bird
46. "Shave and a haircut" follower
48. Withstand temptation
49. Wakens
50. Brag
51. Big time
52. Range up to two under par?
57. Homer's neighbor
58. Workshop items
59. Take the wheel
60. Driller's letters
61. Up
62. Director Kazan

DOWN

1. Purrer
2. What?
3. Corroded
4. "St. Elmo's Fire" actor
5. Foe
6. Wise rival
7. ___ sum
8. 1996 Madonna role
9. Go back
10. Golf shots where you cry "Spud!"?
11. Took
12. Chasm
14. Least delayed
18. Olympic goal
22. Arp's art
23. Actress Massey
24. Driving ranges?
25. Indiana Jones extras
26. ___ free
27. Ben from "Bonanza"
29. Weeps
31. Utterly disgusted
32. What ___ is new?
35. Weakness
36. Collects
39. Hoagies
42. Pique

Par for the Course

Solution on Page 367

1	2	3	4	■	■	5	6	7	8	9	■	10	11	12
13				14	■	15					■	16		
17					18						■	19		
■	■	■	20					■	21		22			
■	23	24					■	25						
26						■	27						■	■
28					■	29				■	30		31	32
33			■	34	35					36	■	37		
38			39	■	40				■	41	42			
■	■	43		44				■	45					
46	47						■	48						■
49						■	50					■	■	■
51			■	52		53						54	55	56
57			■	58					■	59				
60			■	61					■	■	62			

44. Flavia's fest
45. Honey liquor
46. Popcorn concern, if bigger
47. Went after
48. Dean Martin event
50. Actor Lugosi
53. Pilfer
54. Come together
55. Circle of life
56. Period

ACROSS

1. Golf tap-ins
6. ___ Supporting Actor
10. French Sudan, today
14. Onset
15. Hotel door posting
16. Yalies
17. Site of Pago Pago
18. Lot unit
19. 1963 epic role for Liz
20. Midnight
23. Dancer Bruhn
24. Trawling, perhaps
25. Malden of movies
28. Key ___ pie
30. Bungling
34. Hitter stat
35. Small plateau
36. Mideast peninsula
37. Director with a profile
41. Perpetrator
42. Author Ephron
43. Island garland
44. "Don't ___ 58 Across" (old flag motto)
45. Secretary's forte
46. River rowers
47. Mock-up
49. Soon
51. Grasping-at-straws attempt
58. See 44 Across
59. Euro preceder in Italy
60. Bran's stuff
61. Burden
62. Swear
63. Slowly wear away
64. Katie's cohost
65. Giraffe feature
66. "Touched by an Angel" actress

DOWN

1. Alley whisper
2. Where Jews are gentiles
3. Break a bronco
4. Bricklayer's tool
5. ". . . twelve o'clock, we climb the ___"
6. Like undrinkable water
7. ___ and every
8. Crystal lines
9. High schoolers
10. Car doctor
11. Half a British greeting
12. Stead
13. "Is You ___ Is You Ain't My Baby?"
21. Like a mosaic
22. Japanese entertainer
25. TV "Music Hall" sponsor
26. More capable
27. Long gun
29. Stephen King's home
31. ___ Gay
32. Old AMC model
33. Polynesian carvings
35. Repaired
38. Car dealer's offer
39. Cherokee chopper

Stubborn Itch

Solution on Page 367

1	2	3	4	5	■	6	7	8	9	■	10	11	12	13
14					■	15				■	16			
17					■	18				■	19			
20					21					22				
■	■	■	23				■	24				■	■	■
25	26	27		■	28		29		■	30		31	32	33
34			■	35				■	■	36				
37			38					39	40					
41					■	■	42				■	43		
44					■	45				■	46			
■	■	■	47		48		■	49		50		■	■	■
51	52	53					54					55	56	57
58				■	59				■	60				
61				■	62				■	63				
64				■	65				■	66				

40. Hag
45. Reason why
46. Selling like hotcakes
48. La Scala locale
50. Proposal
51. Large sewing device
52. Tolstoy's Karenina
53. Blue material
54. Gator kin
55. Double reed
56. Cincinnati team
57. Alder or elder

ACROSS

1. 59 Across, e.g.
6. Dry-cleaning dilemma
10. Identical
14. Come to terms
15. Mute's sound effect
16. Gunk
17. One way to bet
20. Zone
21. They might be martial
22. Classic
23. Socially inept
25. Parisian street
26. Monikers
29. Outdo
33. "___ Male War Bride"
34. Throb
36. Gillespie genre
37. Bar order
41. Boston cream ___
42. Stash
43. Civil War side
44. Attacks with ack-acks
47. Motionless
48. "Norma ___"
49. It uses dits and dahs
51. "What's Up, Doc?" star
54. ___ vinegar
55. Victor's wife
59. Stanwyck/MacMurray film
62. Chief Justice Warren
63. Actress Bancroft
64. "Beauty and the Beast" heroine
65. Brogue or brogan
66. Shed item
67. Hasta la vista

DOWN

1. Fake fanfare
2. Lab aide
3. "___ Grit"
4. Like pilaf
5. Sushi fish
6. Pen's inferior
7. Bash
8. Has
9. Chinese "way"
10. Annoying distance
11. Extra dry
12. Local bond type
13. Advantage
18. Husking bee needs
19. ___ of duty
24. Oater actor
25. Regretted
26. Moves like a weak plot
27. Expect
28. Entertainer Josephine
29. "Rich Man, Poor Man" author
30. Radical Hoffman
31. Arias
32. Totally worn out
34. Army members
35. Business VIP
38. Gotcha
39. An inning has six
40. Without limits
45. Fit for farming

Mixed Doubles

Solution on Page 367

1	2	3	4	5	■	6	7	8	9	■	10	11	12	13
14					■	15				■	16			
17					18					19				
20				■	21				■	22				
■	■	■	23	24				■	25			■	■	■
26	27	28				■	■	29				30	31	32
33					■	34	35			■	■	36		
37					38					39	40			
41			■	■	42				■	43				
44			45	46			■	■	47					
■	■	■	48			■	49	50				■	■	■
51	52	53			■	54				■	55	56	57	58
59					60					61				
62				■	63				■	64				
65				■	66				■	67				

46. Autumn
47. "Laugh-In" comic
49. Heavenly gift
50. Less junior
51. Nice things to say
52. Couples' cruise director
53. New currency
54. It gets shafted
56. "___ Marlene"
57. D-Day battle site
58. Yes votes
60. Munch
61. Many a 35 Down

ACROSS

1. "Maltese Falcon" actress
6. Yadda-yadda
9. Newton who was knighted
14. Hindu mystic
15. Marker
16. Long thin country
17. Exemplar
19. Helped out
20. Blemishes
22. "___ a Small World"
23. Deposit
24. Theater thoroughfares
29. "The rooster crows at midnight," e.g.
33. "Bring in the ___ suspects"
34. ___ and bear it
36. Received
37. Sci-fi film of '55
41. Bran source
42. Word-processing pioneer
43. Actress Garbo
44. Muckraked
47. Pamper
48. The Dead ___ Scrolls
49. It's mined
51. They signed Dolly, Reba, and The Platters
59. Itch relievers
60. Pesky
62. "The Stick" on "Cheers"
63. Doubling cube
64. Motown misfire
65. Pub missiles
66. Ingested
67. Alms getters

DOWN

1. Pyramid pest
2. Crossed the Channel
3. O'Hara home
4. Actor Sharif
5. Eliminates
6. Dick Van Patten's limit
7. Big books
8. Talk a blue streak
9. He got too much sun
10. 9-to-5 and graveyard
11. Verdi opera
12. Guinness of "Kind Hearts and Coronets"
13. Give up
18. "How sweet ___!"
21. Turn over
24. Jam need?
25. Jones of jazz
26. Neil Simon's "California ___"
27. Vegas opener
28. Wallach of "Baby Doll"
29. Flash's merciless foe
30. Come to terms
31. Reached
32. Patriot Allen
34. Happy
35. Vied for office
38. Take an oath
39. The "I"
40. Author Buchwald

Planetary Efforts

Solution on Page 367

45. Rise
46. Puts it another way
47. After 40 Down, '20s style
49. Go around
50. Actress Zellweger
51. Anti-DWI gp.
52. Lamb's pseudonym
53. Emulate a mouse in a film title
54. "Star Wars" mystic
55. The yoke's on them
56. Carnie's specialty
57. 10 cc, e.g.
58. Took to court
61. Conniving

Answers

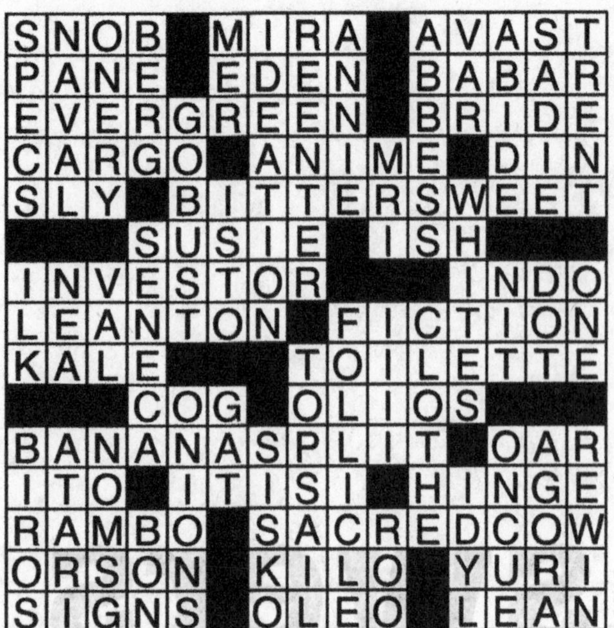

Give Peas a Chance

All about Me

Follow the Money

What the Dickens?

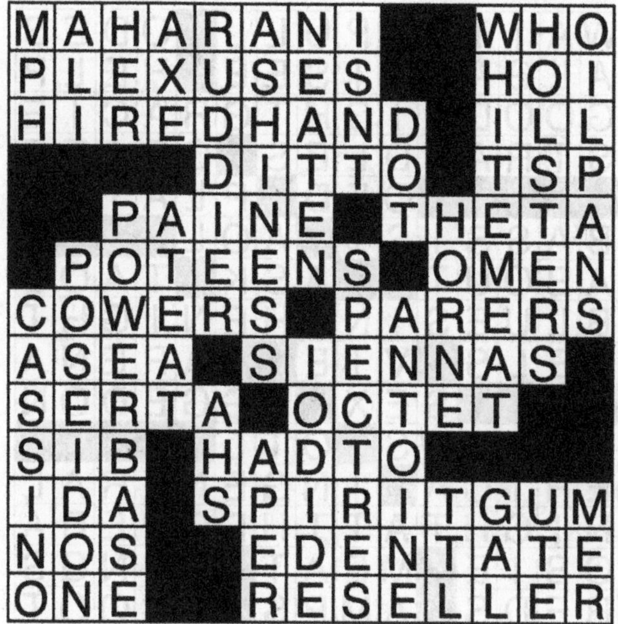

Have a Ball

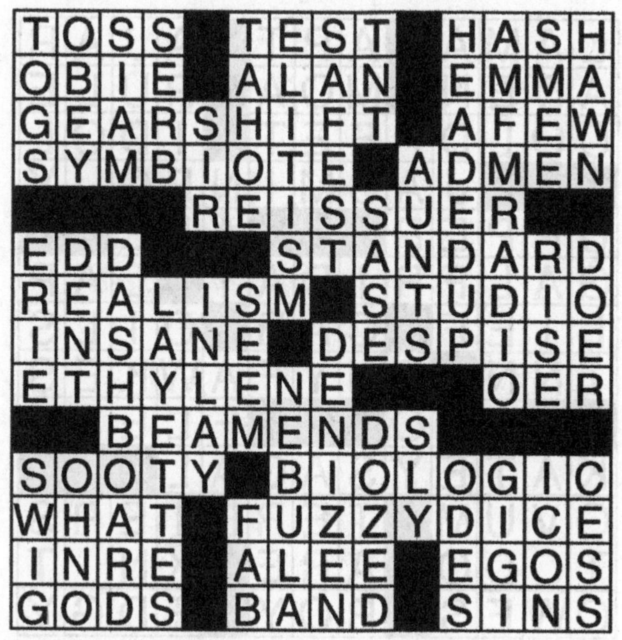

By the Driver

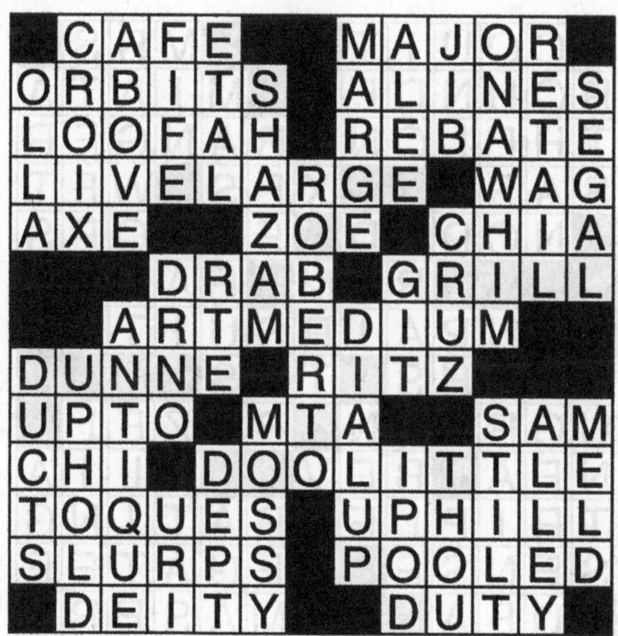

Size Up

Twosomes

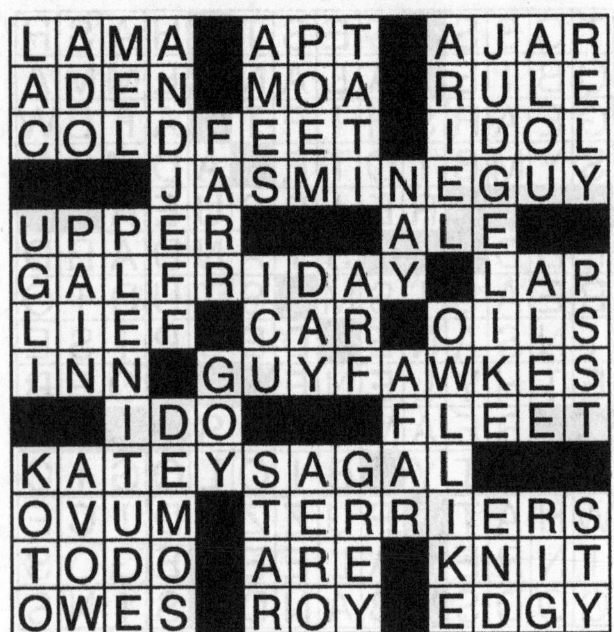

L	A	M	A	■	A	P	T	■	A	J	A	R
A	D	E	N	■	M	O	A	■	R	U	L	E
C	O	L	D	F	E	E	T	■	I	D	O	L
■	■	■	J	A	S	M	I	N	E	G	U	Y
U	P	P	E	R	■	■	■	A	L	E	■	■
G	A	L	F	R	I	D	A	Y	■	L	A	P
L	I	E	F	■	C	A	R	■	O	I	L	S
I	N	N	■	G	U	Y	F	A	W	K	E	S
■	■	I	D	O	■	■	■	F	L	E	E	T
K	A	T	E	Y	S	A	G	A	L	■	■	■
O	V	U	M	■	T	E	R	R	I	E	R	S
T	O	D	O	■	A	R	E	■	K	N	I	T
O	W	E	S	■	R	O	Y	■	E	D	G	Y

Guys and Gals

W	A	I	T	S	■	P	U	L	L	■	O	D	E	S
A	L	G	A	E	■	I	S	E	E	■	H	E	L	P
G	O	O	D	N	I	G	H	T	G	R	A	C	I	E
S	T	R	A	D	D	L	E	S	■	O	R	A	T	E
■	■	■	■	■	O	E	D	■	P	L	A	Y	E	D
B	A	S	S	I	S	T	■	A	O	L	■	■	■	■
A	B	O	U	T	■	■	A	S	K	■	T	A	O	S
B	L	U	E	S	I	N	T	H	E	N	I	G	H	T
E	E	L	S	■	V	I	E	■	■	A	R	E	N	A
■	■	■	■	S	E	X	■	E	G	G	E	D	O	N
S	T	R	A	W	S	■	O	I	L	■	■	■	■	■
E	R	I	C	A	■	I	N	G	E	N	E	R	A	L
N	I	G	H	T	A	T	T	H	E	O	P	E	R	A
O	B	I	E	■	M	E	A	T	■	D	I	N	G	S
R	E	D	S	■	A	M	P	S	■	S	C	O	O	T

Several Nights

A	P	O	P	■	O	F	F	S	■	P	R	I	M	A
H	O	P	E	■	C	L	U	E	■	R	I	D	E	R
A	L	E	C	■	T	O	R	T	R	E	F	O	R	M
B	A	C	K	B	A	Y	S	H	U	F	F	L	E	■
■	■	■	■	A	N	D	■	■	M	A	S	■	■	■
B	E	L	A	T	E	■	W	E	B	B	■	R	C	A
A	L	E	R	O	■	S	I	L	L	■	M	E	A	L
B	E	G	I	N	T	H	E	B	E	G	U	I	N	E
E	N	I	D	■	H	O	L	A	■	R	I	G	O	R
S	A	T	■	F	E	E	D	■	H	O	R	N	E	T
■	■	■	A	R	T	■	■	P	A	P	■	■	■	■
■	I	N	D	I	A	N	L	O	V	E	C	A	L	L
B	R	E	A	D	S	A	U	C	E	■	O	K	I	E
A	M	I	G	A	■	S	T	U	N	■	M	I	N	G
D	A	L	E	Y	■	H	E	S	S	■	O	N	T	O

Artie Shaw Hits

A	C	Q	U	I	T	■	■	■	M	R	S	■
R	O	U	N	D	E	R	■	M	I	A	T	A
T	H	E	L	O	N	E	R	A	N	G	E	R
S	A	S	E	■	■	X	E	S	■	W	E	T
■	N	O	D	E	D	■	F	S	T	O	P	S
■	■	■	■	R	U	M	■	E	A	R	L	Y
■	A	U	P	A	I	R	S	U	I	T	E	■
A	N	K	H	S	■	T	I	S	■	■	■	■
U	G	R	I	A	N	■	B	E	Z	E	L	■
N	E	A	■	B	E	V	■	■	E	L	I	A
T	R	I	P	L	E	A	R	A	T	I	N	G
S	E	N	S	E	■	L	E	G	A	T	E	E
■	D	E	A	■	■	■	M	A	S	E	R	S

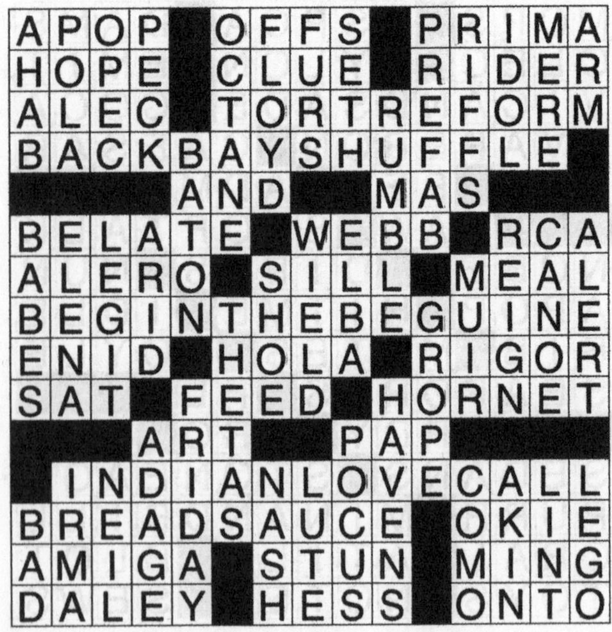

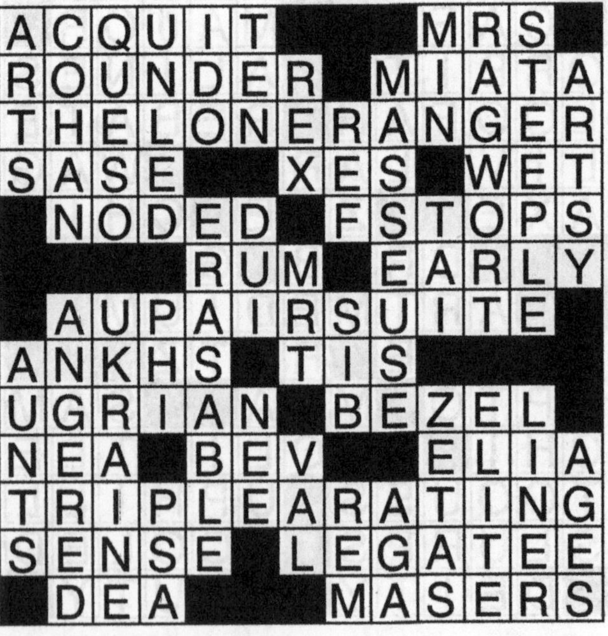

Easy As 1-2-3

Featured Star

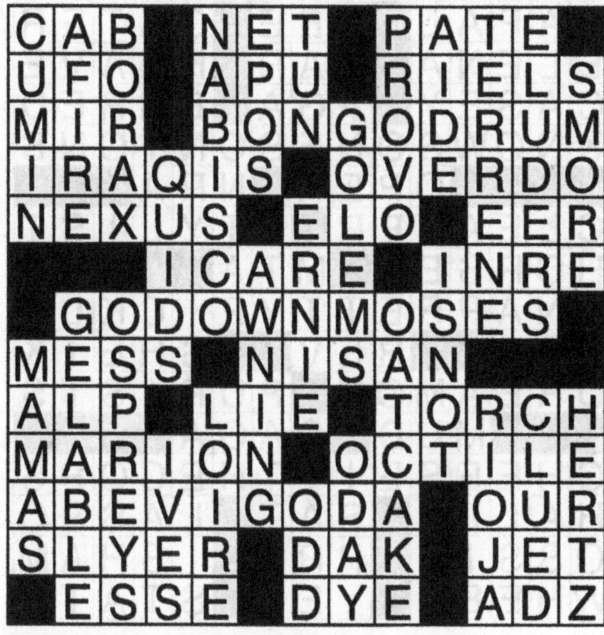

Divine Inspiration

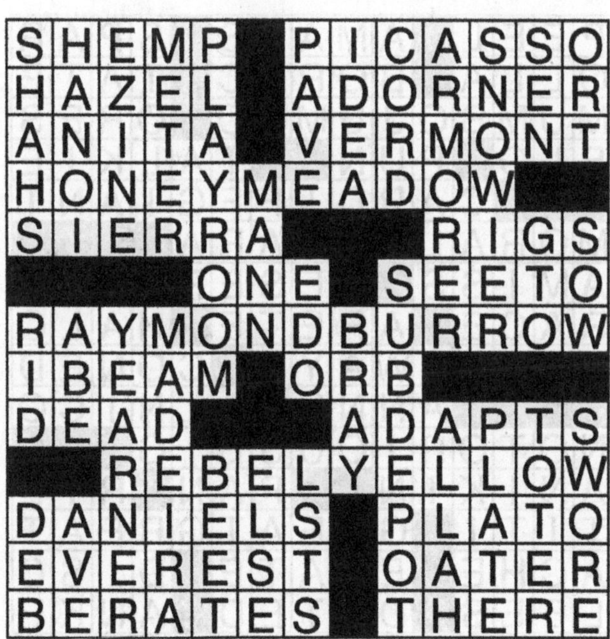

Pain at the End

He's in His Films

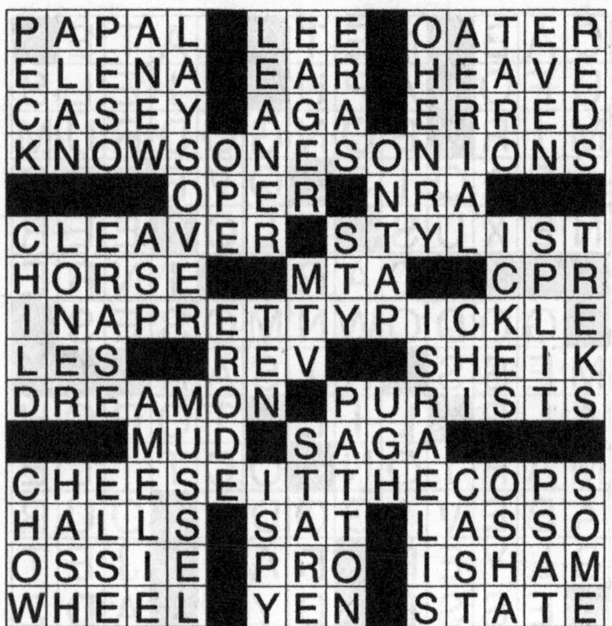

Burger Time

It's a Mad, Mad, Mad, Mad World

Li'l Abner

At Large

Slots

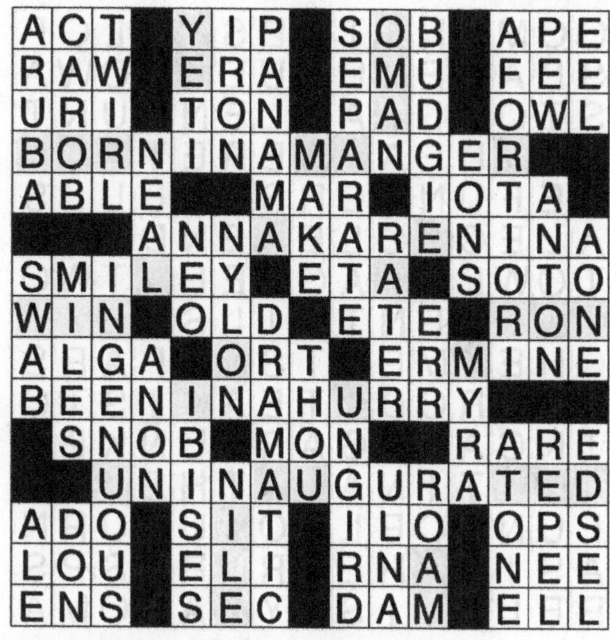

Al Hirschfeld Tribute

Leave It to Beaver

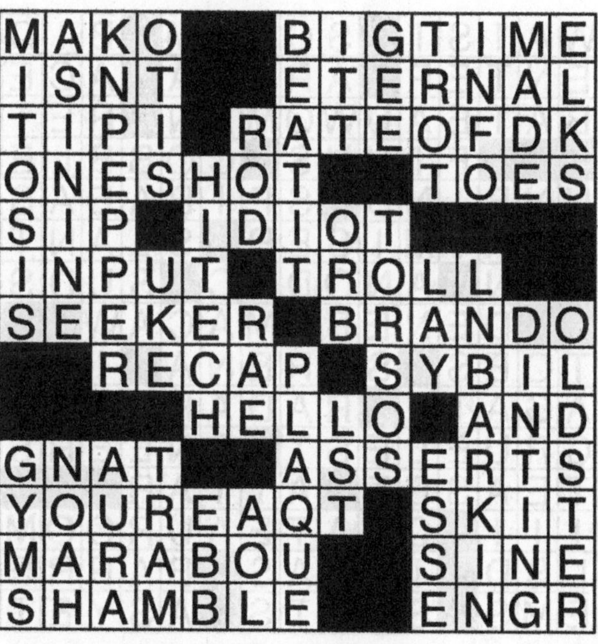

A Couple of Letters

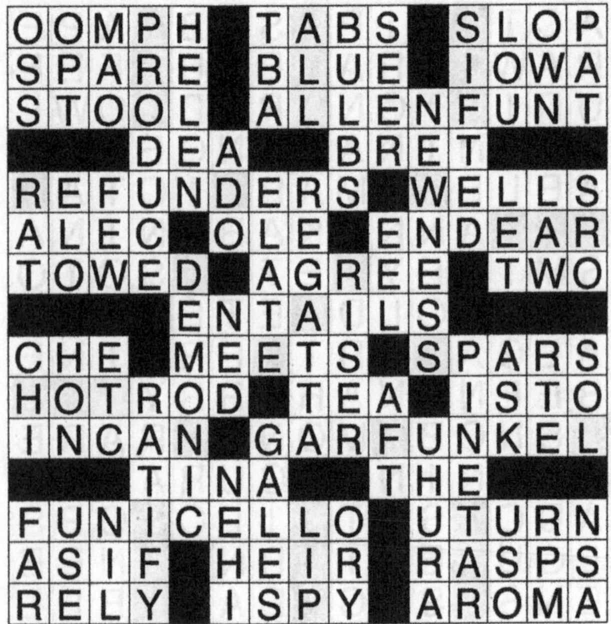

Ain't We Got Fun?

Natural Settings

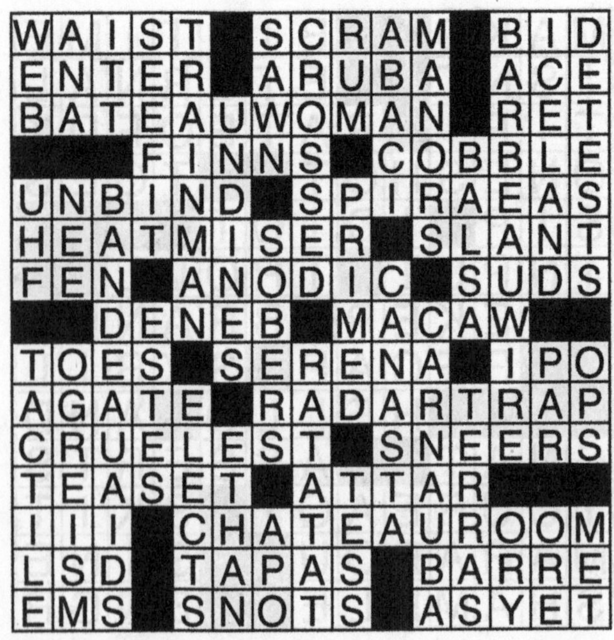

Just Add Water

Spanish Count

Hidden Doors

I Love Ewe

That Smarts

Choice of Beverage

HH

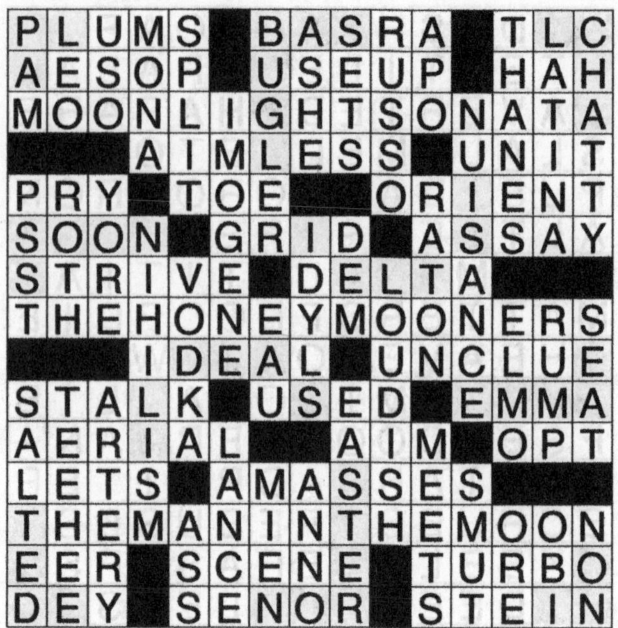

PLUMS BASRA TLC
AESOP USEUP HAH
MOONLIGHTSONATA
AIMLESS UNIT
PRY TOE ORIENT
SOON GRID ASSAY
STRIVE DELTA
THEHONEYMOONERS
IDEAL UNCLUE
STALK USED EMMA
AERIAL AIM OPT
LETS AMASSES
THEMANINTHEMOON
EER SCENE TURBO
DEY SENOR STEIN

Moon Music

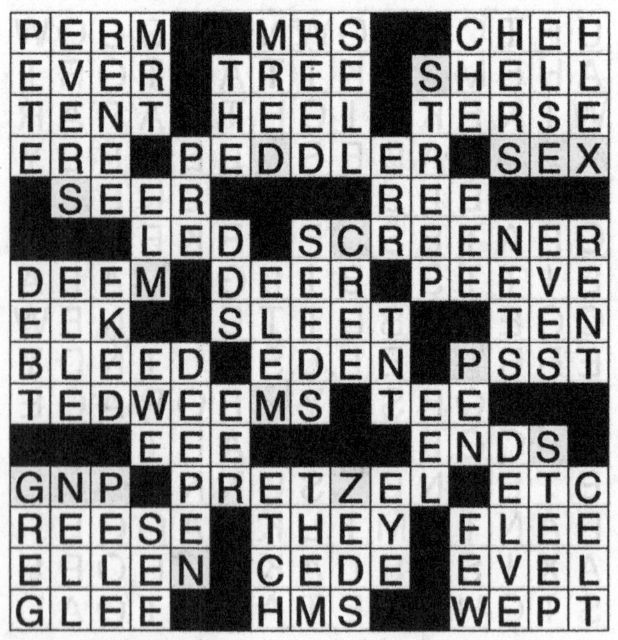

Life of Es

End Count

H	B	O	M	B		B	M	W		C	H	E
A	U	D	I	O		R	A	Y		H	U	G
D	R	E	S	S	S	I	Z	E		E	R	G
			O	C	T	A	D		L	S	T	S
T	A	G		P	A	R	A	D	E	S		
S	U	R	F	E	R	S		R	A	S	T	A
A	R	A	R	A	T		R	E	V	E	A	L
R	A	S	E	R		R	O	S	E	T	T	E
		S	Y	S	T	E	M	S		S	E	X
I	L	S	A		R	U	P	E	E			
R	U	E		J	O	S	S	S	T	I	C	K
A	B	E		A	P	E		U	N	T	I	E
Q	E	D		Y	E	S		P	A	S	T	A

Triple SSS

I	N	S		H	A	S	P		M	U	T	E
P	I	T		U	C	L	A		E	T	A	L
A	C	E		S	H	O	R	T	T	E	R	M
S	H	R	E	K	Y	G	R	E	E	N		
S	E	N	S	E				C	O	S	T	A
			T	R	A	Y	S	H	R	I	E	K
E	O	N			P	E	A			L	E	A
T	R	E	E	W	R	E	C	K	S			
C	U	P	P	A				E	U	L	E	R
		H	O	N	E	Y	B	R	E	E	Z	E
P	O	R	C	E	L	A	I	N		T	I	P
U	H	O	H		A	L	E	E		O	N	O
T	O	N	S		M	E	N	D		N	E	T

Write In, You Say?

O	M	A	R		A	B	B	I	E		A	S	E	A
R	E	N	E		C	R	A	W	L		C	L	A	N
B	A	Z	O	O	K	A	J	O	E		C	O	R	N
I	R	A		N	A	S	A		M	A	R	P	L	E
T	A	C	T	I	C	S		L	E	G	U	P		
			A	O	K		J	A	N	E	E	Y	R	E
C	A	J	U	N		C	E	N	T	S		J	O	T
L	O	O	T		M	A	S	K	S		S	O	S	O
O	N	E		T	A	S	T	Y		O	C	E	A	N
G	E	N	I	U	S	E	S		F	L	U			
		A	N	N	O	Y		N	E	S	M	I	T	H
D	A	M	P	E	N		B	A	L	E		W	O	E
O	V	A	L		J	O	E	M	O	N	T	A	N	A
R	I	T	A		A	L	L	E	N		U	S	E	D
A	S	H	Y		R	E	A	D	S		G	A	R	Y

A Cup of Joe

D	U	N	C	E	C	A	P			W	A	C
S	T	A	R	W	A	R	S			A	D	A
L	E	T	T	E	R	M	A	N		T	O	R
					B	I	T	E		E	R	E
		A	G	G	I	E		A	R	R	A	S
A	F	F	O	R	D	S		T	O	M	B	S
L	O	T	T	I	E		R	E	S	A	L	E
A	R	E	A	S		M	E	S	S	I	E	R
N	E	R	T	S		A	S	T	I	N		
A	R	M		O	B	I	T					
L	U	A		M	E	T	E	R	M	A	I	D
D	N	S			R	A	R	E	B	I	R	D
A	S	H			M	I	S	N	A	M	E	S

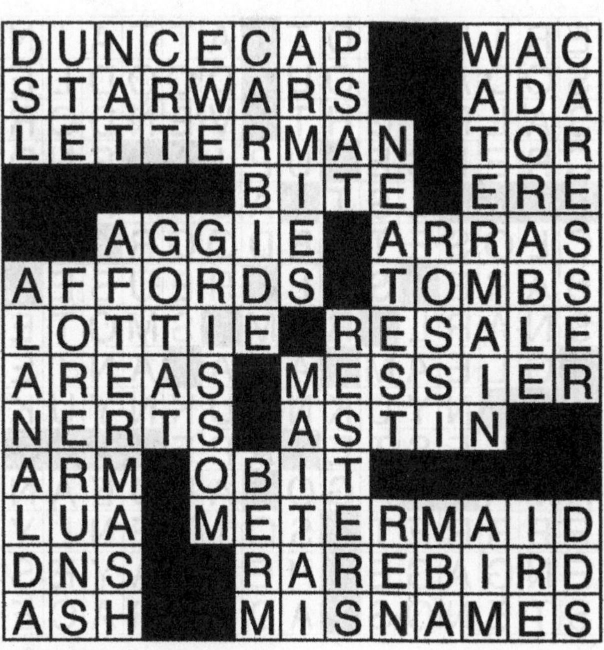

Terminology

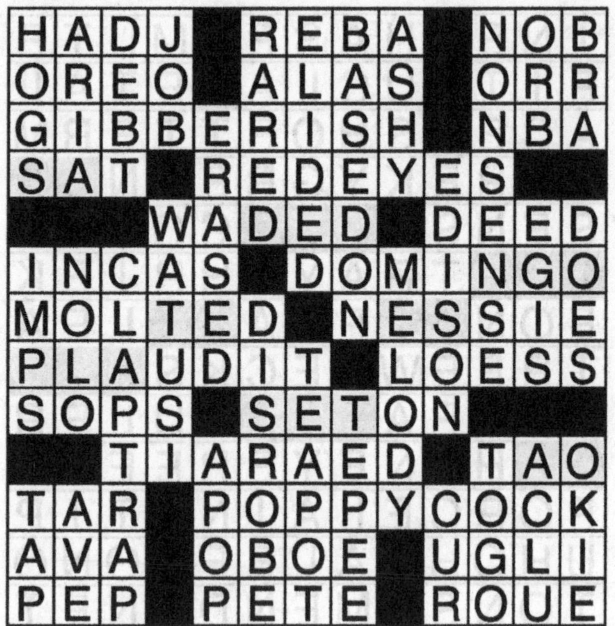
HADJ REBA NOB
OREO ALAS ORR
GIBBERISH NBA
SAT REDEYES
WADED DEED
INCAS DOMINGO
MOLTED NESSIE
PLAUDIT LOESS
SOPS SETON
TIARAED TAO
TAR POPPYCOCK
AVA OBOE UGLI
PEP PETE ROUE

Balderdash

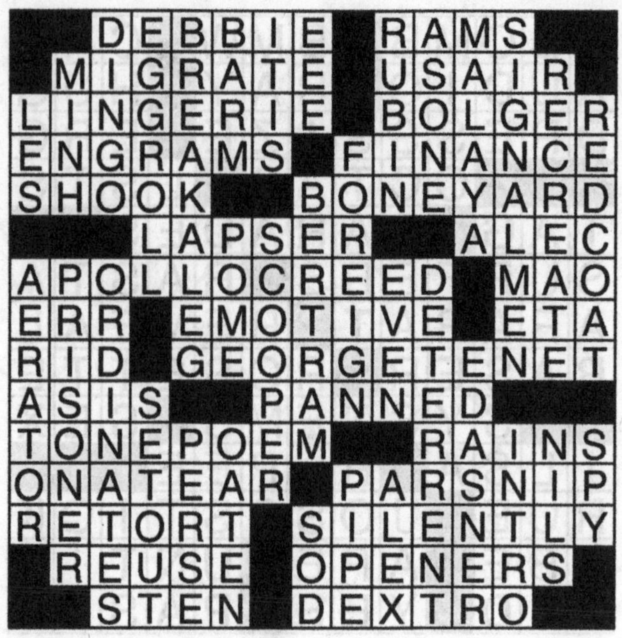
DEBBIE RAMS
MIGRATE USAIR
LINGERIE BOLGER
ENGRAMS FINANCE
SHOOK BONEYARD
LAPSER ALEC
APOLLOCREED MAO
ERR EMOTIVE ETA
RID GEORGETENET
ASIS PANNED
TONEPOEM RAINS
ONATEAR PARSNIP
RETORT SILENTLY
REUSE OPENERS
STEN DEXTRO

I'm a Believer

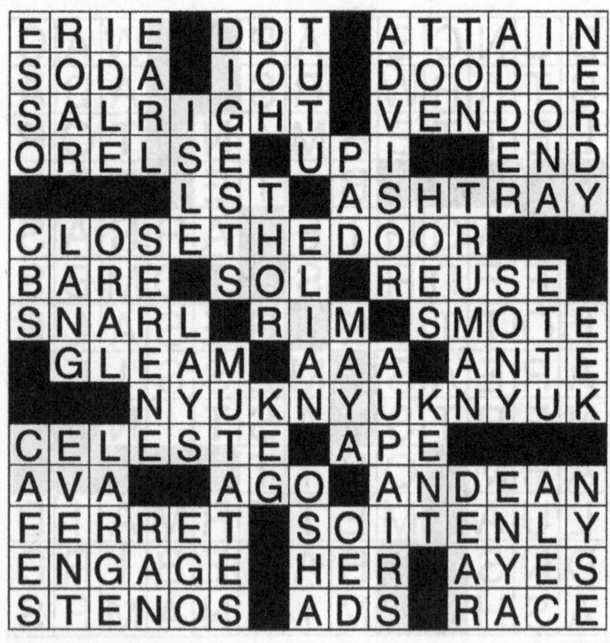
ERIE DDT ATTAIN
SODA IOU DOODLE
SALRIGHT VENDOR
ORELSE UPI END
LST ASHTRAY
CLOSETHEDOOR
BARE SOL REUSE
SNARL RIM SMOTE
GLEAM AAA ANTE
NYUKNYUKNYUK
CELESTE APE
AVA AGO ANDEAN
FERRET SOITENLY
ENGAGE HER AYES
STENOS ADS RACE

Two Bits

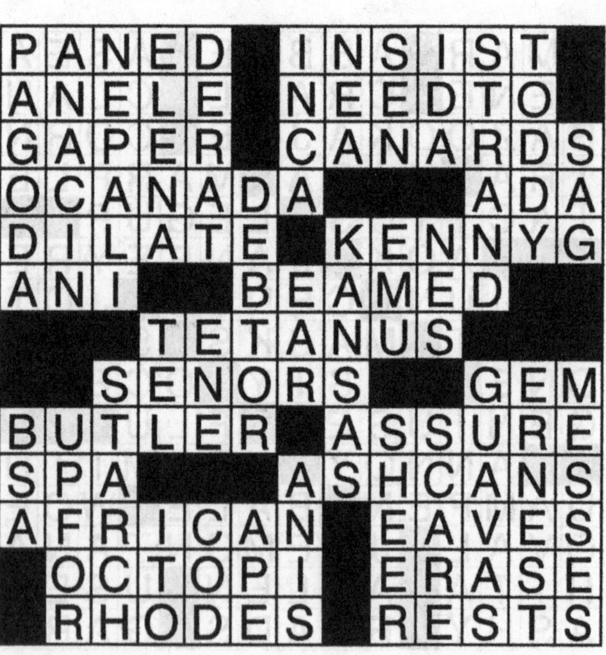
PANED INSIST
ANELE NEEDTO
GAPER CANARDS
OCANADA ADA
DILATE KENNYG
ANI BEAMED
TETANUS
SENORS GEM
BUTLER ASSURE
SPA ASHCANS
AFRICAN EAVES
OCTOPI ERASE
RHODES RESTS

Can-Do

Hirsute

Keep Your Eye on the Ball

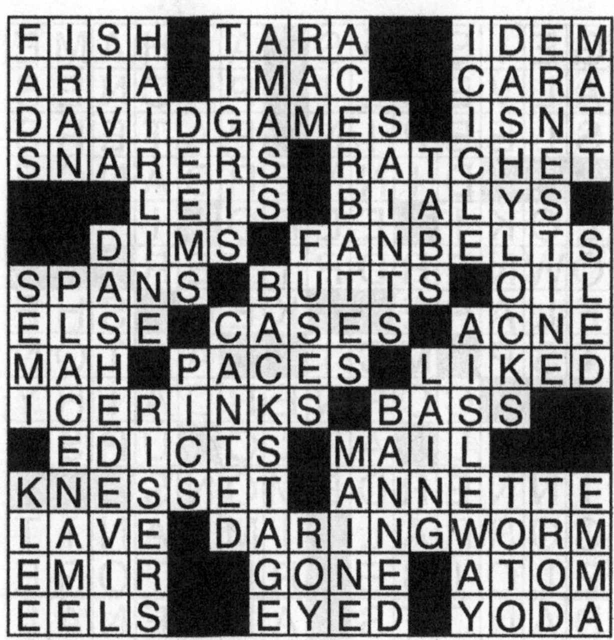

Assistant D.A.

The Nose Knows

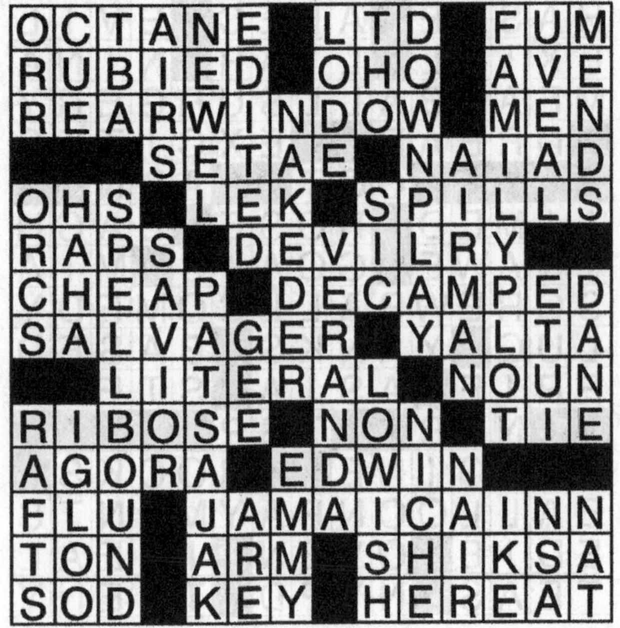

Hitch

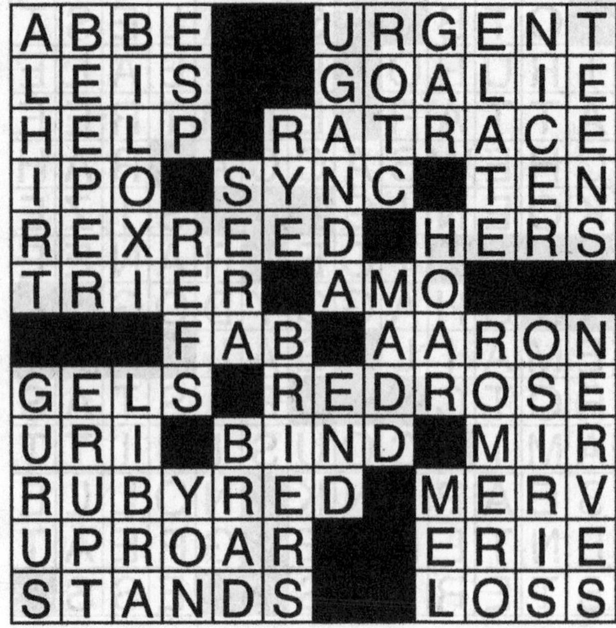

RR Crossing

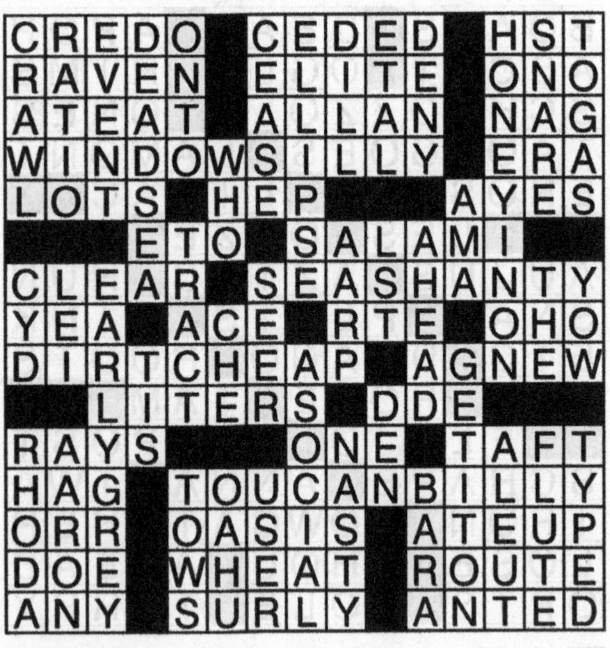

Y Me?

G	E	I	S	H	A	S		A	S	H	A	M	E
A	L	V	E	O	L	I		P	H	O	N	E	S
S	L	E	E	P	I	N		P	A	T	E	R	S
			D	I	N	N	E	R	D	A	N	C	E
L	O	K	I		E	E	R	O		I	T	I	S
O	W	N	E	R	D	R	I	V	E	R			
F	L	A	R	E			K	E	G		S	H	E
T	S	P		M	C	I			A	C	T	O	N
			C	O	R	N	E	R	D	A	I	R	Y
R	E	E	L		A	R	L	O		U	R	S	A
I	N	N	E	R	D	E	M	O	N	S			
C	O	R	R	A	L		I	M	E	A	N	I	T
E	L	O	I	S	E		R	E	S	T	O	R	E
D	A	N	C	E	S		A	R	S	E	N	A	L

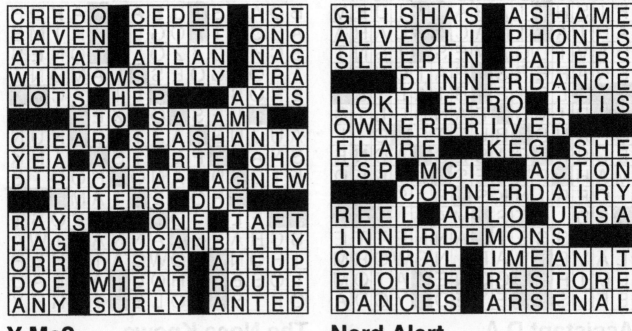

Nerd Alert

Fingered

OO!

It's All Relative

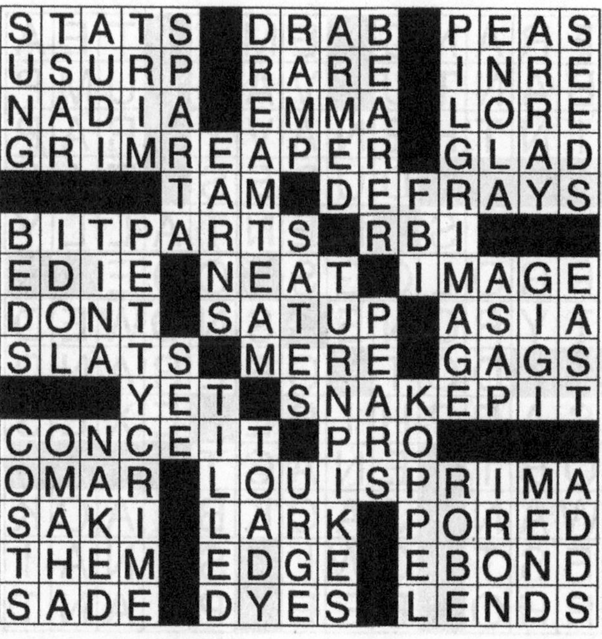

Rim Shots

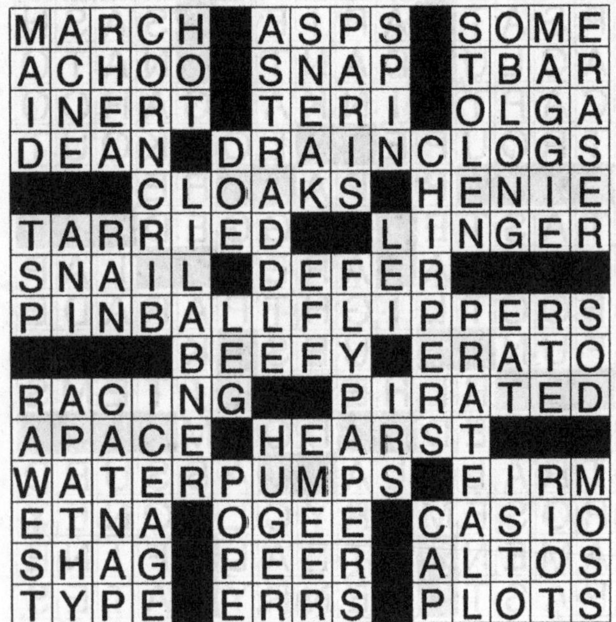

Fancy Footwear

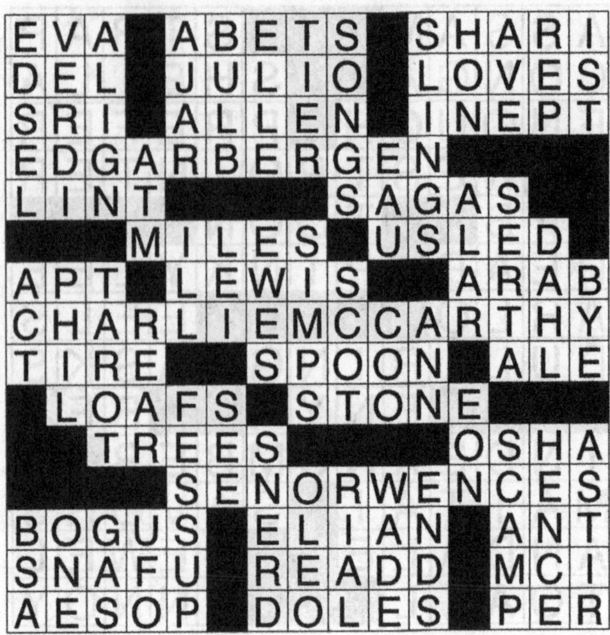

Ventriloquism

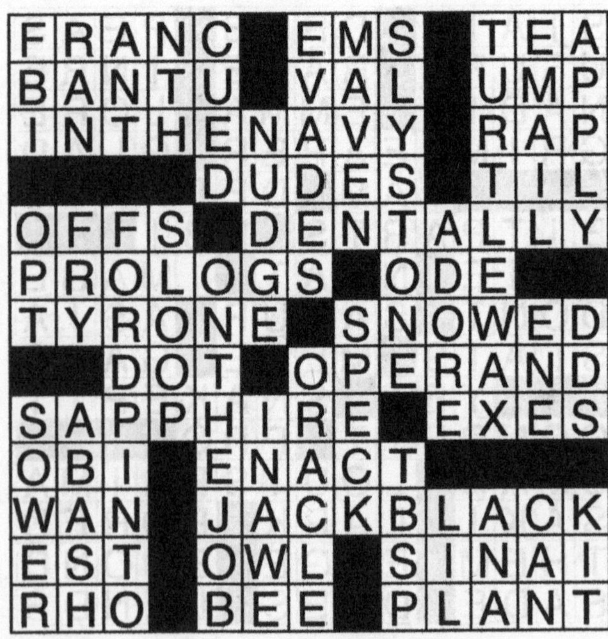

Bean There, Done That

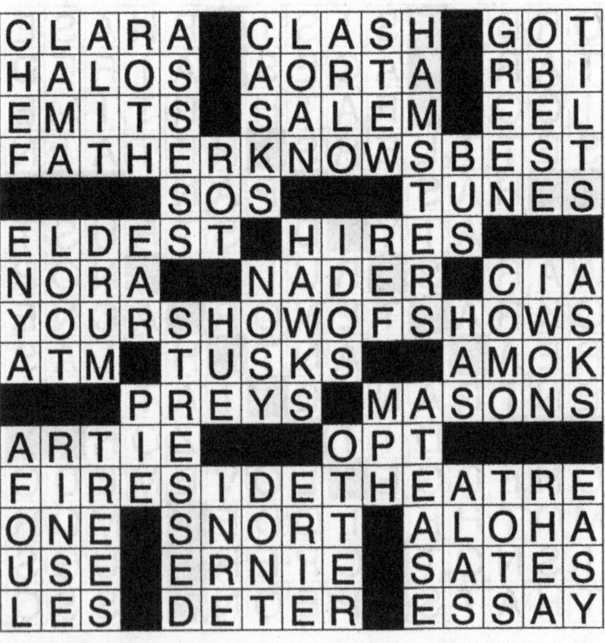

Classic TV

R	A	F	T	S		S	P	A	R		L	U	N	A
A	P	R	I	L		H	I	D	E		O	R	A	L
C	H	O	C	O	L	A	T	E	M	O	U	S	S	E
K	I	N	S	W	O	M	A	N		I	S	A	A	C
S	S	T		E	M	U	S		P	L	Y			
		B	O	D	E	S		S	U	I		B	A	R
I	T	E	M				L	I	T	E	R	A	T	I
V	A	N	I	L	L	A	E	X	T	R	A	C	T	S
A	U	C	T	I	O	N	S				S	K	Y	E
N	T	H		E	O	N		H	E	L	P	S		
			B	L	T		B	A	B	A		T	B	A
M	E	T	R	O		C	A	T	A	M	A	R	A	N
S	T	R	A	W	B	E	R	R	Y	B	L	O	N	D
R	A	I	N		U	R	G	E		D	A	K	A	R
P	L	O	D		D	E	E	D		A	N	E	L	E

The Neapolitan

S	A	L	E		A	L	L	O	T		Q	T	I	P
O	V	E	N		M	O	O	R	E		A	H	S	O
D	A	Y	T	R	I	P	P	E	R		N	E	E	D
A	S	T	R	I	D	E			R	I	D	G	E	S
S	T	E	A	L	S		M	A	I	T	A	I		
			N	E	T		O	R	B	S		P	T	S
D	E	B	T	S		V	I	O	L	A		P	E	P
A	V	I	S		F	O	S	S	E		M	E	R	E
L	E	G		E	L	I	T	E		A	U	R	I	C
I	N	D		D	A	L	E		A	I	L			
		I	C	E	M	A	N		M	O	T	T	O	S
A	L	P	I	N	E			R	E	L	I	A	N	T
R	A	P	T		N	O	S	E	N	I	P	P	E	R
T	H	E	E		C	O	P	E	D		L	E	N	A
E	R	R	S		O	P	A	L	S		E	D	D	Y

Zipper Closing

S	I	P	S		D	E	L	L		S	C	I	F	I
E	S	A	U		E	D	I	E		C	O	M	E	T
E	A	R	P		M	A	L	T		R	O	P	E	S
M	A	K	E	N	O	M	I	S	T	A	K	E		
S	C	A	R	Y				G	A	M		T	A	B
			B	L	O	S	S	O	M		F	U	M	E
E	P	A		O	L	I	N			A	D	O	P	T
S	A	N	A	N	D	R	E	A	S	F	A	U	L	T
S	U	C	K	S			E	T	A	L		S	E	E
A	S	E	A		W	I	R	E	T	A	P			
Y	E	S		P	B	S				M	A	P	L	E
		T	R	I	A	L	A	N	D	E	R	R	O	R
E	E	R	I	E		E	V	E	R		S	O	U	R
R	E	A	C	T		T	O	R	E		E	S	S	O
A	L	L	E	Y		S	N	O	W		D	E	E	R

Goofy

C	A	R	T		F	R	O	M		E	R	R	O	R
A	L	O	U		R	A	T	E		L	E	A	V	E
C	L	O	T		O	P	T	S		E	D	G	E	S
T	A	K	E	I	N	T	O	A	C	C	O	U	N	T
I	N	S	E	R	T			S	I	T				
				S	I	F	T		A	R	A	B	I	A
A	N	N	A		E	R	O	S		I	C	O	N	S
B	A	C	K	G	R	O	U	N	D	C	H	E	C	K
E	M	A	I	L		S	T	A	R		E	R	A	S
L	E	A	N	O	N		S	P	A	S				
				M	A	D			M	O	D	E	S	T
L	O	S	E	O	N	E	S	B	A	L	A	N	C	E
I	N	C	A	N		G	O	A	T		T	O	R	A
S	T	A	R	T		A	U	D	I		E	L	A	M
T	O	R	S	O		S	P	E	C		D	A	M	S

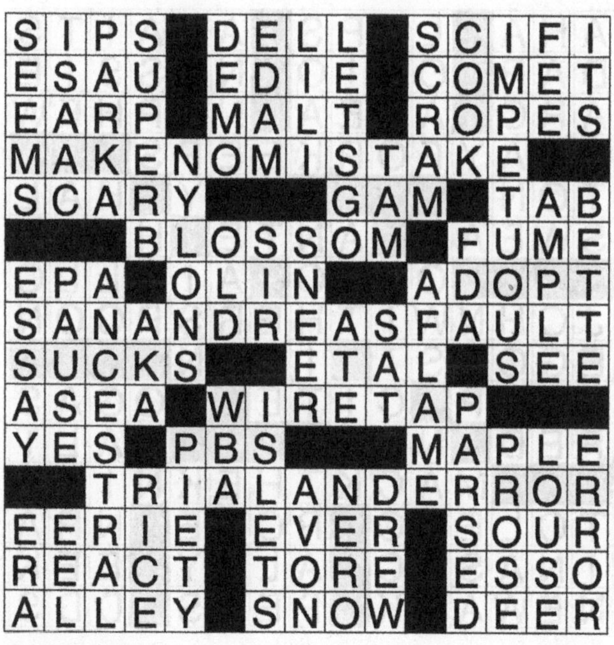

You Can Bank on It

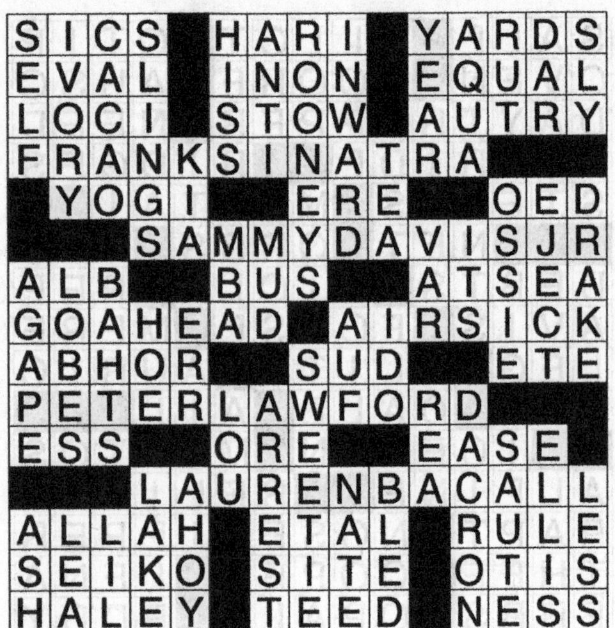

Rat Pack

All That Jazz

J.J.

Setting Pieces

D	R	E	A	R	■	A	L	D	O	■	A	S	A	P
E	A	G	L	E	■	P	E	E	P	■	M	O	O	R
B	E	G	I	N	T	H	E	B	E	G	U	I	N	E
■	■	■	G	O	B	I	■	T	R	O	L	L	E	Y
C	L	A	N	■	A	D	S	■	A	T	E	■	■	■
H	U	M	I	D	■	S	T	A	T	■	T	A	D	A
O	P	E	N	U	P	■	A	L	O	U	■	N	A	P
K	I	N	G	P	O	R	T	E	R	S	T	O	M	P
E	N	D	■	E	S	A	U	■	S	E	R	I	A	L
R	O	S	A	■	S	P	E	C	■	S	I	N	G	E
■	■	■	T	H	E	■	S	A	P	■	A	T	E	S
P	R	O	T	E	S	T	■	C	A	L	L	■	■	■
H	O	N	E	Y	S	U	C	K	L	E	R	O	S	E
E	V	E	S	■	E	T	A	L	■	N	U	T	T	Y
W	E	S	T	■	D	U	N	E	■	O	N	C	U	E

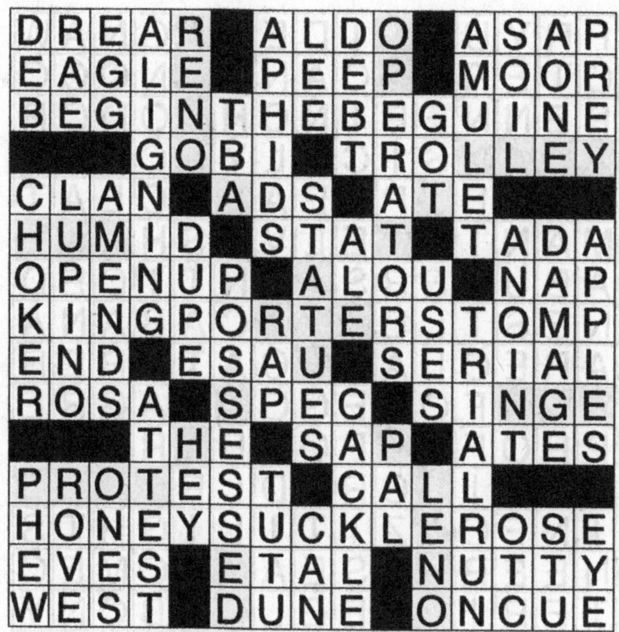

Classic Big Band Songs

F	A	T	■	W	W	I	■	A	N	G	S	T
A	M	A	■	E	O	N	■	S	O	R	T	A
C	N	N	N	E	W	S	■	T	I	E	U	P
T	O	G	O	■	S	A	F	I	R	E	■	■
S	T	O	O	L	■	N	O	R	■	X	E	S
■	■	■	D	O	R	E	N	■	E	A	R	L
G	A	U	L	L	E	■	D	I	S	M	A	Y
N	A	P	E	■	B	L	A	N	C	■	■	■
P	A	C	■	B	E	E	■	D	O	T	E	D
■	■	C	O	L	L	A	R	■	R	E	N	O
A	D	O	R	E	■	S	A	T	T	E	S	T
M	I	D	A	S	■	E	V	E	■	T	U	T
P	E	E	L	S	■	S	E	T	■	H	E	Y

Say It Again

M	A	W	■	A	L	A	R	■	D	A	B	S
E	L	I	■	R	E	N	E	■	O	L	E	O
O	F	T	■	H	I	G	H	H	O	P	E	S
W	A	H	■	A	G	L	E	A	M	■	■	■
■	■	H	O	T	H	E	A	D	■	L	A	M
A	H	O	Y	■	■	S	T	I	M	U	L	I
G	A	L	E	N	A	■	S	T	I	N	G	S
H	Y	D	R	A	N	T	■	■	S	C	A	T
A	S	S	■	T	A	R	N	I	S	H	■	■
■	■	■	E	C	L	A	I	R	■	H	I	S
H	A	S	H	H	O	U	S	E	■	O	N	E
E	X	P	O	■	G	M	A	N	■	U	T	E
Y	E	A	H	■	S	A	N	E	■	R	O	D

All Wet

G	W	E	N	■	G	O	L	D	■	A	C	T	O	R
A	W	A	Y	■	O	H	I	O	■	H	A	R	P	O
W	I	S	E	■	O	N	L	Y	■	S	T	I	E	S
K	I	T	T	Y	F	O	Y	L	E	■	B	A	N	S
■	■	■	S	O	B	■	P	E	N	P	A	L	S	■
A	H	A	■	W	A	W	A	■	G	A	L	■	■	■
D	U	S	K	■	L	A	D	Y	■	C	L	O	U	D
D	R	E	I	D	L	S	■	A	S	T	O	U	N	D
S	L	A	T	E	■	H	U	L	A	■	U	S	D	A
■	■	■	T	S	P	■	P	E	R	M	■	T	O	Y
■	S	A	Y	K	I	D	S	■	A	A	A	■	■	■
B	A	C	H	■	C	A	T	S	T	E	V	E	N	S
O	N	T	A	P	■	N	A	T	O	■	A	L	O	E
S	T	O	W	S	■	C	R	A	G	■	I	M	I	N
S	A	N	K	A	■	E	T	N	A	■	L	O	R	D

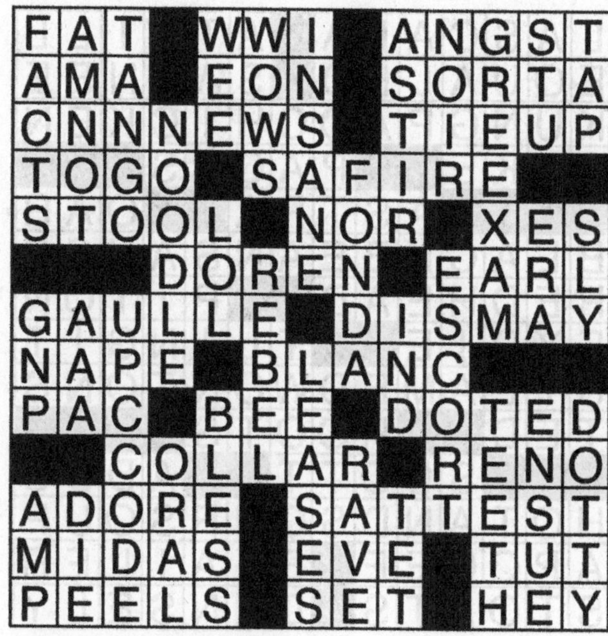

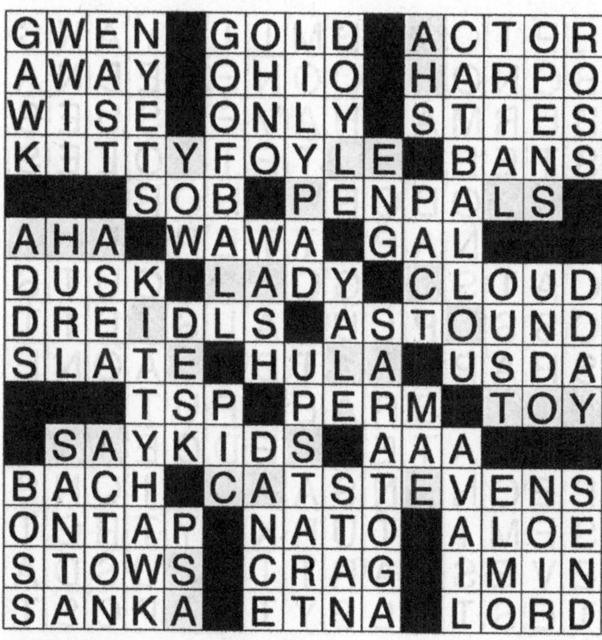

Feline Foibles

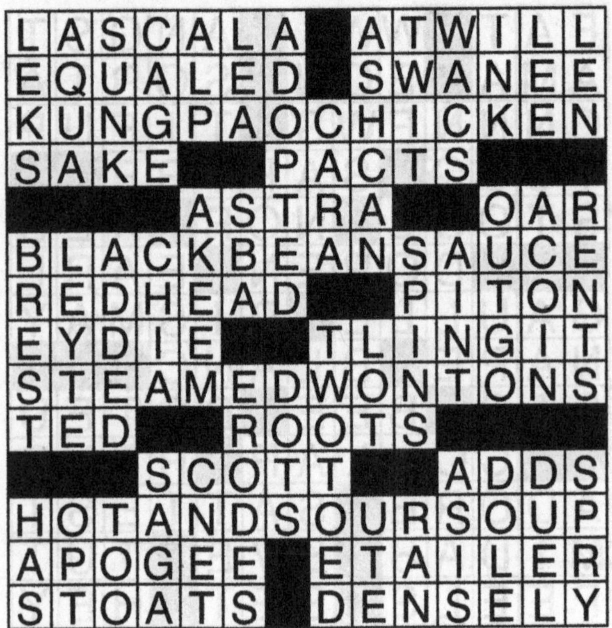

Chinese Food

Using Your Noodle

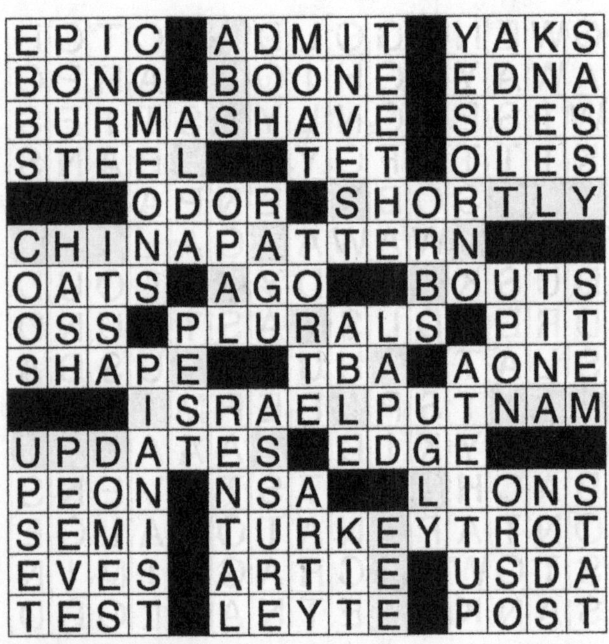

National Leaders

The In Crowd

Gene Kelly

Astronomy 101

Takeout Food

Father's Day

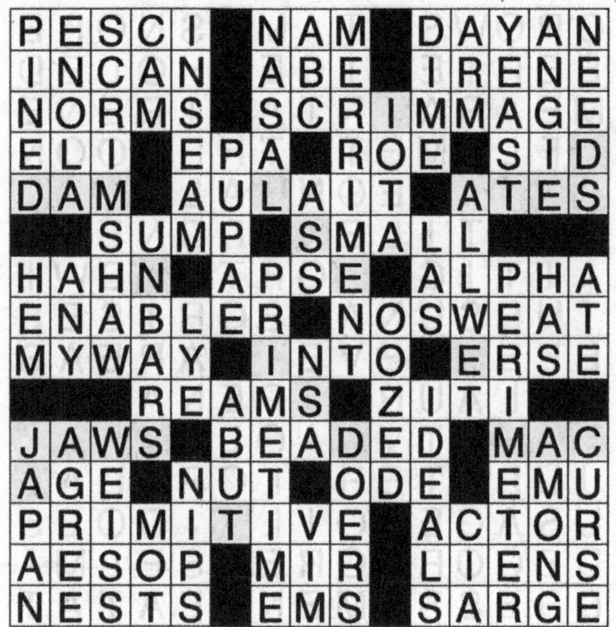
PESCI NAM DAYAN
INCAN ABE IRENE
NORMS SCRIMMAGE
ELI EPA ROE SID
DAM AULAIT ATES
SUMP SMALL
HAHN APSE ALPHA
ENABLER NOSWEAT
MYWAY INTO ERSE
REAMS ZITI
JAWS BEADED MAC
AGE NUT ODE EMU
PRIMITIVE ACTOR
AESOP MIR LIENS
NESTS EMS SARGE

Around the Rim

HEADS HST GUS
ULNAE ETA RNA
PLAYEDCUP ADA
ONEUP SNOB
ARF ABATED
MORAVIA MARIN
OPENER MALAGA
RENEE TENSPOT
CARFUL SRO
LAHR ALOHA
ORB HEANDSEEK
OAR URN THONG
TBA EYE VENDS

ID Theft

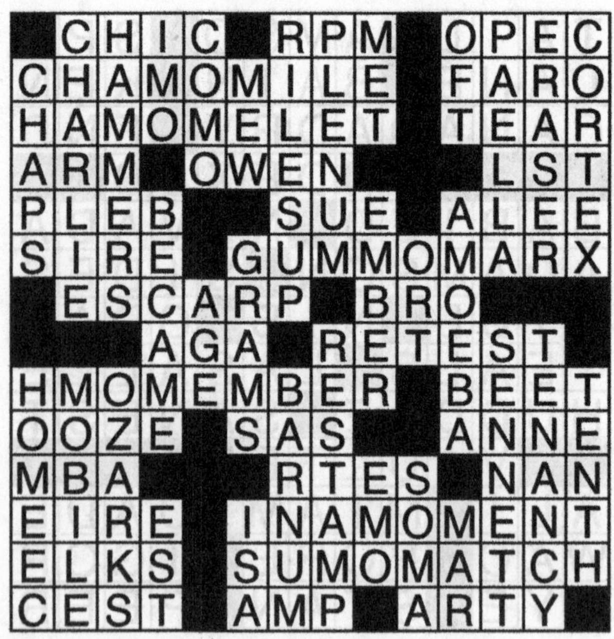
CHIC RPM OPEC
CHAMOMILE FARO
HAMOMELET TEAR
ARM OWEN LST
PLEB SUE ALEE
SIRE GUMMOMARX
ESCARP BRO
AGA RETEST
HMOMEMBER BEET
OOZE SAS ANNE
MBA RTES NAN
EIRE INAMOMENT
ELKS SUMOMATCH
CEST AMP ARTY

Mommie Dearest

ELAM POET SPAR
TOMATILLO ERSE
NOPLACELIKEOHM
ASSAI LAMP
DNA GEYSERS
SPLITVOLTS LET
ALOE EMO ALPO
TAUS IAN PERI
END WATTSUPDOC
RAMRODS APO
OURS PILAF
JOULEOFTHENILE
ANTE ROBERTSON
BOHR BRAY SPUD

Shocking!

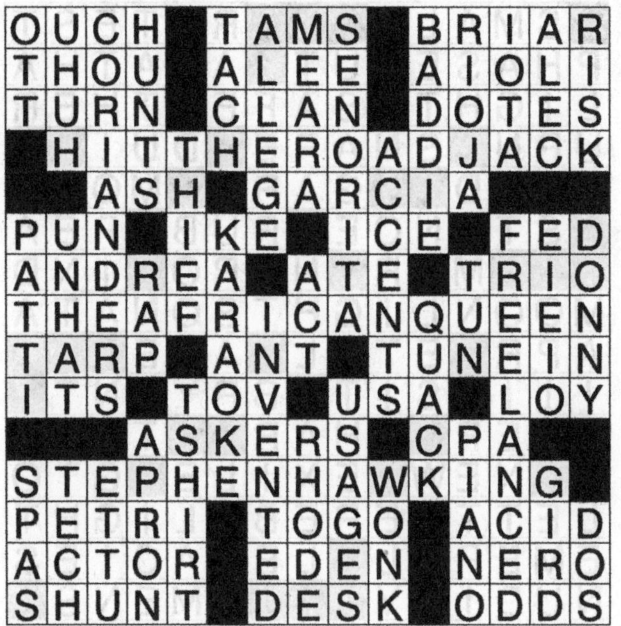

Face Cards

Because I Have To

Christmas Colors

MUSIC BORIS
MANACLE NUMERAL
INBREED OREGANO
SARATOGASPRINGS
OMEN LIMES SIRE
SAD HANES STAIR
FEIGN ELENA
TRANSISTORS
BREVE TAROS
BEADY RIGUP ODD
EMMA FEELS PARE
TOLLHOUSECOOKIE
TAILORS SAMPLED
ANNETTE SNIPERS
SENSE STAYS

Let the Chips Fall Where They May

F	L	I	E	R	■	S	A	L	A	D	■	S	A	D
R	O	D	E	O	■	A	B	A	T	E	■	H	O	E
Y	E	L	L	O	W	S	U	B	M	A	R	I	N	E
E	W	E	■	T	E	S	T	■	■	R	I	V	E	R
R	E	D	■	B	A	Y	■	P	A	I	N	■	■	■
■	■	■	P	E	N	■	R	E	N	E	G	A	D	E
S	M	O	R	E	■	V	I	C	E	■	S	L	U	R
P	A	P	E	R	B	A	C	K	W	R	I	T	E	R
E	L	A	M	■	I	N	K	S	■	I	D	O	L	S
D	E	L	I	C	A	C	Y	■	A	C	E	■	■	■
■	■	■	E	L	S	E	■	R	I	O	■	V	C	R
S	P	I	R	O	■	■	Z	I	N	C	■	I	R	E
H	E	R	E	C	O	M	E	S	T	H	E	S	U	N
A	L	A	■	K	I	O	S	K	■	E	R	A	S	E
M	E	N	■	S	L	O	T	S	■	T	A	S	T	E

Beatles Music

■	S	M	A	L	L	■	■	■	R	E	T	E	S	T
P	H	A	S	E	O	U	T	■	A	G	A	T	H	A
L	I	G	H	T	A	S	A	F	E	A	T	H	E	R
U	R	N	■	S	N	A	R	E	■	D	U	I	■	■
S	E	E	D	■	■	G	A	R	B	■	M	O	L	T
■	S	T	A	N	C	E	■	R	U	B	■	P	E	A
■	■	■	M	I	R	■	N	E	R	O	■	I	N	D
M	O	O	N	L	I	G	H	T	S	O	N	A	T	A
A	P	R	■	E	T	A	L	■	A	T	E	■	■	■
I	I	I	■	S	I	T	■	B	R	Y	A	N	T	■
D	E	E	P	■	C	H	A	R	■	■	T	O	I	L
■	■	N	E	W	■	E	X	I	L	E	■	G	T	O
L	E	T	T	H	E	R	E	B	E	L	I	G	H	T
E	M	E	R	I	L	■	L	E	G	A	C	I	E	S
N	U	D	I	T	Y	■	■	■	O	M	E	N	S	■

Illuminating

F	A	Y	E	■	G	N	P	■	P	I	E	R
A	R	E	S	■	L	O	O	P	H	O	L	E
T	E	N	T	■	I	N	L	I	E	U	O	F
W	A	T	E	R	M	E	L	O	N	■	■	■
A	S	L	E	E	P	■	■	T	O	P	E	D
■	■	■	M	A	S	T	E	R	M	I	N	D
A	H	A	■	■	E	O	S	■	■	A	G	E
C	E	N	T	E	R	M	O	S	T	■	■	■
T	R	O	U	T	■	■	T	I	A	R	A	S
■	■	■	B	U	T	T	E	R	M	I	L	K
S	I	D	E	D	O	O	R	■	T	O	T	O
A	K	U	R	E	Y	R	I	■	A	J	A	R
W	E	D	S	■	S	A	C	■	M	A	R	T

Midterms

O	F	F	■	L	T	D	■	■	S	K	A	T
D	R	L	A	U	R	A	■	■	M	I	L	O
D	E	E	R	X	I	N	G	■	E	M	M	E
S	E	A	M	■	A	G	O	■	E	N	O	L
■	■	■	O	D	D	I	S	H	■	O	N	E
■	■	F	R	O	S	T	H	E	A	V	E	S
B	O	O	E	D	■	■	■	L	I	A	R	S
E	N	D	R	O	A	D	W	O	R	K	■	■
N	E	D	■	S	M	O	O	T	H	■	■	■
A	T	E	S	■	O	R	R	■	E	G	G	O
T	O	R	E	■	R	E	S	T	A	R	E	A
A	G	E	R	■	■	M	E	L	D	E	R	S
R	O	D	E	■	■	I	N	C	■	W	E	T

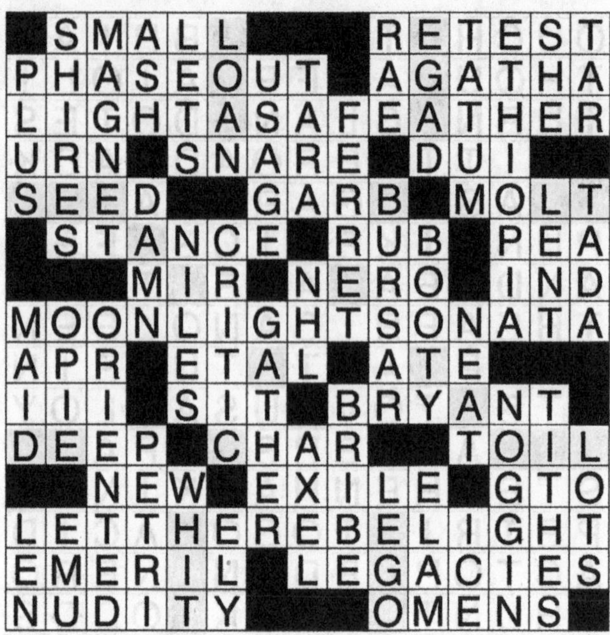

Road Rules

Q&A

Oops!

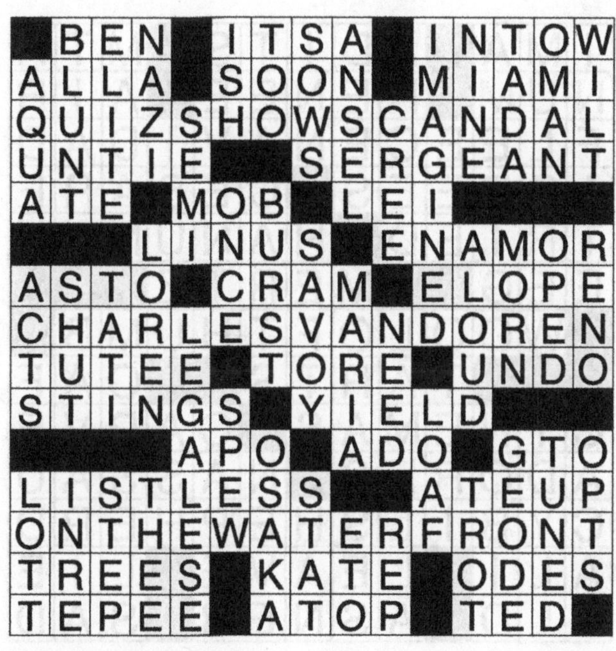

Notorious

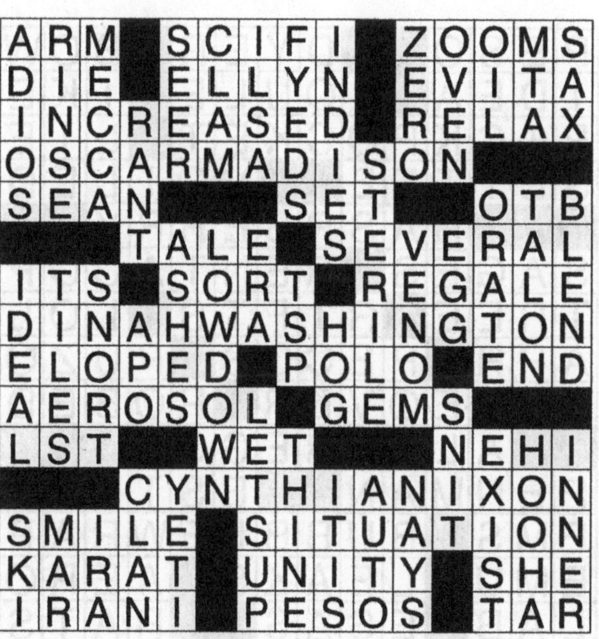

Presidential Pretenders

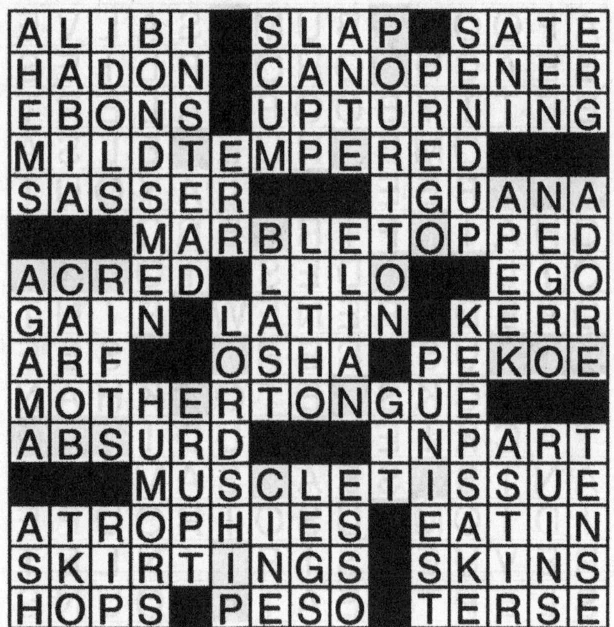

A	L	I	B	I	■	S	L	A	P	■	S	A	T	E
H	A	D	O	N	■	C	A	N	O	P	E	N	E	R
E	B	O	N	S	■	U	P	T	U	R	N	I	N	G
M	I	L	D	T	E	M	P	E	R	E	D	■	■	■
S	A	S	S	E	R	■	■	■	I	G	U	A	N	A
■	■	■	M	A	R	B	L	E	T	O	P	P	E	D
A	C	R	E	D	■	L	I	L	O	■	■	E	G	O
G	A	I	N	■	L	A	T	I	N	■	K	E	R	R
A	R	F	■	■	O	S	H	A	■	P	E	K	O	E
M	O	T	H	E	R	T	O	N	G	U	E	■	■	■
A	B	S	U	R	D	■	■	■	I	N	P	A	R	T
■	■	■	M	U	S	C	L	E	T	I	S	S	U	E
A	T	R	O	P	H	I	E	S	■	E	A	T	I	N
S	K	I	R	T	I	N	G	S	■	S	K	I	N	S
H	O	P	S	■	P	E	S	O	■	T	E	R	S	E

MT–Headed

S	C	A	T	■	M	A	R	I	O	■	H	E	L	D
U	L	N	A	■	I	P	A	N	A	■	O	L	E	O
P	U	T	T	I	N	O	N	T	H	E	R	I	T	Z
S	E	S	A	M	E	■	■	O	U	T	R	A	G	E
■	■	■	■	P	R	O	S	■	■	N	O	N	O	S
S	M	I	L	E	■	D	O	G	E	A	R	■	■	■
H	O	N	E	D	■	D	O	U	G	■	■	A	D	O
A	N	N	I	E	G	E	T	Y	O	U	R	G	U	N
W	A	S	■	■	O	S	H	A	■	R	E	E	S	E
■	■	■	G	O	T	T	E	N	■	B	A	S	K	S
R	A	N	U	P	■	■	D	A	T	A	■	■	■	■
A	D	A	M	A	N	T	■	■	O	N	E	M	A	N
G	O	D	B	L	E	S	S	A	M	E	R	I	C	A
E	R	I	E	■	S	A	U	C	E	■	G	L	I	B
S	E	A	L	■	T	R	E	E	S	■	O	D	D	S

Irving Berlin

P	E	S	O	■	■	D	Y	E	R	■	B	O	W
I	D	E	A	■	J	O	U	L	E	■	I	K	E
P	I	C	K	P	O	C	K	E	T	■	L	I	E
S	E	T	T	E	E	■	■	M	O	I	L	E	D
■	■	■	R	A	S	P	B	E	R	R	Y	■	■
S	A	G	E	S	■	R	E	N	T	A	C	O	P
T	R	E	E	■	R	I	F	T	S	■	L	O	L
A	P	R	■	P	E	C	O	S	■	P	U	Z	O
G	A	M	E	O	V	E	R	■	R	O	B	E	D
■	■	A	L	T	E	R	E	G	O	S	■	■	■
P	E	N	M	A	N	■	■	E	S	T	A	T	E
E	M	S	■	B	U	B	B	L	E	W	R	A	P
E	M	U	■	L	E	A	K	S	■	A	E	R	O
L	A	B	■	E	S	A	S	■	■	R	A	T	S

Sandwich Orders

I	M	A	■	A	D	I	T	S	■	M	T	A
N	U	M	■	R	E	N	E	E	■	A	I	R
F	L	E	E	C	E	N	A	V	I	D	A	D
A	G	R	E	E	S	■	C	E	S	A	R	E
T	R	I	E	D	■	H	A	N	U	M	A	N
E	E	G	■	■	M	E	R	T	Z	■	■	■
■	W	O	O	L	O	F	T	H	U	M	B	■
■	■	■	T	A	R	T	S	■	■	O	A	F
C	I	N	E	M	A	S	■	C	A	R	V	E
A	D	O	R	E	S	■	N	A	S	S	A	U
C	Y	B	I	L	S	H	E	P	H	E	R	D
A	L	I	■	L	E	A	V	E	■	L	I	E
O	L	D	■	A	S	N	E	R	■	S	A	D

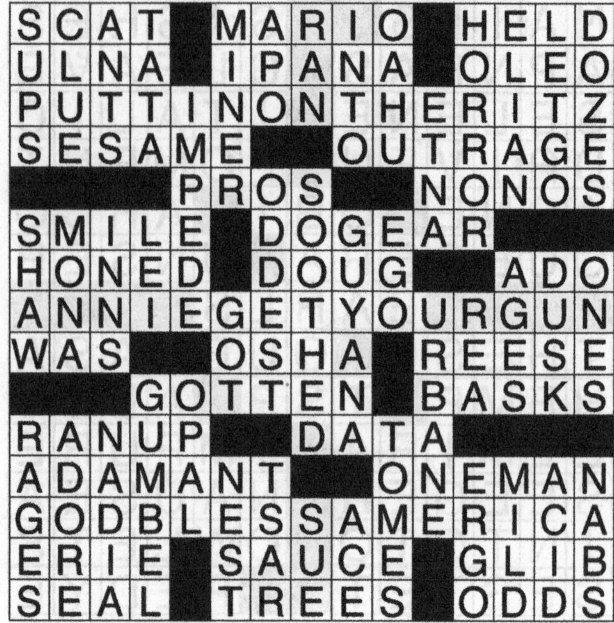

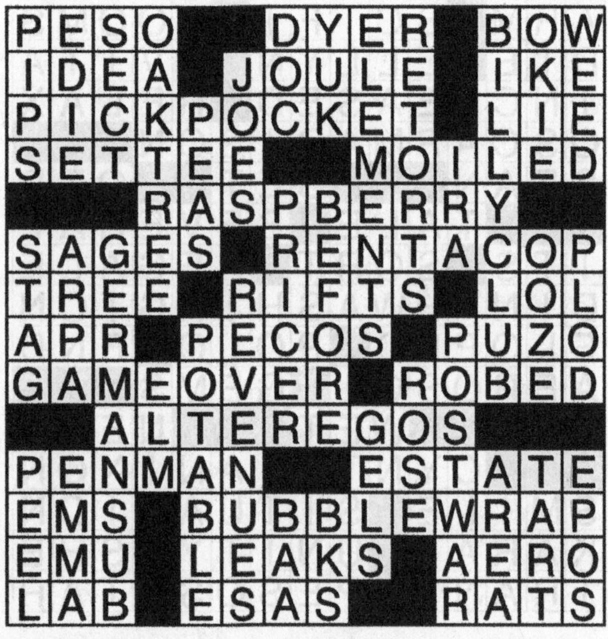

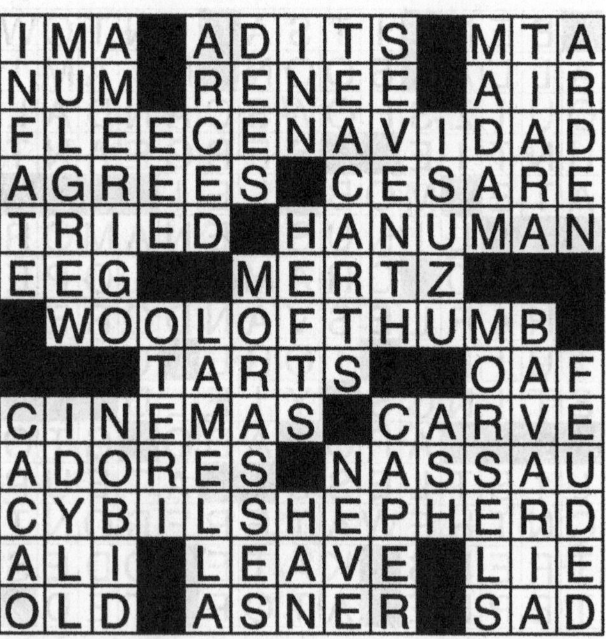

I See Ewe

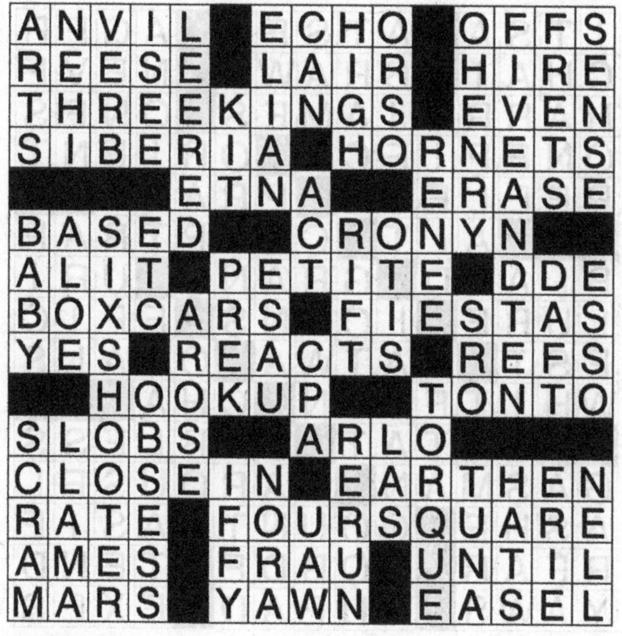

3 to 6

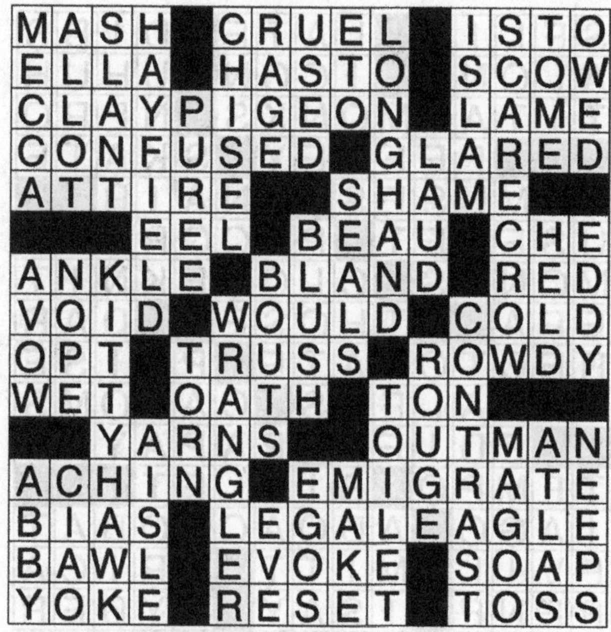

Frequent Flyers

One-Hit Wonders

DRIPS ABBA ODOR
RUNUP FOOL SEAT
AMANA RUDE MAKE
MONTREALEXPO
ARE SLID ANGST
GEODESICDOME
AGE RAKE FIX
FREEBIE DESSERT
OUT ABLE IRK
RBUCKMINSTER
MAPLE LIEN SIT
ARCHITECTURE
SEMI LAVA ORGAN
PEAR OVER DEANS
ALOE DENS EERIE

Fuller Experience

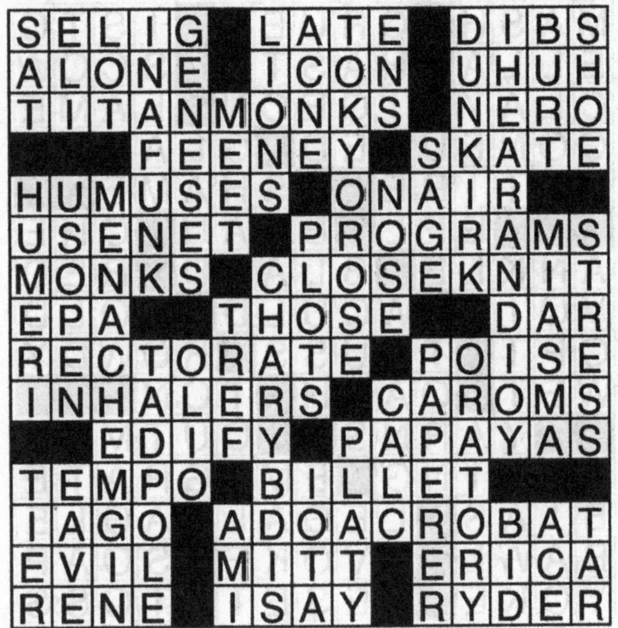

Begone

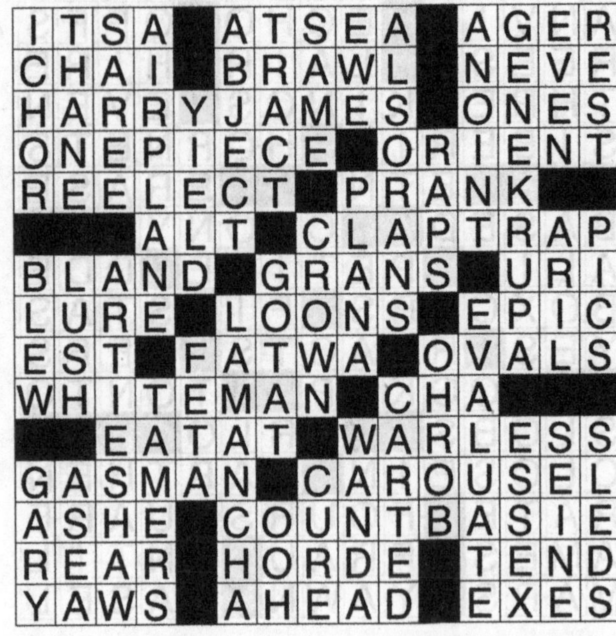

Bandleaders of Yesteryear

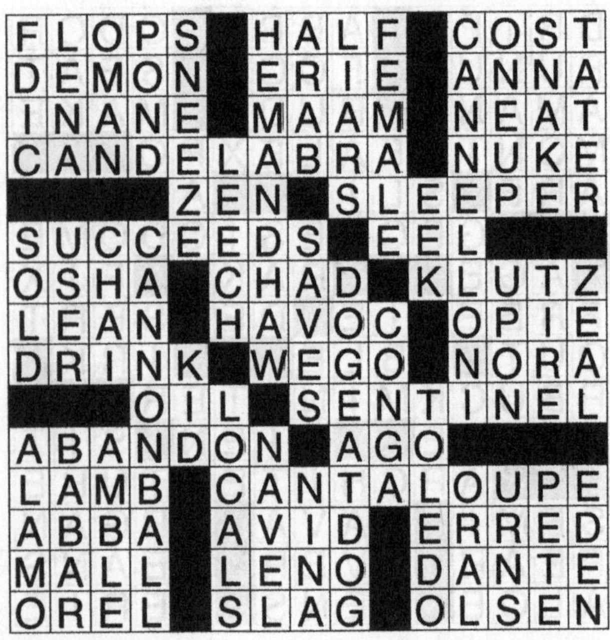

Can-Can

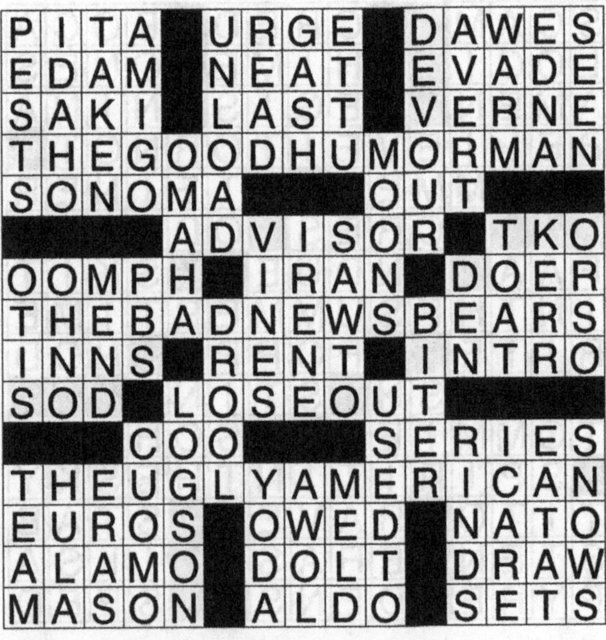

The Good, the Bad and the Ugly

One of Hitchcock's Classics

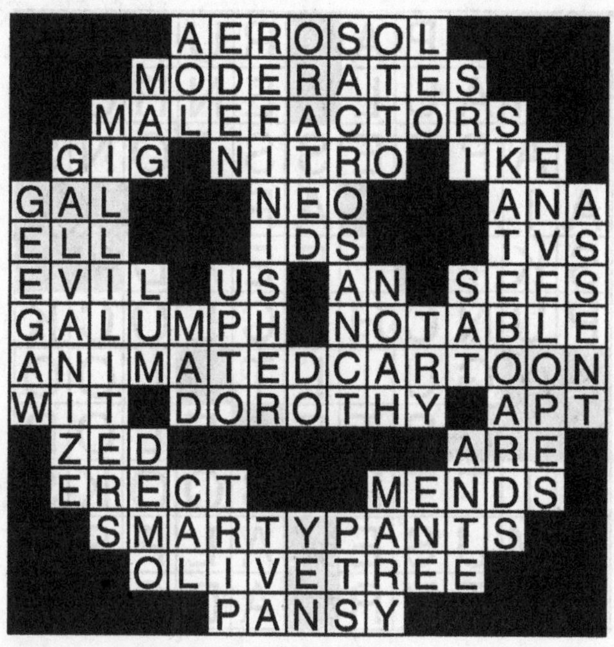

Be of Good Cheer

The Dick Van Dyke Show

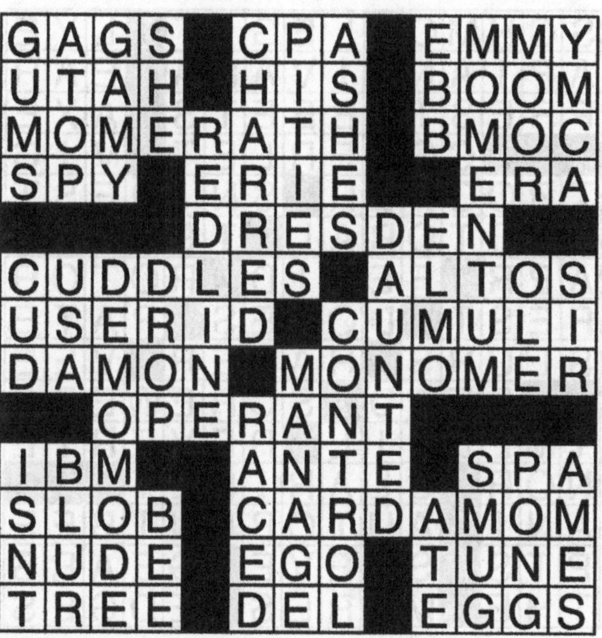

Mother's Day

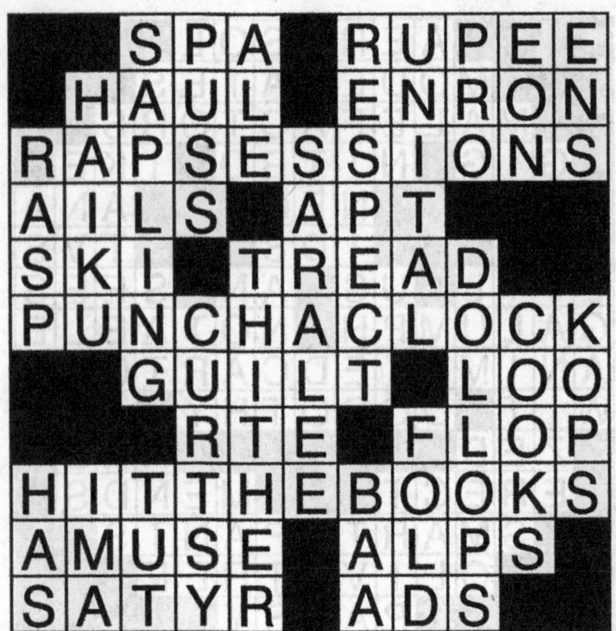
SPA RUPEE
HAUL ENRON
RAPSESSIONS
AILS APT
SKI TREAD
PUNCHACLOCK
GUILT LOO
RTE FLOP
HITTHEBOOKS
AMUSE ALPS
SATYR ADS

Wallop

PELOTA EDGING
TONIGHT NEEDER
CONSOLES DENOVO
HACKNEYED POLIO
ASHY RAWS CALM
ITO ZEE ENTITLE
TEX BLOODRED
CABCALLOWAY
BOOKREST DEL
ANNEALS DSL TAB
TECH SERE BAIO
STEEN TAXIDERMY
MIDAIR STRUTTED
AMERCE ERECTED
NESTED ROSTER

Let It Ride

SCHMO LEGIT LYE
APIAN IVANA EAR
PRESTOBEETS AXE
COVERLET VIC
TROOPER SNIDEST
SECTORAL TERI
APR FETID ROTOR
REST DOMES PATE
SLURS RASER VEE
READ SCREWERS
IMPERIL REVERIE
NOR CLARINET
ANI AUTOBENTBEE
PTS STEVE GEARS
THE MERES EDGES

To Be or Not to Be

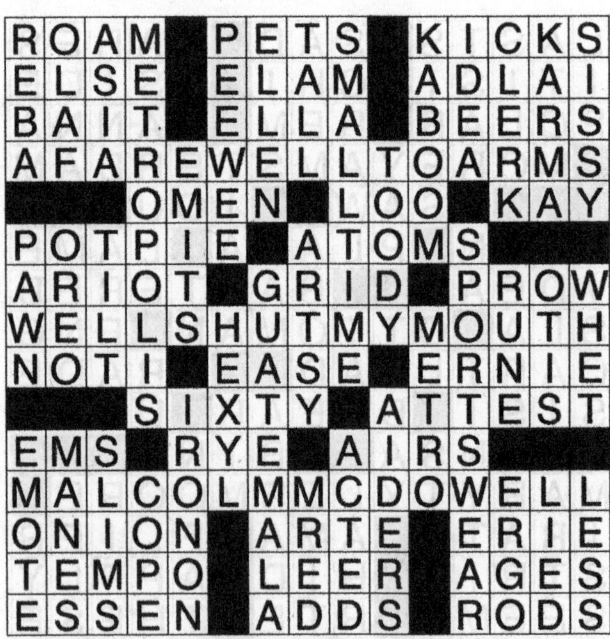
ROAM PETS KICKS
ELSE ELAM ADLAI
BAIT ELLA BEERS
AFAREWELLTOARMS
OMEN LOO KAY
POTPIE ATOMS
ARIOT GRID PROW
WELLSHUTMYMOUTH
NOTI EASE ERNIE
SIXTY ATTEST
EMS RYE AIRS
MALCOLMMCDOWELL
ONION ARTE ERIE
TEMPO LEER AGES
ESSEN ADDS RODS

Well, Well, Well

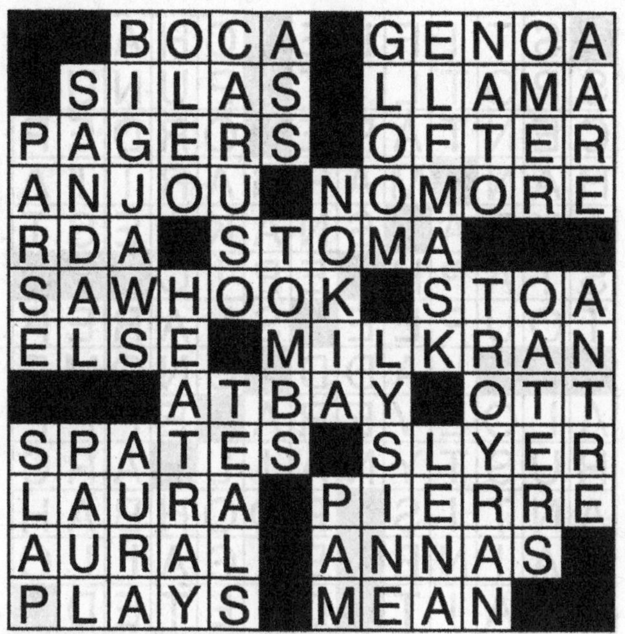

Double Features

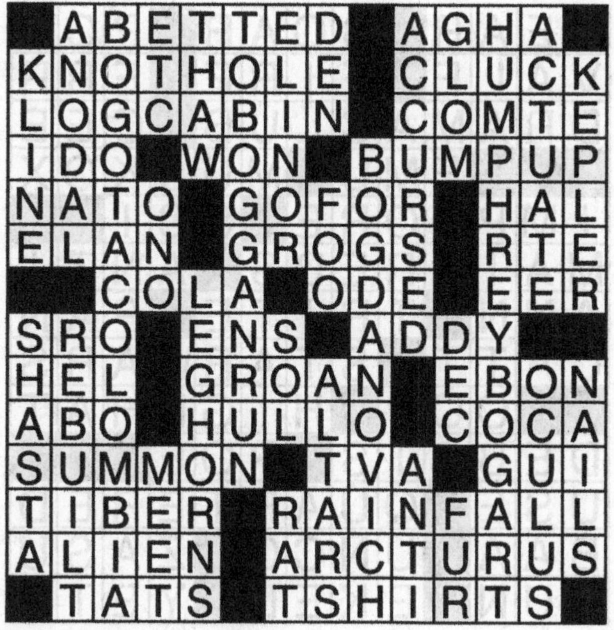

Bogged Down

How Long Has It Been?

You're So Vain

Measure for Measure

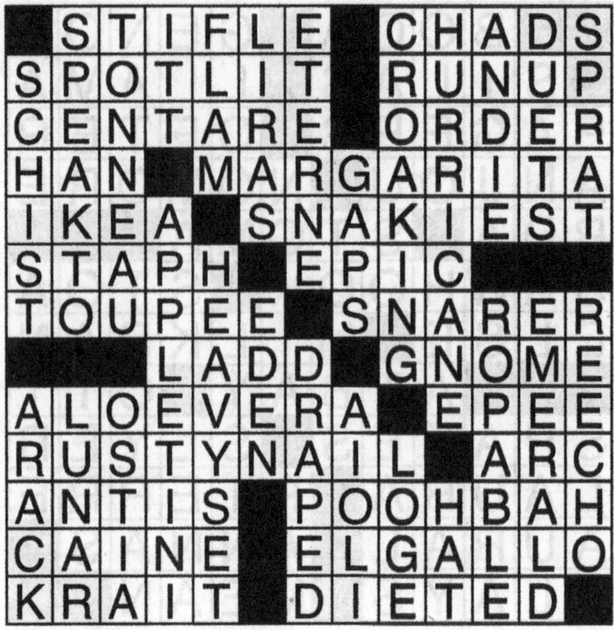

Drinks at 9

Top Cards

Old Lines

Hit Parade

Wear 'em on the End

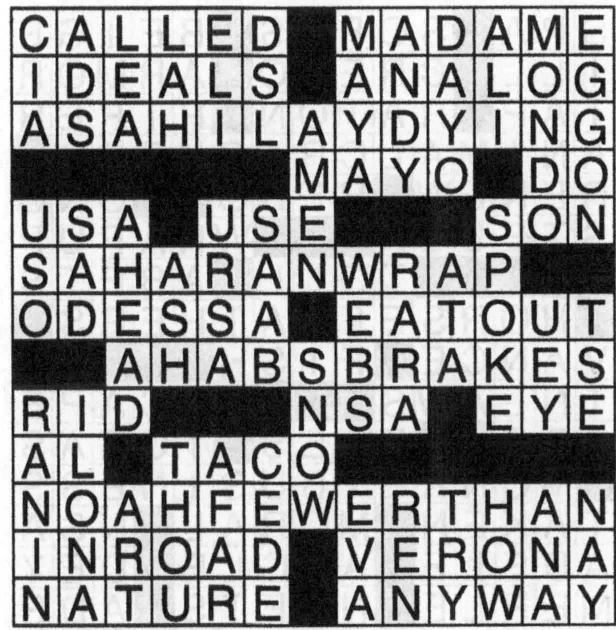

Open Wide and Say "Ah"

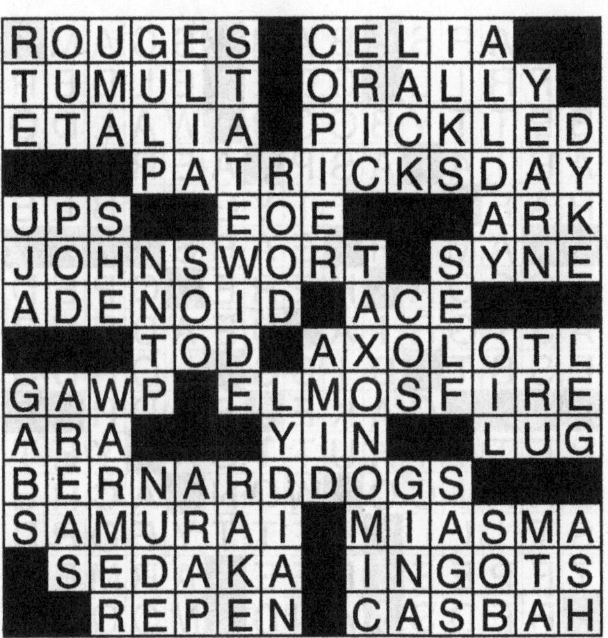

Losing My Religion

T	A	P	I	R	■	S	D	I	■	S	H	Y
S	N	A	F	U	■	P	A	C	■	T	E	A
P	I	N	S	T	R	I	P	E	■	R	A	W
■	■	■	■	A	D	E	P	T	■	I	V	E
F	A	S	T	B	A	L	L	■	E	K	E	D
A	L	P	H	A	■	S	E	R	V	E	■	■
A	L	L	E	G	E	■	S	E	E	O	F	F
■	■	I	W	A	S	A	■	I	N	U	R	E
C	O	T	S	■	C	R	A	N	S	T	O	N
A	B	E	■	L	A	M	P	S	■	■	■	■
R	E	N	■	S	P	A	R	E	T	I	R	E
B	A	D	■	T	E	N	■	R	A	T	O	N
O	H	S	■	S	D	I	■	T	O	T	E	S

Bowl-a-Rama

B	E	A	■	A	Q	U	A	■	P	A	C	K	S	■
R	E	M	■	C	U	R	L	■	O	B	R	I	E	N
A	L	P	A	C	I	N	O	■	U	S	E	D	T	O
■	■	■	M	E	N	■	H	E	N	■	E	D	I	T
A	S	L	A	N	T	■	A	L	C	A	P	O	N	E
T	W	O	S	T	E	P	■	G	E	T	■	■	■	■
S	E	T	S	■	T	H	O	R	■	A	G	O	G	O
E	A	T	E	N	■	R	T	E	■	D	E	C	O	R
A	R	O	S	E	■	A	B	C	S	■	N	E	R	D
■	■	■	■	H	A	S	■	O	N	S	T	A	G	E
A	L	L	E	I	T	E	R	■	O	P	E	N	E	R
S	O	A	R	■	O	D	E	■	W	O	E	■	■	■
H	O	R	N	I	N	■	A	L	J	O	L	S	O	N
E	N	G	I	N	E	■	C	O	O	L	■	A	A	A
■	S	E	E	D	S	■	H	U	B	S	■	T	R	Y

You Can Call Me Al

B	O	A	R	S	■	B	A	R	■	S	C	A	M	■
A	P	R	I	L	■	O	D	E	■	E	L	D	E	R
B	E	T	T	Y	B	O	O	P	■	W	A	L	D	O
A	R	I	A	■	A	S	P	■	A	E	R	I	A	L
R	A	F	■	B	E	T	T	Y	G	R	A	B	L	E
■	■	A	M	E	R	■	E	A	R	S	■	■	■	■
C	O	C	O	A	■	H	E	R	E	■	O	P	E	D
A	S	T	O	R	I	A	■	D	E	A	D	E	N	D
P	S	S	T	■	D	I	B	S	■	L	O	R	D	S
■	■	■	■	C	A	K	E	■	F	A	R	R	■	■
B	E	T	T	Y	H	U	T	T	O	N	■	Y	E	T
E	N	R	I	C	O	■	W	O	N	■	A	C	R	E
S	T	I	L	L	■	B	E	T	T	Y	F	O	R	D
T	E	P	E	E	■	E	E	E	■	A	R	M	E	D
■	R	E	D	S	■	A	N	D	■	M	O	O	D	Y

Same Name

S	P	A	■	S	O	F	A	S	■	B	E	I	G	E
I	L	L	■	C	R	E	D	O	■	A	R	M	O	R
T	A	P	■	R	A	T	O	N	■	R	I	P	E	R
A	N	I	M	A	L	C	R	A	C	K	E	R	S	■
R	E	N	E	W	■	H	E	R	O	■	■	O	N	O
S	T	E	L	L	A	■	■	■	W	R	A	P	U	P
■	■	■	■	■	T	O	L	L	■	A	B	E	T	S
■	H	O	R	S	E	F	E	A	T	H	E	R	S	■
V	A	N	C	E	■	F	I	S	H	■	■	■	■	■
I	N	L	A	W	S	■	■	■	E	S	C	A	P	E
A	D	O	■	■	E	W	E	S	■	T	O	G	A	S
■	M	O	N	K	E	Y	B	U	S	I	N	E	S	S
T	A	K	E	N	■	M	O	R	A	L	■	N	S	A
A	D	E	L	E	■	A	N	G	L	E	■	D	E	Y
M	E	R	L	E	■	N	Y	E	T	S	■	A	D	S

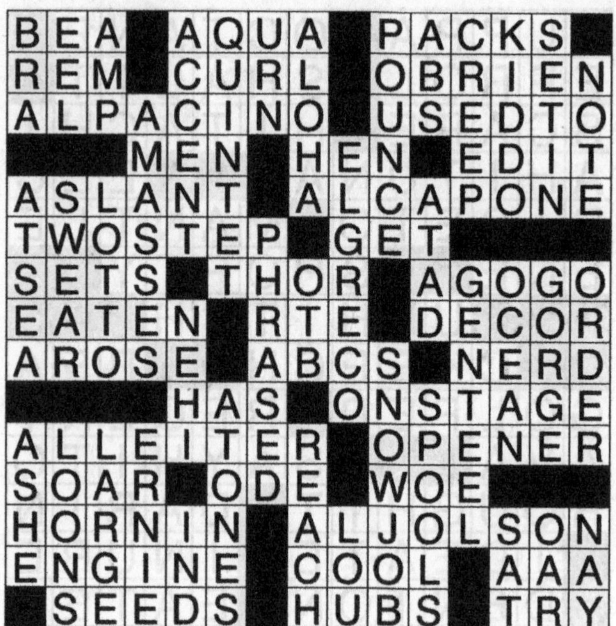

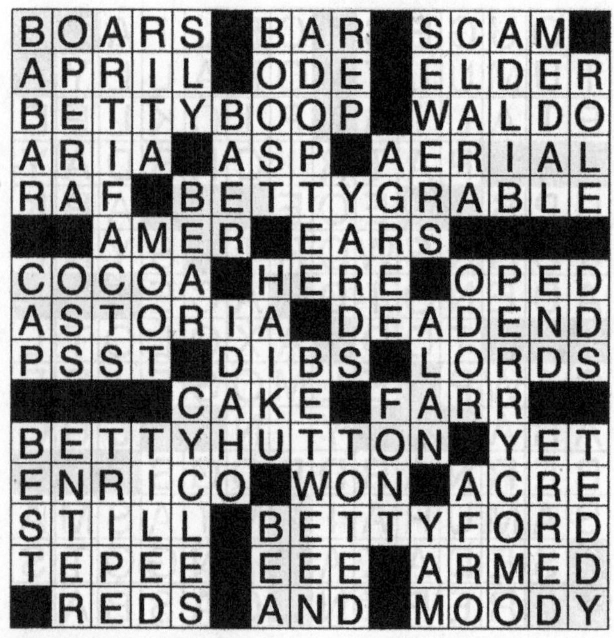

Marx Brothers Movies

DAWN BODS SEDAN
OLIO OREO ARENA
GOLDWATER GRAND
MEDEA PEA TIE
ASS REDENBACHER
DYNES SIRS
PATE RUT EDITED
STIGMAS ENSNARE
IMPROV OPT GREW
PERI GEESE
GREENSTREET CPA
AIR HOE YOURS
PSALM PINKERTON
EERIE ISEE CUBE
DRYER CHEN APER

Colorful People

LOGOS SAFE MATS
IMEAN DULL IDOL
FATHAHINES LURE
ENSURE TEA ELSE
LYRIC FSTOP
OMIT DEEMED
MATILDA SAVANNA
ARETOO REVEAL
REMOVES SCRIMPS
PERISH SOSO
BOGUS GUESS
ACRE ANT EATING
SEAN COUNTBASIE
RAFT EURO IPANA
ANTE STEW NEWER

Men of Jazz

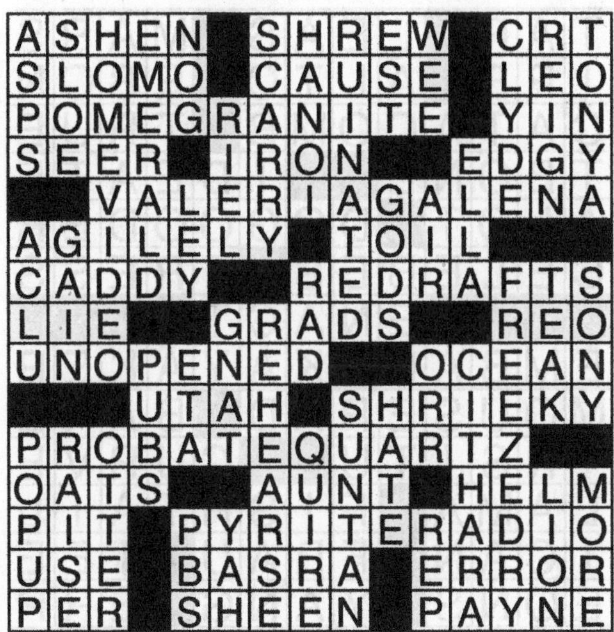
ASHEN SHREW CRT
SLOMO CAUSE LEO
POMEGRANITE YIN
SEER IRON EDGY
VALERIAGALENA
AGILELY TOIL
CADDY REDRAFTS
LIE GRADS REO
UNOPENED OCEAN
UTAH SHRIEKY
PROBATEQUARTZ
OATS AUNT HELM
PIT PYRITERADIO
USE BASRA ERROR
PER SHEEN PAYNE

Turning to Stone

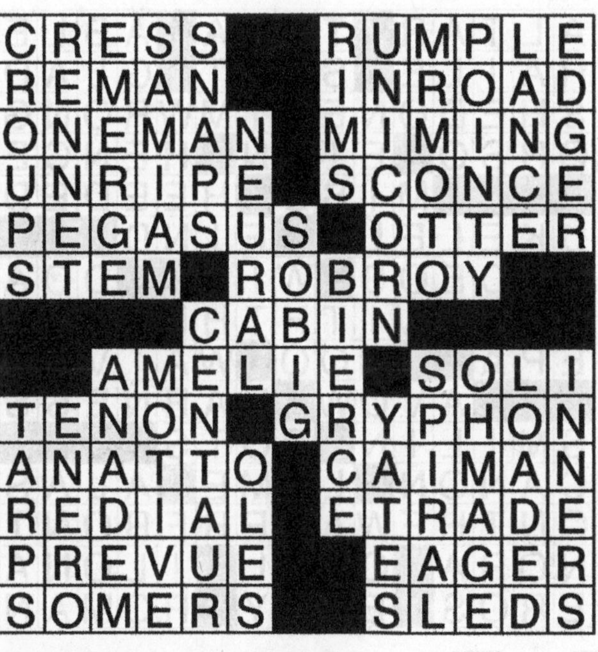
CRESS RUMPLE
REMAN INROAD
ONEMAN MIMING
UNRIPE SCONCE
PEGASUS OTTER
STEM ROBROY
CABIN
AMELIE SOLI
TENON GRYPHON
ANATTO CAIMAN
REDIAL ETRADE
PREVUE EAGER
SOMERS SLEDS

Mythical Critters

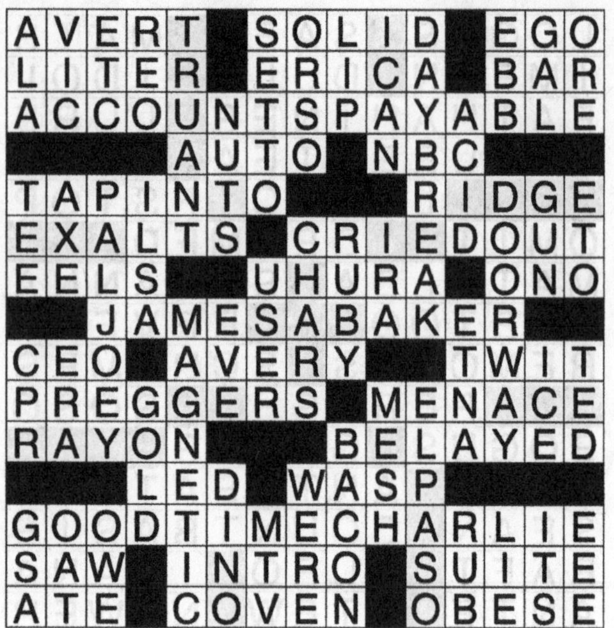

Military ABCs

Singin' in the Rain

Top Films

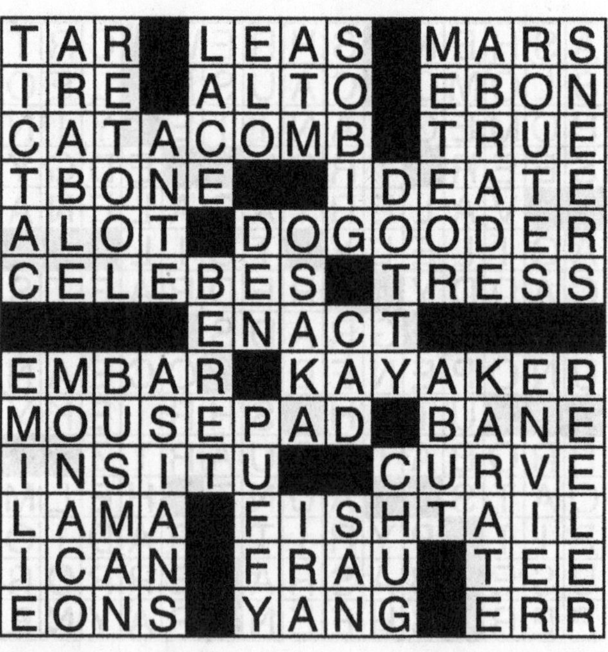

Pets

T	A	C	K	S	■	M	O	T	E	L	■	T	S	P
I	N	L	E	T	■	R	O	U	T	E	■	O	H	O
S	T	O	N	E	S	T	H	R	O	W	■	M	A	P
■	■	S	T	E	P	■	■	E	N	D	G	A	M	E
A	P	E	■	D	A	N	T	E	■	■	O	T	A	Y
R	E	D	O	■	R	H	I	N	E	S	T	O	N	E
C	R	I	B	S	■	L	E	S	L	I	E	■	■	■
S	U	N	S	E	T	■	■	■	I	N	V	A	D	E
■	■	■	C	A	N	A	D	A	■	S	E	G	A	L
M	I	N	E	S	T	R	O	N	E	■	N	I	N	A
I	N	O	N	■	■	M	E	N	D	S	■	T	A	M
S	C	R	E	E	C	H	■	■	E	L	I	A	■	■
L	I	T	■	B	L	O	W	O	N	E	S	T	O	P
E	T	O	■	B	A	L	E	D	■	P	L	E	A	T
D	E	N	■	S	P	E	E	D	■	T	E	S	T	S

Nesting Nests

A	C	E	S	■	A	L	T	O	■	W	A	F	E	R
S	L	A	T	■	L	O	A	N	■	A	G	I	L	E
W	A	T	E	R	F	A	L	L	■	N	O	B	I	D
I	R	A	N	I	■	F	L	Y	N	N	■	■	■	■
M	A	T	■	P	R	E	Y	■	E	A	T	E	R	S
■	■	■	W	E	A	R	■	B	A	B	A	L	O	O
A	F	F	I	R	M	■	W	A	T	E	R	L	O	O
C	R	A	G	■	■	L	A	Y	■	■	M	I	T	T
H	O	T	W	A	T	E	R	■	G	R	A	S	S	Y
E	S	T	A	T	E	S	■	O	P	E	C	■	■	■
S	T	Y	M	I	E	■	B	R	A	N	■	M	O	M
■	■	■	■	S	N	O	R	E	■	E	B	O	N	Y
B	A	R	N	S	■	G	O	L	D	W	A	T	E	R
S	N	A	F	U	■	L	O	S	E	■	B	E	A	N
A	D	E	L	E	■	E	D	E	N	■	E	L	L	A

Desert Cry

P	T	S	■	■	T	O	P	P	S	■	C	A	R	S
L	A	U	D	■	A	W	A	I	T	■	A	N	E	W
E	M	M	E	T	K	E	L	L	Y	■	E	T	N	A
A	P	A	C	H	E	■	M	A	M	A	S	B	O	Y
■	A	C	R	O	S	S	■	F	I	N	A	L	■	■
■	■	■	E	R	U	P	T	■	E	N	R	A	P	T
L	O	B	E	■	P	L	E	A	S	E	■	B	O	O
I	V	E	S	■	■	I	N	D	■	■	T	B	S	P
L	E	E	■	G	E	T	S	U	P	■	E	Y	E	S
I	N	A	J	A	M	■	E	L	I	T	E	■	■	■
■	■	R	U	L	E	R	■	T	R	U	T	H	S	■
A	N	T	L	E	R	E	D	■	A	T	E	O	U	T
N	E	H	I	■	G	N	A	T	T	U	R	N	E	R
T	R	U	E	■	E	E	R	I	E	■	S	O	D	A
S	O	R	T	■	S	E	E	P	S	■	■	R	E	M

Buggy People

S	K	I	E	R	■	■	N	I	B	B	E	D	■
P	E	N	N	E	■	■	A	R	E	O	L	A	R
R	I	V	E	T	■	T	Z	A	T	Z	I	K	I
I	L	O	■	E	G	O	I	S	T	■	C	O	D
E	L	G	A	L	L	O	■	■	E	L	I	T	E
S	O	U	V	L	A	K	I	■	R	A	T	A	■
T	R	E	E	■	S	A	N	E	S	T	■	■	■
■	■	■	R	E	S	I	S	T	■	E	S	S	E
■	C	A	S	A	■	M	O	U	S	S	A	K	A
T	A	P	E	R	■	■	L	I	T	T	L	E	S
O	N	O	■	H	O	P	E	S	O	■	T	E	T
D	O	L	M	A	D	E	S	■	U	N	I	T	E
D	E	L	I	R	I	A	■	■	T	O	N	E	R
■	S	O	R	T	E	R	■	■	S	T	E	R	N

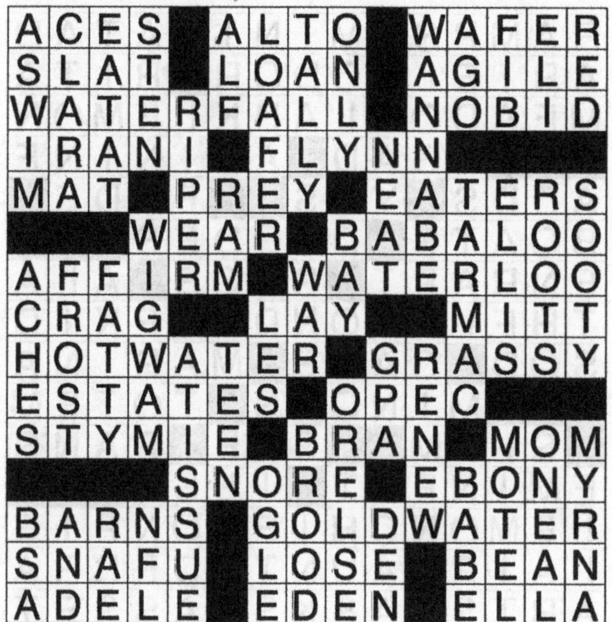

It's All Greek to Me

What Life Hands You

Final Measures

Polarity

Singing to the Choir

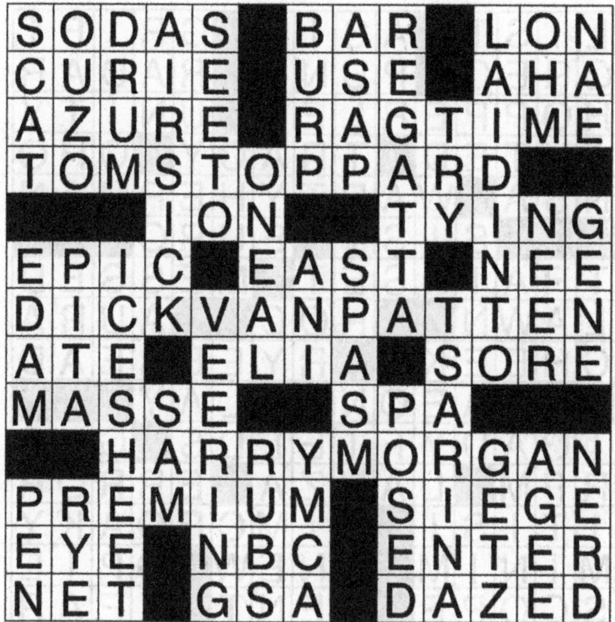

S	O	D	A	S	■	B	A	R	■	L	O	N
C	U	R	I	E	■	U	S	E	■	A	H	A
A	Z	U	R	E	■	R	A	G	T	I	M	E
T	O	M	S	T	O	P	P	A	R	D	■	■
■	■	■	I	O	N	■	■	T	Y	I	N	G
E	P	I	C	■	E	A	S	T	■	N	E	E
D	I	C	K	V	A	N	P	A	T	T	E	N
A	T	E	■	E	L	I	A	■	S	O	R	E
M	A	S	S	E	■	■	S	P	A	■	■	■
■	■	H	A	R	R	Y	M	O	R	G	A	N
P	R	E	M	I	U	M	■	S	I	E	G	E
E	Y	E	■	N	B	C	■	E	N	T	E	R
N	E	T	■	G	S	A	■	D	A	Z	E	D

Tom, Dick, and Harry

D	U	M	B	■	■	C	H	E	A	P	■	P	R	E
I	S	A	A	C	■	O	O	M	P	H	■	H	A	M
M	E	R	C	H	A	N	D	I	S	E	■	O	T	B
■	■	A	H	A	B	■	■	L	E	A	R	N	E	R
T	O	T	■	R	E	F	S	■	■	S	E	E	D	Y
L	A	H	R	■	T	O	U	C	H	A	N	D	G	O
C	H	O	I	R	■	S	P	O	O	N	■	■	■	■
■	U	N	D	O	E	S	■	R	E	T	I	N	A	■
■	■	■	■	A	V	I	A	N	■	S	K	U	L	L
C	H	A	N	D	E	L	I	E	R	■	E	T	T	U
O	U	G	H	T	■	■	M	A	Y	A	■	H	O	G
U	S	E	L	E	S	S	■	■	A	L	P	O	■	■
G	T	O	■	S	U	C	H	A	N	D	S	U	C	H
A	L	L	■	T	R	A	S	H	■	O	S	S	I	E
R	E	D	■	S	E	R	T	A	■	■	T	E	A	M

Holding Hands

A	B	C	S	■	A	D	D	U	P	■	T	U	N	A
M	E	A	L	■	V	E	R	S	E	■	U	N	I	X
B	E	N	I	T	O	M	U	S	S	O	L	I	N	I
I	P	E	C	A	C	■	G	R	A	V	I	T	A	S
■	■	■	E	T	A	T	■	■	C	O	P	■	■	■
R	A	M	■	A	D	O	L	F	H	I	T	L	E	R
E	T	A	L	■	O	P	A	L	■	D	R	I	V	E
M	O	N	A	■	■	E	T	A	■	■	E	V	E	N
A	N	N	U	L	■	K	E	M	P	■	E	I	R	E
P	E	A	R	L	H	A	R	B	O	R	■	D	Y	E
■	■	■	E	A	U	■	■	E	R	O	S	■	■	■
P	R	E	A	M	B	L	E	■	T	A	K	I	N	G
Y	A	L	T	A	C	O	N	F	E	R	E	N	C	E
R	I	M	E	■	A	D	D	E	R	■	I	R	A	N
E	N	O	S	■	P	E	A	R	S	■	N	E	A	T

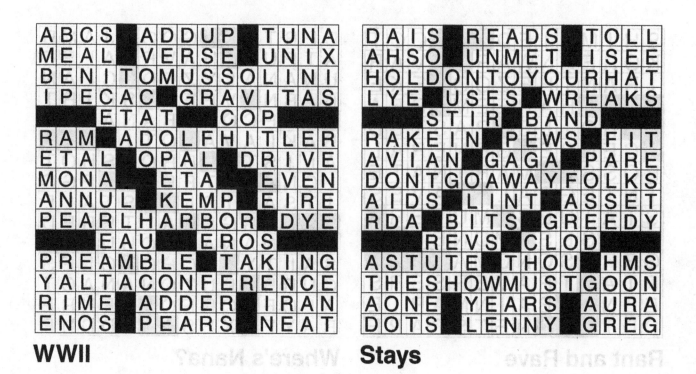

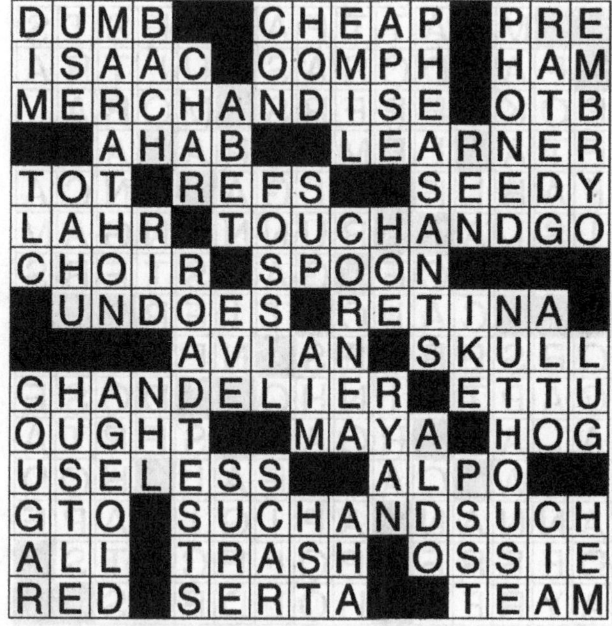

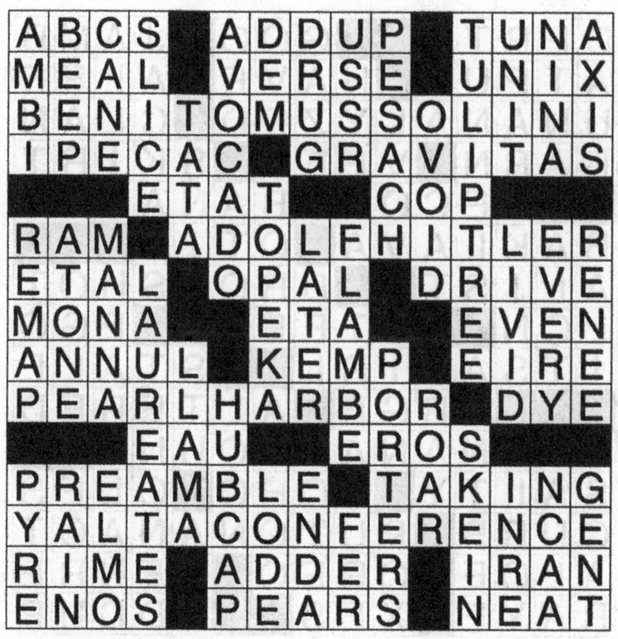

WWII

D	A	I	S	■	R	E	A	D	S	■	T	O	L	L
A	H	S	O	■	U	N	M	E	T	■	I	S	E	E
H	O	L	D	O	N	T	O	Y	O	U	R	H	A	T
L	Y	E	■	U	S	E	S	■	W	R	E	A	K	S
■	■	■	S	T	I	R	■	B	A	N	D	■	■	■
R	A	K	E	I	N	■	P	E	W	S	■	F	I	T
A	V	I	A	N	■	G	A	G	A	■	P	A	R	E
D	O	N	T	G	O	A	W	A	Y	F	O	L	K	S
A	I	D	S	■	L	I	N	T	■	A	S	S	E	T
R	D	A	■	B	I	T	S	■	G	R	E	E	D	Y
■	■	■	R	E	V	S	■	C	L	O	D	■	■	■
A	S	T	U	T	E	■	T	H	O	U	■	H	M	S
T	H	E	S	H	O	W	M	U	S	T	G	O	O	N
A	O	N	E	■	Y	E	A	R	S	■	A	U	R	A
D	O	T	S	■	L	E	N	N	Y	■	G	R	E	G

Stays

Not Okay

Froggy Mountain High

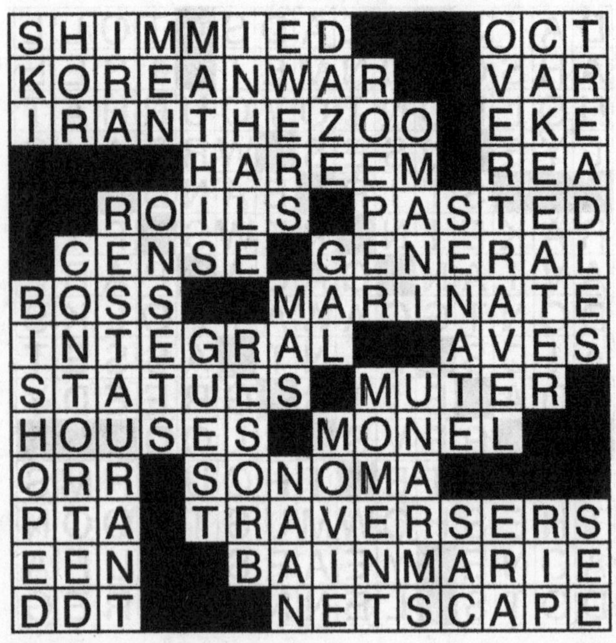

Rant and Rave

Where's Nana?

Par for the Course

Stubborn Itch

Mixed Doubles

Planetary Efforts

160 SUPER-SIZED PUZZLES!

Packed with 160 puzzles in an easy-on-the-eyes format, this collection features puzzles with a variety of themes, including pop stars, sports, favorite foods, movies, pets, outer space—and more! *The Everything® Jumbo Book of Large-Print Word Searches* is everything a puzzler could want!

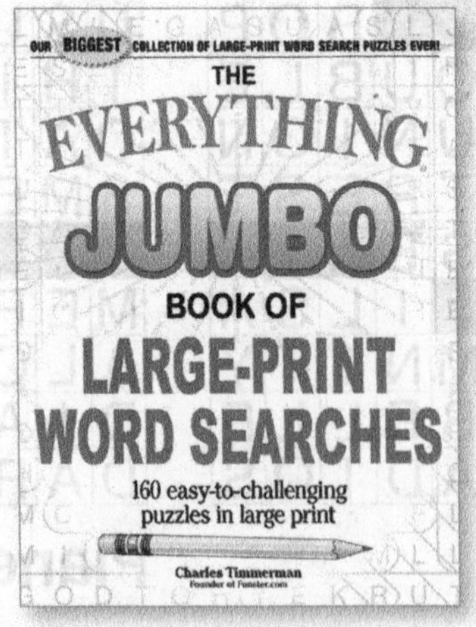

The Everything® Jumbo Book of Large-Print Word Searches
978-1-5072-0917-2